always up to date

The law changes, but Nolo is always on top of it! We offer several ways to make sure you and your Nolo products are always up to date:

1 **Nolo's Legal Updater**

We'll send you an email whenever a new edition of your book is published! Sign up at **www.nolo.com/legalupdater**.

2 **Updates @ Nolo.com**

Check **www.nolo.com/update** to find recent changes in the law that affect the current edition of your book.

3 **Nolo Customer Service**

To make sure that this edition of the book is the most recent one, call us at **800-728-3555** and ask one of our friendly customer service representatives. Or find out at **www.nolo.com**.

3rd edition

Nolo's Deposition Handbook

by Attorneys Paul Bergman & Albert J. Moore

Third Edition	May 2005
Editor	Stephanie Bornstein
Illustrations	Mari Stein
Cover Design	Toni Ihara
Book Design	Stephanie Harolde
Production	Sarah Hinman
Proofreading	Emily K. Wolman
Index	Janet Perlman
Printing	Consolidated Printers, Inc.

Bergman, Paul, 1943-
    Nolo's deposition handbook / by Paul Bergman & Albert J. Moore.--3rd ed.
      p. cm.
    Includes index.
    ISBN 1-4133-0178-9 (alk. paper)
    1. Depositions--United States--Popular works. 2. Discovery (Law)--United
States--Popular works. I. Title: Deposition handbook. II. Moore, Albert J. III. Nolo (Firm)
IV. Title.
KF8900.B44 2005
347.73'072--Dc22

                                                      2005040657

For information on bulk purchases or corporate premium sales, please contact the Special Sales department. For academic sales or textbook adoptions, ask for Academic Sales. Call 800-955-4775 or write to Nolo at 950 Parker St., Berkeley, CA, 94710.

Dedication

To all the nonlawyers who seek to understand the civil justice system and to use it to vindicate their legal rights.

—PB, AJM

Acknowledgments

Thank you to Meredith Master, a UCLA law student, and Kevin Gerson, a UCLA law librarian, for helping us with legal research.

We are grateful to Jake Warner and Steve Elias, who established and have continued a tradition of excellence at Nolo and who pushed us (occasionally painfully!) to produce a book that might be consistent with that tradition. Thank you also to Lulu Cornell and all the Nolo employees for using their design and production skills on our behalf.

Thank you to David Binder (our esteemed UCLA law school colleague) and Sherrill Johnson, excellent lawyers whose wisdom and years of deposition practice are reflected throughout the book.

Thank you to UCLA law student Audrey Lustgarden for cheerfully helping us to prepare the third edition.

—PB, AJM

Table of Contents

Introduction: How to Use This Book

PART ONE: BEING DEPOSED

1: An Overview of Deposition Procedures

2: Using Depositions in a Lawsuit

3: Preparing to Give Deposition Testimony

4: Responding to Questions

5: Beginning a Deposition: "The Usual Admonitions"

6: Background Questions

10: Defending a Deposition

11: Taking a Deposition: Deposing a "Hostile" Witness

12: Taking a Deposition: Responding to a Defending Attorney's Roadblocks

13: Taking a Deposition: Deposing a "Friendly" Witness

14: Videotaped Depositions

Glossary

Appendix 1: Excerpts From the Federal Rules of Civil Procedure (FRCP)

Appendix 2: State Discovery and Deposition Rules

Appendix 3: Sample Forms

Index

Introduction

How to Use This Book

Depositions enable the parties to a lawsuit (people who are suing, called "plaintiffs," and people who are being sued, called "defendants") to question each other and other witnesses before going to court. A deposition is like testimony in court—under oath—but it occurs before trial, outside the courtroom, and without a judge or jury present. While depositions have a number of uses, parties take depositions primarily in the hope of uncovering information that supports their legal claims and undermines the other side's legal claims.

This book explains and illustrates deposition rules, procedures, and strategies in civil cases (legal disputes between private parties). It does not cover criminal cases. Depositions are one of several methods of investigating the facts of a case before trial that together constitute what lawyers call "formal discovery" (other methods of formal discovery are covered in Chapter 9). This book, however, focuses on depositions for a number of important reasons:

- Information uncovered during depositions is often the key to a case's outcome, whether the case is resolved through a voluntary settlement by the parties (as is usually true), a summary judgment (a decision by a judge before the trial begins), or a trial.

- While other formal discovery methods rely on written questions and answers drafted mainly by lawyers, depositions consist of live, oral testimony by deponents (people who are questioned at depositions), including plaintiffs, defendants, and nonparty witnesses (witnesses with case-related information but no formal involvement in a lawsuit). Parties often have days or even weeks to respond to written discovery requests, while deponents must answer deposition questions immediately. Depositions, therefore, tend to be far more stressful than other forms of formal discovery, so you'll want to know in advance exactly what will happen and how to prepare.

- Because depositions typically take place in private conference rooms rather than in public courtrooms, only people who have testified at deposition before are likely to understand what will happen at a deposition and the importance of their testimony.

- Depositions are usually the most expensive discovery tool. If you're a party and you hire an attorney, you'll incur attorney's fees if your attorney takes or defends a deposition. If you're the party taking the deposition, you'll also have to pay for a court reporter to transcribe the testimony, a videographer to videotape it, or both.

A. Part One: Being Deposed

This book is divided into two parts. Part One (Chapters 1 through 8) provides information primarily for the person who is being deposed (questioned under oath at a deposition). Part Two (Chapters 9 through 14) explains how to take a deposition or defend a party or witness on your side who is being deposed.

Part One explains deposition rules and procedures from the perspective of a deponent (the person being asked questions). You may be a deponent because:

- You're a party (plaintiff or defendant) to a lawsuit. For example, you're a plaintiff suing the defendant, your former employer, for wrongful termination; the employer's lawyer deposes you.

- You're a nonparty witness who knows case-related information. For example, you're a bystander who observed a collision between two cars whose drivers are now the parties to a lawsuit. The driver of either car might depose you.

- You're an expert witness who has been hired by a party to investigate a case and render opinions based on your specialized knowledge. For example, you are a medical expert who has been retained by the plaintiff in a medical malpractice case to explain why the defendant doctor's treatment of the plaintiff was substandard; the defendant chooses to depose you.

No matter what type of deponent you are, and whether or not you are represented by a lawyer, you should read Part One to learn:

- what to do (and not do) in preparation for your deposition (see Chapter 3)

- what to do if you're asked to bring documents to the deposition (see Chapter 3)

- how far you can be required to travel for a deposition and whether you are entitled to be paid for time spent testifying (see Chapter 1)

- the three "Golden Rules" for answering deposition questions (see Chapter 4)

- what questions you have a legal right to refuse to answer (see Chapter 7)

- whether you have to answer questions that your lawyers objects to (see Chapter 4)

- how to deal with "trick" questions that many lawyers love to ask during depositions (see Chapter 4)

- what to do if the deposing lawyer is verbally abusive (see Chapter 4)

- what warnings you'll probably be given at the beginning of the deposition (see Chapter 5), and

- if you're an expert witness, what your role will be in the process before trial and what types of questions you're likely to be asked at deposition (see Chapter 8).

B. Part Two: Taking and Defending Depositions

Part Two explains deposition rules and procedures from the perspective of a party who does not have a lawyer and is representing him- or herself. Most people in the legal system refer to people who represent themselves as "pro per" or "pro se" litigants. ("Pro se" means "in one's own behalf" in Latin; a "litigant" is a party engaged in the process of a lawsuit, also called "litigation.")

When representing yourself, you may be either:

- The deposing party, the party who arranges for and conducts the deposition questioning. For example, you're a pro se defendant in an auto accident case and you depose the plaintiff, the driver of the other car.

- The defending party, the party who is present at a deposition arranged for and conducted by your adversary (the other side). As a defending party, you are entitled to be present at depositions taken by your adversary and (among other things) to question the deponent after your adversary finishes his or her questioning. For example, you're a pro se defendant in an auto accident case and you defend the deposition the plaintiff takes of a nonparty witness—your friend who was a passenger in your car at the time of the accident.

If you're representing yourself and either taking or defending a deposition, you'll need to read both Parts One and Two of this book. In Part Two, you'll learn about such issues as:

- how depositions compare to the other methods of formal discovery (see Chapter 9)

- how to arrange for a deposition, including how to require the deponent to produce case-related documents (see Chapters 9 and 10)

- how to depose a "hostile" witness—one whose testimony goes against you and who may not want to discuss the case with you (see Chapter 11)

- how and when to depose a "friendly" witness—one who supports your legal claims (see Chapter 13)

- how to respond when an opposing lawyer engages in intimidating or other improper behavior (see Chapters 10 and 12)

- how to make and respond to objections (see Chapters 10 and 12)

- how to take and defend videotaped depositions (see Chapter 14), and

- whether to bring out helpful information that your adversary has overlooked (see Chapter 10).

C. The Federal Rules of Civil Procedure (FRCP)

The deposition rules and procedures described in this book primarily come from a set of laws known as the Federal Rules of Civil Procedure. (Everyone with a law degree calls them the "FRCP," so you'll need to remember this bit of alphabet soup.) The FRCP establishes general procedures for civil cases in all federal district courts (trial courts), from the time you file the case initially through the final judgment. Rules 26 through 30, 32, 37, and 45 are the main rules that govern depositions. The text of these rules, current as of the date this book was published, is set forth in Appendix 1.

This book focuses on the FRCP not only because they dictate federal court procedures but also because state rules follow them closely. The whole American system of formal discovery before trial (including depositions) began when Congress enacted the FRCP into law in 1938. These rules were then gradually adopted by the states. Through many amendments over the years, the FRCP has remained the basis for all states' discovery practices. In fact, many states have adopted the FRCP more or less intact as their own, down to the FRCP's numbering system and headings. States that have not adopted the FRCP generally have rules that closely mimic FRCP procedures.

D. Finding the Deposition Rules That Apply to You

If you're representing yourself in a lawsuit and about to take or defend a deposition, you'll need to be familiar with the most current version of the discovery and deposition rules in your court. The sections below will help you find those rules.

1. Federal Court Cases

If you're representing yourself in a federal court case, begin by reading through the FRCP discovery and deposition rules set out in Appendix 1. Of course, you'll want to check to see whether those rules have been amended since the date of

this book's publication. One way to do so is to go to a library. If you live or work near a law library that's open to the public, that's the best place to go to find the current version of the FRCP. However, even a large general public library is likely to stock the latest version of the FRCP.

You can also access the FRCP online. One website that provides the current version of the FRCP is maintained by the Cornell University Law School Legal Information Institute at www.law.cornell.edu/rules/frcp/?. A second website through which you can access the full text of the FRCP is the Law Library Resource Xchange, at www.llrx.com/courtrules. Or you can use Nolo's Self-Help Law Center at www.nolo.com.

 Always check for amendments to the FRCP.

The FRCP is often amended. For example, "voluntary disclosure" requirements (discussed in Chapter 9) first came into being in the 1990s and were substantially modified in 1999. Thus, if you're representing yourself in a federal case, you must make sure that you have the current version of the FRCP before embarking on depositions and other forms of discovery.

2. State Court Cases

If you're representing yourself in a state court case, you'll undoubtedly find that, as mentioned above, your state's procedures will closely resemble those set forth in the FRCP. Nevertheless, you'll want to consult your state's deposition rules before testifying at, arranging for, or defending a deposition, because some procedures may vary. For example, such issues as how much advance notice you have to give a deponent before taking a deposition and how much money you may have to give to a nonparty witness whose deposition you want to take can vary from one state to another.

Failure to follow your state's rules exactly can have serious consequences. For example, if your failure to make proper arrangements causes a deposition to be canceled at the last minute, you might have to reimburse your adversary for the expenses of rescheduling. Repeated mistakes might even lead a judge to order that you not be allowed to conduct discovery at all.

Follow the instructions in Appendix 2 for finding your state's rules, either in the library or online.

Icons Used in This Book

Look for these icons to alert you to certain kinds of information.

 This icon warns you of potential problems.

 This icon alerts you to a practical tip or a good idea.

 This icon refers you to helpful books and other resources for further information.

■

Part One:
Being Deposed

Part One (Chapters 1 through 8) gives all the information you will need to prepare to have your deposition taken. Whether you are deposed as a party to a lawsuit, a nonparty witness, or an expert witness, Part One has information that will help you testify effectively and accurately. (For an overview of the topics addressed in Part One, please see Section A of the introduction.)

Chapter 1

An Overview of Deposition Procedures

This chapter will familiarize you with deposition procedures. Unless you have had your deposition taken, these procedures will likely be unfamiliar: Most depositions take place in private conference rooms rather than in public courtrooms. (You may have seen depositions depicted in films like *Class Action* and *The Rainmaker,* but please don't base your expectations on those depictions!) Along with other information, this chapter describes how depositions are organized, how you might be able to alter the arrangements if necessary, and what role each person at the deposition will play.

A. Depositions in a Nutshell

A deposition normally consists of a lawyer (or a person representing him- or herself) asking the deponent (the person being deposed) questions. The deponent may be a party to the lawsuit or a nonparty witness (someone who may have case-related information, such as a bystander who observes an auto accident). Depositions may seem informal, since they typically take place in conference rooms with no judge present. Yet do not be fooled—they share many characteristics with testimony in court during a trial.

For example, as the deponent you'll be placed under oath, and your testimony will be recorded and transcribed by an official court reporter. (Increasingly, depositions are videotaped as well. See Chapter 14.) Moreover, since the overwhelming percentage of cases settle prior to trial, your deposition may be your only chance to testify. Thus, lawyers often prepare as carefully for depositions as for trial. And because what is said at a deposition can have a major impact on the eventual resolution of a dispute, deponents should be as careful and as accurate in giving deposition testimony as they would be in testifying in a courtroom at trial.

B. Providing Notice of a Deposition

A deposing party (a party planning to take a deposition) has to give you advance written notice of the deposition's time and place. This section explains these notice procedures.

1. Types of Deposition Notices

Your deposition process will start when you receive one of two types of notices. If you're a bystander or other nonparty witness, you'll be personally served with a court order usually called a "Subpoena re Deposition." (See Sample Form #1 in Appendix 3.) A subpoena is a court order requiring you to show up at the deposition.

If you're a party (plaintiff or defendant), your adversary will provide you a more basic form of notice by mailing you (or your attorney, if you have one) what is usually called a "Notice of Deposition." (See Sample Form #4 in Appendix 3.) No subpoena is necessary to require a party to attend a deposition.

2. Significance of a Deposition Notice

Whether you're a party or a nonparty witness, you must comply with a deposition notice. As a party, if you fail to cooperate, you can be "sanctioned" (penalized) by a judge for failing to appear at the time and place established in the Notice of Deposition. The sanction can range from a monetary fine that you must pay to your adversary to dismissal of your legal claims or defenses if you repeatedly fail to attend.

Though a Notice of Deposition is somewhat informal, a subpoena is a court order. If you are a nonparty witness and you fail to obey a Subpoena re Deposition, you can be held in "contempt of court" (in violation of a court order) and a bench warrant can be issued for your arrest. And if a judge finds you to be in contempt of court, you may be ordered to pay a chunky fine.

3. Contents of a Deposition Notice

Whether you receive a Notice of Deposition or a Subpoena re Deposition, the document will indicate the place and time of your deposition. In addition, both forms of notice generally include the following information:

- The name, telephone number, and address (including probably the email address) of the attorney taking the deposition, and which party the attorney represents (for example, "Attorney for Plaintiff").

- The title of the court in which the lawsuit is pending (for example, "Central District Court, Cook County").

- A "caption" indicating the names of the parties (for example, *"York vs. Lancaster"*) and the official case number.

- Whether you are to bring documents to the deposition. For party deponents, this information may be included in the notice or in an attached separate document often called a "Request for Production of Documents." For nonparty deponents, this information will be included in a form of subpoena usually called a "Subpoena Duces Tecum re Deposition." (See Sample Form #2 in Appendix 3.)

- Whether the deposition will be audio or video recorded instead of (or, more likely, in addition to) being transcribed by a court reporter (stenographer).

- Where the deposition will be held. Usually, the attorney who schedules a deposition holds it on his or her home turf, in a conference room in the attorney's law offices. However, an attorney might also take a deposition in a conference room provided by a court reporting service, especially if the deposition will require equipment which the deposing attorney lacks (such as a videotape setup or a video-conferencing facility for a "remote" deposition).

C. Deposition Scheduling Requirements

The sections below describe the rules that parties must follow when serving deposition notices.

1. Travel Requirements

As a general rule, as a nonparty witness you can't be forced to attend a deposition more than 100 miles away from your home or place of business. (FRCP 45(c)(3)(A)(ii).) Parties may have to submit to depositions in more distant locales. If you're a party and you think that having to be deposed in a distant locale will cause you an undue burden or financial hardship, however, see Section D, below.

2. Length of Advance Notice

Whether you are a party or nonparty witness, a deposition notice must give you "reasonable" advance warning that your deposition is to be taken. (See FRCP 30(b)(1).) Although there is no precise definition of "reasonable," except in rare cases of emergency, fewer than ten days notice is probably unreasonable. As a courtesy, many deposing lawyers will contact you or your attorney (if you have one) before scheduling your deposition to ensure that the chosen date is convenient.

3. Witness Fees

If you're a party, you are not entitled to any payment for testifying at deposition.

If you're a nonparty witness, you can be paid, but in most localities you'll receive a pittance (perhaps $40) as a witness fee, often accompanied by one-way mileage from your home to the deposition site (at a rate of about 30¢ per mile).

Normally, a check for your witness fee will be attached to the Subpoena re Deposition. If not, demand your witness fees from the person who serves you with the subpoena. If your demand for payment is ignored at the time of service, repeat the demand when your deposition begins. If you are again turned down, you may refuse to testify until the fee is paid.

Expert Witness Fees

Unlike ordinary nonparty witnesses, if you've been retained as an expert, you are entitled to your "usual professional fees" for the time you spend testifying at deposition. Experts' deposition fees may amount to hundreds of dollars per hour. For additional discussion of expert witness fees and expert deponents in general, see Chapter 8.

D. Rescheduling Your Deposition

If the chosen date, time, or place of your deposition is inconvenient, you can usually get it changed. To do so, contact your attorney, if you have one. If you're not represented by an attorney, contact the attorney who will depose you. (Remember, the attorney's name and telephone number will be on the Notice of Deposition or the Subpoena re Deposition.) Tell the attorney why the chosen date, time, or place is inconvenient. If possible, suggest alternatives that will work for you. Attorneys routinely agree to requests to change inconvenient deposition arrangements if you ask far enough in advance and have a reasonable justification for making the request. (Examples of a reasonable justification would include a previously scheduled vacation or an important business meeting.)

If the deposing lawyer refuses to change the deposition arrangements, send the lawyer a letter (or email message) explaining why you want to change the deposition arrangements. If you believe that the deposition notice failed to comply with any of the requirements described in Section C, above (for example, you were given only five days advance notice), your letter should state that as well. Finally, state that you will not appear for the deposition. Keep a copy of the letter for your files.

Sample Letter to Schedule Your Deposition

October 21, 20xx

Dear Mr. Blasi,

This letter is to follow up on our telephone conversation of a couple of days ago. In that conversation, I told you that I am not able to appear for a deposition next Wednesday, October 28. As I told you, I had previously scheduled an important business meeting with three other people on that date, and it simply cannot be rescheduled.

In addition to the inconvenience of the October 28 date, I was served with a subpoena on October 20, only eight days before I was supposed to be deposed. I don't think that's reasonable advance notice, especially for a businessperson such as myself.

I repeat here what I told you on the phone. I will make myself available for a deposition if you give me reasonable advance notice, especially if you select any of the dates discussed: November 17 or 18 or December 1 or 2. Otherwise, please be advised that I will not appear for a deposition on October 28.

Sincerely,

Carson Taylor

Carson Taylor

Such a letter may finally convince the deposing lawyer that you are serious. If so, the lawyer may agree to reschedule your deposition. However, if the lawyer continues to refuse to change the date and you don't appear, the lawyer might go to court and ask a judge to sanction (penalize) you for failing to show up. (See Section B2 for more on sanctions.)

If you do not want to run this slight risk of incurring sanctions, you can go to court before the scheduled deposition date and seek a "protective order" rescheduling your deposition. A protective order is an order that a judge may make to protect any party or person from "annoyance, embarrassment, oppression, or undue burden or expense" in connection with any discovery procedure, including depositions. (See FRCP 26(c). For more information about how to seek a protective order, see Chapter 10.)

Example

You observed an automobile accident while on vacation in Florida and gave your name and address to a police officer. Several months after returning home to New York, you receive a Subpoena re Deposition ordering you to attend a deposition in Florida. The subpoena is invalid under Florida Rule of Civil Procedure 1.410, which provides that you can be subpoenaed for examination only in the county where you reside or are employed.

First, you should contact the party that subpoenaed you and indicate that you will not attend the deposition. The party might respond by offering to reimburse you for any expenses you *incur in traveling to Florida. You are free to accept or reject the offer. If you reject the offer to go to Florida, the party could come to New York and subpoena you under New York state law.*

If the party insists that you come to Florida at your own expense, you have the right to ignore the subpoena and simply fail to show up. Or you could retain a Florida attorney and have the attorney move to "quash" the subpoena (have it declared invalid). The order should be granted, and you should be reimbursed for your attorney's fees.

E. Avoiding a Deposition Altogether

As a nonparty witness, you may believe that you shouldn't be deposed at all. For example, you may know so little about a case that a deposition is likely to waste everyone's time, most of all yours. If so, your best bet is to contact the attorney who issued the subpoena and try to discuss the case informally. (Send an email, fax, or letter if the attorney doesn't return your calls.) Attorneys usually don't want to waste their time and their clients' money taking unproductive depositions. An informal interview may convince the attorney that you are not worth deposing.

If after discussing what you know with the attorney—or unsuccessfully attempting to do so—the attorney insists on deposing you, you may refuse to appear for your deposition. However, you run a substantial risk that a judge will hold you in contempt of court. Therefore, you should probably seek legal advice before refusing to be deposed at all. Alternatively, you could go to court and seek a protective order relieving you from having to be deposed.

Example

An independent bookseller has brought suit for unfair business practices against All Books, a book wholesaler, claiming that All Books discriminates against the independent bookshop and in favor of a nearby recently opened bookstore that is part of a national bookstore chain. All Books notices the deposition of Fay Perback, who owns the only other independent bookshop in town.

Since she orders books from a different wholesaler, Fay has no involvement in the lawsuit and knows nothing about it. Fay thinks that the only reason All Books wants to depose her is to get back at her for not doing business with All Books by exposing her business practices to the other bookstores, making it more difficult for her to compete.

If the deposing lawyer refuses Fay's request to cancel her deposition, Fay may go to court and seek a protective order. Fay would explain to the court her lack of information and how her answers to deposition questions would waste her time and hurt her business. If the wholesaler can't satisfactorily explain to a judge what information Fay has that might have a bearing on the case, the judge will quash the subpoena and order that Fay's deposition not be taken.

F. Duration of Depositions

If you are a party to a lawsuit, FRCP 30(d)(2) limits your deposition to "one day of seven hours" unless the time is extended by a court order or you agree to a longer deposition. The seven-hour limit does not include breaks for lunch or recesses for the participants to stretch their legs, make phone calls, or see to other personal needs.

If you are a nonparty deponent, your deposition may last more than seven hours if all the parties agree to an extension or if a court orders a longer deposition. Even though you are the deponent, you do not have the power to prevent the parties from agreeing to extend your deposition. The length of your deposition might vary greatly depending on the complexity of the case and the importance of your testimony, among other things.

Even if your deposition will last longer than a day, you won't necessarily have to be closeted away from your daily life for several days in a row. For example, even if your deposition is scheduled to extend over three days, you might arrange to testify only one day per week for three different weeks if that is all you can fit into your schedule.

If you believe that a deposition is dragging on longer than you expected (perhaps the deposing lawyer shows up to take your deposition carrying pajamas and a toothbrush), you should ask the deposing lawyer how much longer it will last. If the lawyer is evasive or refuses to be pinned down and you have important scheduling conflicts—for example, you're a physician with patients to treat or a parent who must attend a parent-teacher conference at your child's school—politely indicate when you have to leave and when you might be available in the future for additional questioning. If you sincerely believe that you have answered all relevant questions repeatedly and the deposing lawyer is prolonging your deposition excessively, you might consider simply leaving. However, be aware that a lawyer who thinks you are trying to avoid answering important questions might respond by asking a judge to hold you in contempt of court.

What to Do When a Deposing Lawyer Prolongs Your Deposition

If you believe that a deposing lawyer is prolonging your deposition in bad faith (say, by repeatedly asking about things that have nothing to do with the case or by going over the same ground again and again), you can go to court and ask a judge to issue a protective order to stop further questioning. Or, you could simply tell the lawyer that you'll continue with the deposition for a limited amount of additional time only. For example, you might say: "This is the second day of this deposition, and for the last two hours you've been asking about stuff that has nothing to do with the case. I'm willing to stay for another two hours, but that's it."

However, you shouldn't threaten to walk out without good reason. If a judge thinks that you're trying to avoid answering key questions or that you're being excessively impatient or thin-skinned, he or she can require you to reimburse the deposing party for the costs and attorney fees it has to spend seeking a court order to resume your deposition.

G. Deposition Attendees

Who are the people you will encounter in the world of depositions? This section looks at all the significant players who typically are present (and sometimes not present) at a deposition.

1. The Deponent

The star of the show is the deponent, who may be a party or a nonparty witness who has information concerning the parties' dispute. The deponent's testimony will typically influence both parties' strategies for reaching a settlement or going to trial. (See Chapter 2 for information on how deposition testimony is used in litigation.)

2. The Parties

A party can be compelled to attend his or her own deposition when scheduled by the other party. In addition, unless one party gets a court order to bar the other party from attending, parties also have the right to attend all other depositions, which they sometimes do. (You should almost always do so if you are representing yourself.) Parties foot the bills and may want to know how their lawyers are spending their money. Also, a party may want to voluntarily attend a deposition for any of the following reasons:

- The party wants to lend moral support to a deponent who supports the party's version of events or who is a friend or family member. For example, in a personal injury case, a plaintiff (the party suing) may attend her husband's deposition taken by the defendant (the party being sued) if her husband was a passenger in the car at the time it was struck by the defendant's car.

- The party wants to watch the deposition of a deponent who supports the opposing party in order to evaluate the deponent's demeanor and persuasiveness. This evaluation can help the party decide whether to agree to a settlement or go to trial. For example, a personal injury plaintiff might attend the deposition of the defendant's expert witness accident reconstruction in order to evaluate how persuasive the expert's opinions about how the accident took place might be to jurors.

- The party is quite familiar with the issues involved in a case and wants to be able to suggest questions to his or her attorney during breaks in the deposition. For example, assume that the party is a loan officer who is suing the bank that formerly employed her for wrongful termination. The party might attend a deposition of her former supervisor and suggest follow-up questions based on her intimate knowledge of the bank's loan procedures.

- The party is representing him- or herself and may be either the deposing party (the party who arranged for the deposition and conducts most of the questioning) or the defending party (the party who observes and can participate in a deposition arranged for by the other party).

Why a Court Might Bar a Party From a Deposition

A court might prevent a party from attending a deposition if (1) the party is a prisoner; (2) the party has previously harassed and threatened to harm a deponent; or (3) the party is the deponent's business competitor who could use knowledge of the deponent's trade secrets gained by observing the deposition to harm the deponent's business. A party seeking to bar the opposing party's attendance would have to obtain a court order in advance of the deposition. However, since parties presumptively have a right to observe all depositions, it is rare that a judge will bar a party from observing a deposition.

---

3. Experts

A party who has retained an expert witness may bring that expert to observe the depositions of other witnesses. The expert can suggest questions to the party who retained him or her, and can learn factual information to support his or her opinions. For example, in a personal injury case, the accident reconstruction expert for the plaintiff (the party suing) might attend a deposition of the accident reconstruction expert for the defendant (the party being sued), both to suggest questions for the plaintiff's lawyer to ask based on areas of weakness andto find out if the defendant's expert is basing opinions on information not known to the plaintiff. Or a defense medical expert in a medical malpractice case may attend the plaintiff's deposition taken by the defendant to observe the plaintiff's present physical condition first hand.

4. Lawyers for the Parties

Almost always, lawyers representing the two opposing parties will be present at a deposition—one side deposing, the other side defending. If a lawsuit involves many parties (as may occur in lawsuits involving complex property or civil rights issues, for example), the room may be crawling with "Esquires."

Should My Lawyer Attend All Depositions?

If you're a plaintiff or defendant who's represented by a lawyer, you may wonder if you really need to pay for your lawyer's time to defend a deposition taken by the opposing side of a nonparty witness (for example, a bystander to an accident). Normally, the answer is yes, for the following reasons:

- Your lawyer's presence can help ensure that your adversary's lawyer doesn't use overbearing tactics to goad a helpful but timid witness into changing his or her story.

- Your lawyer can make legal objections to improper questions and, by doing so, can preserve those objections if you go to trial. (See Chapter 10 for further discussion of objections.)

- After your opponent's lawyer concludes the deposition, your own lawyer can also question the deponent. Your lawyer thus has a chance to try to elicit helpful testimony that your opponent's lawyer missed or clarify events that became muddled during the opposing lawyer's questioning. At first blush, you might wonder why this is necessary. After all, if your opponent's lawyer misses asking about information that's favorable to you, you may think, "Great, we'll surprise them with it at trial." Think again. Especially if you hope to convince your adversary to settle, having your lawyer bring out additional favorable evidence during a deposition can be quite helpful.

Despite these potential advantages, your lawyer and you may decide that, if a witness has no important information about the case, the lawyer will not defend a deposition taken by your opponent. The reason for such a decision is that you can save hundreds if not thousands of dollars by not paying for your attorney's time to observe depositions. Even if neither you nor your lawyer attends, you can find out what a deponent had to say by purchasing a copy of the deposition transcript from the court reporter who records it. (See Section 6, below, for more on the court reporter.)

5. Lawyers for Nonparty Witnesses

Nonparty witnesses, such as a bystander who observed an auto accident or an employee who overheard an argument between a supervisor and a former employee suing for wrongful termination, have the right to be represented by an attorney of their own choosing when they are deposed. Nonparty witnesses exercise this right rarely. Normally, with little or no stake in a case's outcome, nonparty witnesses have little incentive to pay a lawyer by the hour to sit through a deposition.

If you are a nonparty witness, however, you may want to consider hiring an attorney to attend your deposition in some instances. Here are some circumstances in which, if you are subpoenaed, you may want to ask an attorney to accompany you to a deposition:

- You fear that you might be named as a defendant in the same or a later civil lawsuit, by the same or a different plaintiff. For example, your employer has been sued based on your alleged carelessness or other misconduct.

Example

You work for a piano moving company that has been sued by a homeowner after the piano you were moving careened down a long flight of stairs into the homeowner's garage and car.

- A party (such as your employer) has asked—or strongly suggested—that you lie during your deposition. You are worried that the party will eventually try to shift blame to you, or that perjury charges will be filed against you if you go along with the request.

Example

You supervised a former employee who is now suing your employer for wrongful termination. Your employer has suggested that you testify untruthfully to corroborate the employer's claim that the former employee was insubordinate.

- Criminal charges might be filed against you or someone close to you as a result of the same claims involved in a civil lawsuit.

Example

A city has filed a civil suit against your employer, a contractor, to recover money that the city paid for work that the contractor falsely claimed had been done. Criminal fraud charges may also be filed against several employees, based on the same alleged misdeeds.

In each of these situations, you may want to review your options with an attorney prior to being deposed and possibly have the attorney accompany you to the deposition. In addition to consulting with you during deposition recesses, your attorney can also help protect your legal rights. For example, your attorney can advise you of your Fifth Amendment right not to answer a question if that answer could incriminate you.

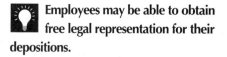
Employees may be able to obtain free legal representation for their depositions.

If your employer is being sued and you receive a deposition notice, you may be able to secure free legal representation at the deposition. Advise your supervisor or your employer's in-house legal counsel that you've received a Subpoena re Deposition and that you'd like the employer to provide you with legal representation at the deposition. Although the employer is not legally obligated to agree to your request, many employers will be happy to ask the lawyer handling the case on the employer's behalf to represent you as well. You and the employer may share the same interests, so you both benefit if a lawyer helps you prepare for your deposition and represents you at the deposition.

6. The Court Reporter

The court reporter places you under oath (makes you swear to tell the truth under penalty of perjury) and records all questions, answers, and comments for the duration of the deposition. Most court reporters transcribe testimony on stenography machines or computers, though some will also audiotape in case they miss a bit of testimony. Within a few weeks after a deposition concludes, the court reporter will prepare a word-for-word transcript of the deposition in a booklet, which you will be asked to review (see Section I).

If a deposition will be videotaped, the court reporter may also operate the video camera and tape machine. Other times, a separate video operator will be present. (See Chapter 14 for more information on videotaped depositions.)

7. Judges

Judges almost never attend depositions. In rare instances, judges appoint judicial officers known as "referees" or "special masters" to preside over depositions. This may happen when one party goes to court claiming that the other party has repeatedly failed to follow proper deposition procedures. If a judge agrees, the judge may appoint a special master to sit in on future depositions and enforce proper procedures. (The judge will also decide which party or parties will pay for the costs of the special master.)

8. The Deponent's Friend or Relative

If you're a deponent, you can probably bring a friend or relative along to a deposition for emotional support. You could do this at trial and, under FRCP 30(c), deposition examinations are supposed to proceed "as permitted at the trial." Even in a locality where the right to have a supporter attend is unclear, the deposing attorney will likely agree to a polite request, especially if the deponent is a child, is infirm, or otherwise may have difficulty testifying without a support person in attendance. The companion may not, however, help the deponent answer questions.

 Don't reveal confidential information to a companion.

Deponents who bring a companion along to a deposition have to be careful about what they say to the companion before and during breaks in the deposition. The deposing lawyer can and sometimes does present a Subpoena re Deposition to the companion, asking the companion to reveal what the deponent said. What deponents say to their attorneys is protected from disclosure by the attorney-client privilege, and, in many states, what one spouse says to another is protected by the spousal privilege. However, no general "friend" or "relative" privilege exists—which means your case-related conversations with a companion are fair game for the opposing lawyer.

9. Other Observers

Under FRCP 30(c), other potential witnesses in a case also have the right to attend depositions. For example, assume that a former employee sues a former employer for age discrimination. The former employee's supervisor would be entitled to attend the employee's deposition, even if the supervisor would be a likely witness if the case went to trial.

In some jurisdictions, even the press and members of the public may be present at depositions. Given the entertainment value of a typical deposition, however, this rarely happens.

Of course, judges have the power to issue protective orders to prevent potential witnesses, the press, and members of the public from attending depositions. For example, if in a widely-reported case, the president of the U.S. or a major rock star were about to be deposed, almost certainly a judge would agree to issue a protective order limiting attendance to the parties and their attorneys.

H. Document Production at Depositions

A Notice of Deposition or Request to Produce Documents (for parties) or a Subpoena Duces Tecum re Deposition (for nonparty witnesses) may indicate that you are to bring designated documents or records to a deposition.

Example

A deposition notice may state as follows: "Deponent Anne Oying is to bring with her to the deposition the following documents and records: all reports, memoranda, records, or documents of any kind in the (employer's) possession relating to the dismissal of Mal Treeted."

If the document request is clear and relatively easy to comply with, simply show up with the documents. Bring original documents if you have them, but do not allow the deposing party to keep the originals. If the deposing party wants to keep a document, ask the party to make a copy of the document and return the original to you.

 Know the rules before turning over documents.

If you've been asked to bring documents to your deposition, be sure to read Chapter 3 before reviewing those documents or bringing them to the deposition. The document request may be improper under the rules of the discovery process, or some of the requested documents may be "privileged" and therefore shielded from disclosure—protected from having to be disclosed.

I. Reviewing and Signing Your Deposition

Some days or weeks after your deposition, the court reporter will make a written, word-for-word transcript of your deposition testimony, which you must review, correct, and return within a set period of time. For procedures relating to reviewing and correcting the written transcript, see Chapter 4, Section H. ■

Chapter 2

Using Depositions in a Lawsuit

Attorneys put depositions to an impressively large number of different uses. This chapter highlights the most common uses of depositions. Knowing how and why depositions are used should help you to understand why you're being deposed, why it's important for you to testify as fully and accurately as you can at your deposition, and why your testimony is likely to be important to a case's outcome whether or not it goes to trial.

A. Using Depositions Before a Trial

Only a small percentage of lawsuits ever make it to an actual trial—a salmon probably has a better statistical chance of finding its spawning ground than a civil lawsuit has of seeing a courtroom. Therefore, if viewed solely as preparation aids for a trial, depositions and other pretrial discovery tools would seem to be of little value. But this misses the point: A major reason why such a small percentage of cases goes to trial is that the exchange of information during discovery often makes going to trial unnecessary. The sections below illustrate the typical uses of depositions before a trial.

1. Summary Judgment Motions

"Summary judgment" is a procedure in which a party files a written "motion" (a formal request for a legal ruling) in court asking the judge to terminate the lawsuit before it goes to a full trial. (Summary judgment procedures are set forth in FRCP 56; most states have very similar rules.) To succeed with a summary judgment motion, a party typically has to convince a judge that:

- no important disputes over the facts of the case exist, and
- under the law that applies to the undisputed facts, the party asking for summary judgment is entitled to a ruling in that party's favor.

Example

Evan Elpus has sued Mackrosoft for breach of contract, claiming that Mackrosoft reneged on a deal to purchase a computer software program that Elpus developed. If Elpus has undisputed factual evidence that Mackrosoft agreed to buy Elpus's program, Elpus can file for summary judgment. If a judge agrees that the evidence is undisputed and if applicable contract law principles support Elpus's claim, the judge should decide the case in Elpus's favor without a trial.

As you can see, a key part of getting a judge to grant summary judgment is to convince the judge that the important facts in a case are undisputed. To do this, parties seeking summary judgment frequently rely on the depositions of key witnesses, as well as on "affidavits" (sworn statements) and documents. In Evan Elpus's case against Mackrosoft, for instance, Elpus might attach the following evidence to his summary judgment motion:

- An excerpt from the deposition of Jenny Daynow, a Mackrosoft vice president, in which Daynow testified that she has the authority to purchase computer programs from software developers and that one of the signatures on a contract with Evan Elpus entitled "Agreement for Software Purchase" is hers.

- Elpus's affidavit in which Elpus asserts that the second signature on the Agreement for Software Purchase is his, and that he signed the agreement immediately after Daynow signed it.

- The signed Agreement for Software Purchase.

Of course, the testimony in depositions can also be used by a party opposing summary judgment. Parties seeking to prevent judges from granting summary judgment motions typically try to show that important factual disputes exist. And attaching excerpts from deposition testimony to what is called a "Motion in Opposition to Summary Judgment" is a typical way that a party seeking to prevent summary judgment establishes the existence of serious factual disputes.

For example, seeking to prevent summary judgment in the Evan Elpus case, Mackrosoft might attach to its opposition motion an excerpt from the deposition of Mackrosoft's president Noah Way, in which Way testified that Mackrosoft had fired Jenny Daynow two months before the date of the Elpus agreement, so she

had no authority to make the deal with Elpus. Another way that Mackrosoft might oppose summary judgment would be to claim that Elpus breached (violated) the agreement himself by being unable to deliver full title ownership of the software program to Mackrosoft. To support this claim, Mackrosoft might attach to its opposition motion excerpts from the deposition of Sara Yayvo, in which she testified that she was a 50% owner of the software program and did not agree to sell it to Mackrosoft.

Why Judges Don't Just Decide Factual Disputes

Judges don't decide factual disputes when ruling on summary judgment motions for two primary reasons. First, since the evidence is all on paper, judges don't have a chance to evaluate witnesses' credibility—for example, who is more reliable if the deposition testimony of two witnesses contradict each other. Second, in many types of civil cases, the parties have a constitutional right to have a jury resolve their factual disputes. Thus, judges will not grant summary judgment when important facts are in dispute.

---

2. Settlement Negotiations

Discussing a possible settlement between the parties is a part of virtually all legal disputes. Often, settlement discussions begin well before a lawsuit is filed. (In some situations, legal rules may require a party to try to resolve a dispute before filing a lawsuit.) And often the very filing of a lawsuit may be largely a negotiation tactic, increasing the pressure on an opponent to settle. Even after a case is filed, your local court rules may require parties to attend settlement conferences and sessions with an outside mediator.

As you no doubt are aware, whether (and when) a case settles depends on numerous factors. For example, whether a party is willing to accept less money now in lieu of more money later often depends on whether the party has an immediate need for money, and how much of the more money later will be eaten up by additional attorney's fees. Likewise, parties vary in their degree of risk averseness— their willingness to take a chance that they'll be happy, or unhappy, with a trial's outcome.

Perhaps the most significant factor affecting settlement negotiations, however, is parties' estimates of how a case is likely to come out if it goes to trial. And it's here that deposition testimony is so important, because deposition testimony is typically a party's best crystal ball as to a trial's likely outcome. Not only does deposition testimony give parties a preview of the content of trial testimony, it also gives them a great chance to judge the credibility of witnesses' testimony.

Example

The following example demonstrates how lawyers commonly use deposition testimony to support their negotiating positions. In this *example, the lawyers are trying to settle a personal injury lawsuit growing out of a traffic accident.*

Plaintiff's attorney: *"Look, if we have to go to trial, a judge or jury is definitely going to decide that your client was driving negligently. After all, when you deposed Jo Smothers, a neutral witness with no ax to grind, she said plainly that your client was turned around talking to someone in the back seat instead of looking at the road just before the accident took place. I think that Smothers's testimony will be more than enough to convince a jury that your client was at fault."*

Defense attorney: *"I don't think that a jury will believe Jo. She may be neutral, but she admitted in her deposition that she'd just had several drinks and that the sun was directly in her eyes when she supposedly observed my client failing to drive carefully. Given that the other witness (the person in the back seat) testified in his deposition that my client was looking forward and driving carefully just before the collision, I think that Jo's testimony will count for very little."*

3. Trial Strategy Planning

One of the main purposes of the discovery tools, including depositions, is to eliminate surprise at trial. Depositions in particular allow attorneys in civil trials to know before a trial starts not only what opposing witnesses are likely to say, but also the demeanor and persuasiveness with which they are likely to say it. Not surprisingly, then, attorneys often base trial strategy on depositions. For example:

- During a deposition, a witness whose testimony generally goes against the deposing party (the parting taking the deposition) may disclose some information that actually supports the deposing party's case. When this happens, the deposing party can plan on asking questions designed to elicit and emphasize this same supportive information at trial. And if at trial the witness says something that contradicts the deposition testimony, the deposing party can raise the conflicting deposition testimony and offer it into evidence (put it before the judge or jury), with the likely result that the witness will lose much credibility. (See Section B2, below.)

Example 1

In a breach of contract case, Ramirez wants to prove that she and Chang made a deal for Ramirez to supply all electrical contracting services in a housing development that Chang was to build. Ramirez deposed White, a waiter who works in a restaurant in which Chang and Ramirez regularly met to conduct many of their negotiations. White testified at the deposition that at the meeting during which Ramirez claims the deal was made, White saw Ramirez and Chang shake hands and click wine glasses. Since this testimony tends to support a conclusion that a deal was made, Ramirez will plan on asking White to repeat this deposition testimony at trial. If White testifies differently at trial, Ramirez

can offer White's conflicting deposition testimony into evidence.

- If a deponent whom an attorney hopes to use as a witness at trial testifies hesitantly and in contradictory fashion during a deposition, the attorney may decide to limit the deponent's testimony at trial, or even not to call that deponent as a witness at all, if the attorney thinks he or she will hurt the case.

Example 2

In the breach of contract case above, Chang had planned to rely on White as a witness at trial after talking to White informally. When deposed by Ramirez, however, White gave contradictory testimony and repeatedly stated that he was unable to recall many details. As a result of the deposition, Chang may decide not to call White as a witness at trial. (Of course, Ramirez could decide to call White as a witness. Ramirez may be hesitant to do so, however, for the same reasons as Chang.)

- If depositions reveal that an adversary's evidence on an important issue is weak, a party may decide to focus on that weakness at trial.

Example 3

In the same breach of contract case, after deposing Ramirez and requesting Ramirez to bring to the deposition any and all documents in Ramirez's possession relating to the alleged contract, Chang realizes that Ramirez has nothing in writing to support the existence of the contract. As a result, Chang's main strategy at trial may be to argue that the lack of a written contract is strong evidence that Chang and Ramirez never finalized the deal.

4. Witness Preparation

Depositions are prime trial preparation tools for witnesses as well as parties. If you've been deposed, you should review your deposition testimony carefully before testifying at trial for the following reasons:

• Your deposition is likely to be an excellent memory refresher, since you will have given it months (and possibly even years) closer to the actual events than you give your trial testimony. As a result, the deposition may well constitute your most complete and accurate account of events.

• If your trial testimony differs from your deposition testimony, the other party can introduce your deposition testimony into evidence (by reading from the deposition transcript) to undermine your credibility. Of course, your trial testimony should reflect what you believe to be the truth at the time of trial, no matter what you said during your deposition. However, if a conflict exists between your deposition and your trial testimony, you should anticipate being confronted with the inconsistency at trial. Your credibility may then depend on whether you have an adequate explanation

for the conflict. (For example, a judge or jury may accept an explanation such as, "I realized that my deposition testimony was inaccurate when I saw a key document that I hadn't seen at the time of my deposition.")

• Evidence rules generally allow an opposing party to examine whatever documents you look at to refresh your recollection before trial. (See Federal Rule of Evidence 612(2).) Since the other side already has access to your deposition, using your deposition to prepare for trial doesn't create a risk that you will have to disclose new information (your preparation materials) to the other party.

B. Using Depositions in a Trial

Though the statistical probability is low, civil disputes do sometimes result in trials. When they do, depositions often play a prominent role. The subsections below explain common trial uses for depositions.

1. To Substitute for Helpful Live Testimony

Parties sometimes depose "friendly" witnesses (witnesses whose testimony supports their versions of events) when they think the deponent will be unavailable to testify in person at the time of trial. (Attorneys commonly refer to such depositions as "depositions to perpetuate testimony.") For example, a party might depose a

friendly witness who is of advanced age and infirm or who plans to leave the country. If the
case does go to trial, and the deposed friendly
witness is in fact unavailable to testify in person,
the party can offer the deposition testimony
into evidence at the trial. (If you are representing yourself, see Chapter 13 for information on
deposing a friendly witness.)

Federal Rule of Evidence 804(a) and FRCP
32(a)(3) set forth situations in which a deponent is considered "unavailable to testify," meaning that deposition testimony can be substituted
for live testimony. For example, a person who is
deceased at the time of trial is obviously unavailable to testify. So too is a witness who is too
ill or infirm to come to court, or one who lives
out of state, beyond the reach of a state's subpoena power.

Once offered into evidence at trial, deposition testimony stands on an equal footing with
live testimony. In other words, judges and jurors
can consider it just as they consider the testimony of live witnesses. But because evidence
rules are much more relaxed at depositions than
at trial (questions that might not be allowed at
trial must be answered during depositions),
judges sometimes exclude portions of depositions that don't comply with the more exacting
evidence rules at trial.

Friendly Depositions Are Often Videotaped

A party who deposes a friendly witness in
order to perpetuate the witness's testimony for
trial may well decide to have the deposition
videotaped. Videotaping may add several
hundred dollars to a deposition's cost.
However, if a friendly witness has important
case-related information, the party undoubtedly wants to maximize its impact on a judge
or jury at trial. And showing a videotape of a
deponent actually testifying is likely to have
greater impact on a judge or jury than the
alternative—a dry reading of a written deposition transcript. (See Chapter 14 for more
information on video depositions.)

---

2. To Impeach a Witness

When a witness's trial testimony is less favorable
to a party's case than the witness's deposition
testimony, the party can read the conflicting
deposition testimony aloud to the judge or jury
during trial. The process is called "impeachment," because evidence that a witness has made
conflicting statements may cause a judge or juror to ignore the witness's trial testimony, or
even to believe that the deposition testimony
constitutes the actual truth.

The following four-step process demonstrates how a party may use a deposition to impeach a witness. Assume that an adverse witness has testified at trial that "the light for east-west traffic was red when the collision occurred." During the same witness's deposition, the witness testified that, "I couldn't see the east-west traffic signals from where I was standing."

Step 1: The pin down. Often, the first part of impeachment of trial testimony with conflicting deposition testimony consists of "pinning down" (having the witness repeat) the trial testimony. Repetition of the trial testimony prevents the witness from trying to weasel out of the impeachment with an explanation such as, "I accidentally misspoke." To pin down the testimony in this example, the questioner could simply ask a single question:

Q: *The light for east-west traffic was red?*

A: *Yes.*

Step 2: Laying the trap. Assuming that it hasn't already been done, the questioner next has the witness verify the witness's deposition transcript. This stage of impeachment may go as follows:

Q: *I have here a booklet entitled "Deposition of Hank O'Hare." Can you please take a look at it and tell me if you recognize what that is?*

O'Hare: Yes, this is a copy of the deposition I gave in this case.

Q: *That's your signature on page 79?*

O'Hare: Yes.

Step 3: Baiting the trap. Especially in jury trials, an impeacher often wants to demonstrate that a witness about to be impeached had every opportunity to answer accurately at the deposition. To do this, the questioner may review some of the warnings ("admonitions") that the witness was undoubtedly given at the outset of the deposition. (For further information about admonitions, see Chapter 5.) This stage of impeachment may unfold along these lines:

Q: *Mr. O'Hare, you were told that you were under oath when your deposition was taken, correct?*

O'Hare: Yes.

Q: *And that was the same oath that you took today in this courtroom?*

O'Hare: Yes.

Q: *I asked you at the deposition whether there was any reason you could not give your best testimony?*

O'Hare: Yes.

Q: *And you told me that there was no reason, right?*

O'Hare: That's true.

Q: *Your deposition was taken just about six months ago, right?*

O'Hare: *That's about right.*

Q: *And would you agree that your memory of the event was probably more accurate and vivid at the time of your deposition than it is now?*

(A witness who smells that impeachment is on the way may try to weasel out of a "yes" answer to this question. However, the question is so firmly based on everyday experience that an attempt to weasel is likely to further erode the witness's credibility.)

O'Hare: *That's probably true.*

Step 4: Springing the trap. With the groundwork laid, the questioner asks permission to read the conflicting deposition testimony to the judge or jury:

Q: *Your Honor, I request permission to read into the record lines 12 throuogh 16 from page 59 of Mr. O'Hare's deposition.*

Judge: *You may do so.*

Q: *"Question: Mr. O'Hare, what color were the traffic signals showing for east-west traffic at the time of the collision? Answer: I couldn't see the east-west traffic signals from where I was standing."*

Q: *Mr. O'Hare, were you asked that question and did you give that answer under oath?*

O'Hare: *Yes.*

At this point the impeachment is concluded and the questioner might move on to other topics. During the impeaching party's final argument, chances are that the party will refer to O'Hare's conflicting versions of key facts and ask the judge or jury to ignore O'Hare's trial testimony or to believe O'Hare's deposition testimony.

3. To Refresh a Witness's Recollection

It is not unusual for witnesses to suffer momentary lapses of memory while testifying at trial. For example, a witness may be asked about, yet commonly forget, such matters as:

- the date of a meeting or the names of all the people who were present at the meeting

- what the witness did immediately after receiving a document in the mail, or

- the exact words of a conversation.

Evidence rules recognize this human frailty and allow questioners to show witnesses nearly every kind of document imaginable to "refresh the witness's recollection." At trial, depositions are one of the most frequently used memory refreshment tools.

Below is a brief example of how a questioner might use a deposition to refresh a forgetful witness's recollection:

Q: *And do you recall what happened next?*

Wit: *Hmm—we either toured the factory right away or ate lunch first. I'm sorry, I'm not sure.*

Q: Might it help you remember if you looked at your deposition?

Wit: It probably will, since it was taken much closer to when this all happened.

Q: Okay, I'm handing you a copy of your deposition that was taken by opposing counsel. Please read the testimony on page 57 to yourself and see if it enables you to recall what happened next. (After the witness reads silently, the questioner removes the deposition from in front of the witness and then continues.)

Q: And is your memory now refreshed as to what happened next?

Wit: Yes, I remember now. We ate lunch before we toured the factory.

Used in this way, a deposition is a catalyst that jogs a witness's recall of past events. The deposition testimony itself is not read to the judge or jury. An adversary can, however, examine a document that a questioner uses to refresh recollection. (See Federal Rule of Evidence 612(2).) Thus, one of the reasons that parties commonly use depositions in preference to other documents to refresh a witness's recollection is that the adversary already has a copy of the deposition. A questioner who refreshes recollection with a deposition thus runs no risk of giving an adversary access to a document that the adversary could not otherwise see. ■

Chapter 3

Preparing to Give Deposition Testimony

This chapter offers suggestions to help you prepare for being deposed (having your deposition taken). Although preparation for anyone being deposed is similar, this chapter's suggestions differ somewhat depending on whether you are:

- a party represented by a lawyer (see Section A, below)

- a party representing yourself (see Section B, below), or

- a nonparty witness (see Section C, below).

Although you may benefit from reading the entire chapter, if you are pressed for time, concentrate on the section that applies to your situation.

A. Parties Represented by Attorneys

If you are a plaintiff or defendant who is represented by an attorney, you may use any or all of the preparation methods suggested in Sections B and C, below. However, because attorneys sometimes follow idiosyncratic practices when it comes to deposition preparation (and some may even disagree with one or more of the suggestions here), consult with your lawyer before beginning to prepare seriously. Then, together, you and your attorney can work out a joint strategy. (If you are a nonparty witness who will be represented by an attorney at your deposi-

tion, like a party, you too should discuss how to prepare for your deposition with the attorney.)

The following subsections address a few subjects that parties should be familiar with even if they are represented by an attorney. Just as educated consumers often get the best deals, educated clients often get the best level of service from their lawyers.

1. Do Not Discuss the Deposition With Your Opponent

Never discuss your deposition with the opposing party or its lawyer. Instead, convey every communication and request, even one as simple as changing the deposition's date or starting time, through your attorney. Especially if your opponent is also represented by a lawyer, contacting the other party personally can be risky, since even a courteous request may be misinterpreted as an attempt to intimidate the party or evade the rules. And if you end up talking about the case, you may unwittingly provide your adversary with additional evidence to use against you. (To encourage parties to settle disputes, evidence rules generally forbid parties from mentioning settlement negotiations or offers and counteroffers at trial. (See Federal Rule of Evidence 408.) However, to avoid any misunderstanding about whether a predeposition conversation you had was a settlement discussion, leave the communications to your attorney.)

2. Meeting Before the Deposition

If you are to testify completely and accurately at your deposition, you'll undoubtedly need to prepare in advance. As a general rule, therefore, expect your attorney to request to meet with you prior to the date of your deposition. Deposition preparation sessions are legitimate and routine: If you're asked at deposition whether you met with your attorney before the deposition to go over your testimony, you can answer "yes" forthrightly. (See Chapter 4, Section B, for more on how to answer this question.)

At the predeposition meeting, the attorney will probably explain what will happen at the deposition, review important documents that you may be asked about, and discuss general strategies as to how you should respond to deposition questions. Many attorneys like to conduct a short "mock" (practice) deposition, so that you can practice answering the types of questions you're likely to be asked at the deposition. During the practice session, your attorney's questions will probably focus on the details of important events.

Your attorney may suggest holding the predeposition meeting only a day or two prior to the deposition. This gives the attorney maximum time to review the file and be up to speed on the issues and the kinds of questions you're likely to be asked. However, your peace of mind should also be a relevant factor. If you're feeling anxious about being deposed, you might ask to meet with your attorney well in advance of the deposition. At this earlier time, the attorney should be able to review the deposition process with you as well as address and hopefully assuage any concerns that are making you anxious.

3. Responding to Requests for Documents

The Notice of Deposition may ask you to bring various documents along to the deposition. If so, review the notice with your attorney. Your attorney may want to refuse the request (at least in part) on the ground that one or more of the sought-after documents is "privileged" (shielded from disclosure). (See Chapter 7.)

Or, the notice may be so broad or vague that you'll need your lawyer's help to know what to bring. For instance, after reading a notice that asks you to bring "all records and memoranda" pertaining to a particular transaction, you may be unsure as to whether an email message obliquely referring to the transaction should be included. If you neglect to bring a document that the deposing party asks—and is entitled—to see, you may have to return with the documents for an additional day of deposition testimony. By checking with your attorney, you can avoid either unnecessarily prolonging your deposition or unwittingly revealing documents the opposing party shouldn't see.

4. Reviewing Documents

Regardless of whether or not a particular document is one that you have been asked to produce at the deposition, it is important that you not read or review any documents in preparation for your deposition until you consult with your attorney. That's because one of the first questions you're likely to be asked at deposition is the following:

Q: *Prior to appearing for this deposition, did you review any documents in preparation for the deposition?*

If you answer "yes," you will probably then immediately be asked to identify all the documents you looked at. Your adversary may then demand to see all these documents. Since deposition rules normally require you to turn over to the opposing party for examination any documents you use to "refresh your recollection" in preparation for a deposition, this demand is usually proper. In fact, in some states, you can even be forced to turn over a document that would otherwise be privileged and thus shielded from disclosure! To avoid having to turn over a document that your adversary may not otherwise have known even existed, you should not review documents before talking to your lawyer.

B. Parties Representing Themselves

If you are representing yourself in a lawsuit, quite possibly the first thing you'll need to do after receiving a Notice of Deposition is to calm down. Check the time, date, and location of the deposition. Remember that depositions are a common feature of civil litigation; that you have been called for a deposition should be seen as neither unusual nor particularly scary.

However, because what you say at the deposition (and how you say it) can significantly influence whether your opponent decides to go all the way to a trial, as well as the terms of any settlement offer it might make you, good preparation is essential. The next sections present some suggestions designed to help you present accurate and credible deposition testimony.

1. Gathering Requested Documents

Review the Notice of Deposition to determine whether you are required to bring specified documents with you to the deposition. Below are issues to consider when deciding how to respond to a document request.

a. Is the Document Request Proper Under the Discovery Rules?

FRCP 26(b)(2) provides that a document request is improper when its "burden or expense ... outweighs its likely benefit, taking into account the needs of the case, the amount in controversy, the parties' resources, the importance of the issues ... and the importance of the proposed discovery in resolving the issues." Typical examples of document requests that may be improper under this rule include:

- a request that is too vague for you to figure out what you're supposed to bring (for example, "produce all records bearing on important accounts")

- a request that is so broad that you would have to fill a 16-wheeler with records in order to comply (for example, "produce all employee records for the past ten years"), or

- a request that seeks hard-to-find documents that you believe have no relevance to the dispute (for example, "produce the last telephone bill you received before installing the new phone system eight years ago").

In all of these situations, FRCP 26(b)(2) probably makes the requests improper. Your initial response should be to contact the deposing party and try to resolve the problem. For instance, if the problem is that the request is too vague, ask the deposing party to specify which documents you are to produce or to narrow the request to a particular period of time. If you and the deposing party agree on what documents you are to bring, it's best to put your understanding in writing in the form of a letter.

Sample Letter Confirming Agreement on Document Request

September 25, 20xx

Dear Mr. Berger,

This letter reflects the agreement we reached during a phone call on September 22. You agreed that I will satisfy the terms of the document request you made in the Notice of Deposition dated September 12 if I produce the following documents at my deposition:

1. Automobile Lease Agreement dated May 17, 20xx.

2. Repair estimate from Fawlty Motor Coach Repair.

3. Fast Lane Insurance Company Automobile Insurance Policy # 768420.

Thank you for your courtesy and cooperation.

Sincerely,

Hamon Rye

Hamon Rye

If you cannot resolve the problem informally, you should bring to your deposition only those documents that you can identify as reasonably related to the case and called for by the document request. For example, if you think that the request to produce "all employee records for the past ten years" is too broad and burdensome, you might bring the records for the past two years if that is the period of time that seems reasonably related to the dispute.

When you're asked at the deposition which documents you've brought, you should respond by identifying what you've brought and explaining why you haven't brought every conceivable document. For example, if you were asked to bring "all records pertaining to important accounts," you might say something like,

"I brought the records for the Hatfield and McCoy accounts. Those are the only ones I brought, because they are the only ones that seem related to this case, and I didn't really know what you meant by 'important accounts' because we have over 500 accounts in the office."

If your adversary's lawyer wants additional records, you might try again to reach an agreement at the deposition. If you cannot reach an agreement, your adversary will have to go to court and seek an order requiring you to produce additional documents. At the court hearing, you can justify your response by pointing out the vague wording of the document request and why additional documents would have no bearing on the case.

b. Are Requested Documents in Your "Possession or Control"?

When complying with a request for documents, you need gather and bring with you to the deposition only those documents that are in your "possession or control." Your adversary cannot force you to obtain documents that are in the possession of someone who is outside your control. At the same time, it is not legally proper for you to give documents away to other people simply to avoid having to comply with a request in a Notice of Deposition.

Example 1

A Notice of Deposition asks you, the owner or manager of a business, to bring a certain written contract to your deposition. The contract is in the office of your assistant manager in a different city. You would have to bring the contract to the deposition. It may not be in your physical possession, but it is under your control because the assistant manager works for you and your company.

Example 2

Again, a Notice of Deposition asks you to bring a certain written contract to your deposition. After receiving the notice, you remove the contract from a file in your office and give it to a friend or relative. Since you voluntarily gave up possession of the contract after you were given notice to produce it at your deposition, the contract remains in your "possession or control" and you would have to produce it at the deposition. (Lawyers would say you have "constructive possession.")

If you don't produce it, the deposing party will surely ask for its whereabouts. You will either have to reveal that you gave it away after receiving the notice to produce it or lie about what happened under oath. Assuming that you tell the truth, you'll have to produce the document anyway. If you're discovered to have lied, you severely damage your credibility and expose yourself to criminal prosecution for perjury.

Example 3

Again, a Notice of Deposition asks you to bring a certain written contract to your deposition. However, the contract was one of a number of documents that you transferred to another company when you sold part of your business. You would not have to produce the contract at your deposition, since it is no longer in your possession or control.

c. Are Requested Documents Privileged?

You also need not and should not turn over to your adversary any documents that are privileged (shielded from disclosure). Examples of documents that you may have a privilege not to reveal include the following:

- Written communications to or from your lawyer. For example, a letter or email message written by you to a lawyer seeking legal representation or an opinion about the merits of your case would be privileged.

- Written communications between you and your spouse. For example, an email message that you send to your spouse describing some aspect of the case would be privileged.

 See Chapter 7 for a fuller explanation of privileges.

Other documents that may be privileged include a letter from your doctor discussing your physical condition, a document that contains confidential business information known as a "trade secret" (such as your company's confidential list of prospective customers), or even a document that might implicate you in criminal activity. Whether documents can be withheld as privileged often depends on the information contained in a document and the legal and factual issues involved in the lawsuit.

Whenever possible, seek legal advice if you think that a possibly important document you do not want to reveal may be legitimately withheld as privileged. If you decide not to seek advice from a lawyer and are still uncertain as to whether the information in question is privileged, you can address the issue at the deposition itself. Tell your opponent's lawyer on the record (taken down by the court reporter after you've been sworn in) which documents you have not produced because you think they are privileged—without revealing too much of their contents. You and the lawyer may then be able to work out an acceptable compromise.

Be careful not to reveal privileged information.

If you voluntarily reveal privileged information, a court might find that you have "waived the privilege" (given up your right to keep the communications confidential). For example, if, in the course of describing a document you withheld because you think it is privileged, you go into such great detail that you reveal the contents of the document, you might have to hand over that document. Err on the side of less detail. It's better to say "I didn't produce correspondence from my lawyer" than "I didn't produce a letter in which my lawyer told me that he thinks I will make a bad witness and will have trouble proving that I have been injured," for example.

Example

You are suing someone for personal injuries they caused you in an auto accident. You get a Notice of Deposition that requires you to produce "all documents that mention or refer to the injuries you claim you suffered as a result of the accident." (These documents would not be privileged, because when you make a legal claim for personal injuries, you waive [give up] the doctor-patient privilege for written and oral communications between you and your physician relating to those injuries.)

On your computer, you have a copy of a letter you sent to the doctor who is treating you for the injuries caused by the accident. In that letter, you briefly refer to the injuries caused by the accident, and then discuss in detail another personal medical problem completely unrelated to the injuries you sustained in the accident. You have decided not to produce the letter because it contains personal information about a medical condition that has nothing to do with the lawsuit, and you assert the doctor-patient privilege as a basis for withholding the letter. At your deposition, the following exchange takes place:

Q (Adversary's lawyer): *Have you brought with you today all the documents I requested in the Notice of Deposition?*

A (You): *With one exception. I have a copy of all the documents that you asked for right here. But there is one document that I am not producing because I believe it is privileged.*

Q: *And what document is that?*

A: *It's a letter I sent to the doctor who's been treating me for injuries I suffered in the accident.*

Q: *Why do you think it is privileged?*

A: *Because it's a letter I sent to my doctor and it's mostly about a personal medical problem I have that has nothing to do with the auto accident.*

Q: *You say this letter is mostly about an unrelated personal medical problem. Does the letter say anything about the injuries you sustained in the accident?*

A: *Yes, it mentions them just very briefly.*

Q: *All right, let me suggest how we might proceed. Use my copy machine and make a copy of the portion of the letter that refers to the injuries you claim to have sustained in the accident. You don't have to copy the rest of the letter. Or if you prefer, you can read to me the portion of the letter that refers to your injuries. But before you do either of those, I want to tell you that I am reserving the right to go to court later in the case to ask the judge to order you to produce the entire letter if I think I need to see it. Can you copy the letter and cover up the portion referring to your medical problem that is unrelated to the accident?*

A: *Yes. I can do that. That sounds fair to me.*

By voluntarily indicating to your opponent that you are withholding a document because you believe it is privileged, you demonstrate to the lawyer (and later to a judge, if necessary) that you are not trying to hide relevant documents. If you are up front about your reasons for withholding documents, you can probably work out solutions with the adversary's lawyer.

What If You Can't Agree on Document Production?

If you and the opposing side's lawyer cannot resolve a dispute about whether you have to produce a document, rules in some localities allow you and the lawyer to telephone a judge or a magistrate directly from the deposition room and resolve the dispute informally. (The clerk of the court in which the lawsuit is filed should be able to tell you if this procedure is available.)

If you cannot resolve the matter via telephone, or if this informal procedure is unavailable in your court, the lawyer may decide to file what is known as a "Motion to Compel Production," asking a judge to order you to turn over the document. You would have a chance to explain to the judge why you don't think you should have to turn it over, either in writing or at a hearing before the judge. You will, of course, have to abide by the judge's order or face a severe penalty.

After gathering the documents you will produce, make photocopies and bring both the originals and the copies to your deposition. (If the documents are many hundreds of pages or more and you want to save the expense of making copies, it's acceptable to bring just the originals to the deposition. The opposing party's lawyer can then pay for any copies he or she wants.) You will ordinarily be allowed to retain the originals, but you should bring them to the deposition in case the lawyer wishes to examine them.

Also bring with you any documents you are withholding based on a claim of privilege, in case after discussing the privilege issue with your adversary's lawyer you decide to reveal unprivileged portions.

2. Refreshing Your Memory About the Facts

Careful preparation is key to giving a successful deposition. Prepare to testify as seriously for your deposition as you would for trial. Thoroughly refresh your memory about the facts of the case so that you can testify accurately and completely. A deposition is not the time to hide the strengths of your case from your adversary. The subsections below explain the many ways you benefit from being well prepared to testify at your deposition.

a. Obtain a Better Settlement Before Trial

As emphasized throughout this book, cases generally settle before they get to actual trials. The terms of a settlement often depend on the parties' assessments of how a case will be decided if they went to a trial. And your opponent's evaluation of the strength of your case will often depend to a significant extent on its assessment of how persuasive a witness you would be in the courtroom.

If at your deposition you can recall and testify completely and convincingly about the facts that underlie your case, you will tend to convince your adversary that you will make a persuasive witness. By contrast, if you repeatedly respond to questions by saying "I don't recall" or "I don't remember" or, even worse, give conflicting accounts of key facts, the other party may well conclude that you are likely to be an unconvincing trial witness.

Consequently, how much you are offered to settle the case (if you are a plaintiff) or how much is demanded from you (if you are a defendant) may depend on how well you testify at your deposition.

b. Look Better Before the Judge or Jury If the Case Goes to Trial

At first blush, you may conclude that you are better off if you go into a deposition with as little recollection of events as possible. Your thinking may go along these lines:

"If I don't refresh my memory in preparation for the deposition, I will honestly be able to answer with 'I don't remember' in response to many deposition questions. That will prevent my adversary from finding out what I'm going to say at trial or getting me to give answers that might damage my case. So, if right before trial I refresh my memory about the facts that I couldn't remember at my deposition, I can really catch my adversary by surprise."

Unfortunately for you, this strategy almost always backfires. One danger is that your opponent may be able to use your "I don't remember" answers in a motion to dismiss your case before trial, on the ground that you do not have enough facts to prove a critical part of your case. A second danger is that your "I don't remember" responses at the deposition can severely damage your credibility at trial. Assume that at trial you are able to testify to a number of facts that you said you couldn't recall at your deposition. The following example illustrates how your adversary can use your "I don't remember" deposition responses to undermine your credibility at trial.

> *Q (Opposing party's lawyer at trial): When you met with Mr. Jones to discuss your work on the Fletcher file, did you tell him that you had been working overtime to try to get all your work done?*
>
> *A (You): Yes, I did.*
>
> *Q: You're sure of that?*
>
> *A: Yes.*

Q: *Your Honor, I ask permission to read into the record a portion of the witness' deposition testimony. This is at page 35, lines 4 through 7.*

Judge: Go ahead.

Q (Lawyer reads from your deposition):

   "Q: When you met with Mr. Jones to discuss your work on the Fletcher file, did you tell him that you had been working overtime to try to get all your work done? A: I don't remember." That was the testimony that you gave at your deposition about a year ago, isn't that true?

A: *Yes.*

Q: *Now, when you met with Mr. Jones to discuss your work on the Fletcher file, did you tell him that you had completed the yearly report on time?*

A: *Yes, I did.*

Q: *Your Honor, I once again ask permission to read into the record another portion of the witness's deposition testimony, this time at page 35, lines 17 through 20.*

Judge: Go ahead.

Q (Lawyer reads from your deposition):

   "Q: When you met with Mr. Jones to discuss your work on the Fletcher file, did you tell him that you had completed the yearly report on time? A: I don't remember." That was also testimony that you gave at your deposition about a year ago, correct?

A: *Yes.*

In most people's experiences, memory is the opposite of fine wine—it usually grows worse, not better, over time. By claiming to be able to remember details at trial that you were unable to recall a year earlier, you give a judge or jury reason to suspect your answers.

Of course, no matter how thoroughly you review the facts of a case in preparation for your deposition, you will probably have to respond to some questions by saying, "I don't remember." Virtually every truthful witness is unable to answer some of the questions posed at a deposition. If you cannot remember the answer to a deposition question, your oath to tell the truth requires that you say just that. Honestly not recalling is a far cry from choosing to remain ignorant on purpose.

3. Methods of Refreshing Your Memory

Most people have their own idiosyncratic methods of recalling past events. (If you doubt this, consider what you do when you lose your keys.) And, of course, the precise sources you will consult to refresh your recollection will necessarily depend on the specific circumstances of your case. Nevertheless, the following general suggestions may be helpful.

a. Determine the Facts in Dispute

Most lawsuits grow out of parties' disputes about how past events unfolded. For example, in an auto accident case, factual disputes might include who had the green light and how seriously the plaintiff was hurt. In a landlord versus tenant case, the factual disputes might be whether the tenant paid the rent on time and whether the landlord adequately fixed a leaking roof promptly after the tenant complained. In a copyright case over ownership of a computer game, the factual dispute may concern whether the software company had access to the game developer's computer files. Were these cases to go to trial, it would be the job of the judge or jury to resolve the factual disputes by deciding what it thinks is most likely the truth. Similarly, in any settlement negotiations, your adversary and you will likely argue about whose version of the disputed facts is correct.

Consequently, you should begin to refresh your memory in anticipation of your deposition by identifying each of the important factual disputes in your case. For example, in a case involving a lawsuit by a restaurant patron who slipped and fell in a restaurant, a factual dispute might consist of the following:

- **Plaintiff's version of events:** Plaintiff slipped on cheese sauce that had been on the restaurant's floor for at least a half hour.
- **Defendant's version:** The cheese sauce was spilled by a customer just moments before the defendant slipped on it.

This dispute about timing can be crucial, because the restaurant may be liable for the customer's injuries only if the cheese sauce was on the floor long enough for the restaurant's employees to have reasonably been expected to clean it up (or put another way, leaving it on the floor for that long amounted to negligence). That's why the deposing party's questions are likely to focus on key factual disputes like this one.

For example, the defendant may ask the plaintiff questions such as:

Q: *Did you see anyone spill the cheese sauce?*

Q: *How long had you been in the restaurant before you slipped?*

Q: *Did you hear any other customers mention that there was cheese sauce on the floor?*

You may be wondering how a person without legal training should go about isolating the key factual disputes in a case. Disputes are normally evident from such sources as:

- The plaintiff's "Complaint" and the defendant's "Answer" (the pleadings that put the legal machinery in motion). While neither you nor your opponent have to set out your full stories in complaints and answers, they often contain enough information for you to identify the principal factual disputes.

- Settlement discussions, either before or after formal court proceedings began.

- Your opponent's use of other discovery methods. For example, if your opponent sends you a set of "interrogatories" (written questions; see Chapter 9, Section H) emphasizing particular parts of your story, those are the parts that your opponent will likely dispute.

b. Review Documents

Reviewing case-related documents is another way to refresh your recollection in anticipation of your deposition. Documents you'll typically want to look at include:

- letters that your adversary and you have exchanged
- business records relating to the transaction involved in a case
- police reports
- witness statements, and
- your answers to any written interrogatories.

There is no need to try to memorize documents. Simply use them to help you remember what happened. Any detail you recall and mention at your deposition might be the one that helps to resolve an important dispute in your favor.

 Don't review privileged or unrequested harmful documents.

Section B3, above, explained the benefits of preparing thoroughly to testify at your deposition. Reviewing documents is an excellent way to help you recall past events. However, you should expect your opponent's lawyer to ask you to identify all documents you used to refresh your memory when preparing for the deposition. The lawyer will probably then ask to see—and you'll

have to hand over—any such documents. As a result, you should not review the following two kinds of documents:

- **Privileged documents.** Even if a document is privileged, you will have to hand it over if you use it to prepare for your deposition. To maintain your claim that a document is privileged, do not use it to refresh your memory. (See Chapter 7 for more information on privileges.)
- **Documents containing harmful information.** You may have a document that contains information that hurts your case. For example, perhaps you wrote a letter to a friend discussing what you thought were weaknesses in your case. If your opponent's lawyer has not asked you to produce that document at the deposition, do not use it to refresh your memory. If you do, and if the lawyer asks to see the documents you used to refresh your memory, you may have to turn it over.

c. Talk to Other Witnesses

You can also refresh your memory by talking to any eyewitnesses who are willing to talk to you informally. You have the right to ask to talk to these people informally, though you can't compel them to speak to you. Remember, however, that your opponent's lawyer can ask you whom you've talked to about the case, and what you talked about. The lawyer may even choose to depose whomever you identify and find out what you said. Therefore, you should be careful not to say anything to a witness or discuss any facts or legal theories you don't want revealed to the other side.

Example

Your landlord is seeking to evict you for non-payment of rent. Your defense is that, as authorized by your state's laws, you deducted from the rent the amount you paid to a roofer to repair a leaky roof after your landlord refused to do so. After receiving a Notice of Deposition from the landlord, you might contact the roofer to refresh your recollection about the extent of the roof problems and what repairs were done. But don't say anything to the roofer that would give the landlord more ammunition to use against you if the landlord were to depose the roofer, such as telling the roofer about the unauthorized mail-order business you've been conducting in your apartment in violation of your lease.

 Never suggest that a witness conceal or withhold information.

Suggesting that a witness conceal or withhold information can amount to the crime of witness tampering or obstructing justice. And if the judge or jury hearing your civil case finds out that you tried to conceal information, your credibility and that of the witness can be ruined. So if you do talk to witnesses, be careful never to say anything like, "I hope you won't tell the other side anything about what I told you the day after the accident. I just wasn't myself that day, so I hope you'll keep that off the record."

d. Visit the Scene of Important Events

According to an old saying, "seeing is believing." For many of us, however, seeing is also remembering. That's why you may be able to enhance your recollection of important events by revisiting the scene where events took place. For example, you might want to visit the scene where an auto accident took place to remind yourself of the layout of the intersection and exactly how the accident happened. If the scene has changed dramatically since the events took place, or if revisiting it is not feasible, consider reviewing any photographs of the scene taken before it was altered.

e. Make Notes

Most people find it hard to keep detailed information in their heads. Writing down your story can help you retain what you have remembered, recall the order of events better, and stimulate your memory even further. Here are a few steps you can take to maximize your recall of key events:

- As you begin preparation, organize your overall story into a chronological outline. If you are like most people, organizing a story according to when events took place will help you remember those events and recall additional details. Leave room in your outline for additional information. (A computer is ideal for this task, because you can easily insert new information into an existing outline.)

- Write down your version of important disputed events, as well as all the information you can think of that indicates that your version is correct.

When representing yourself, any notes you take in preparation for a deposition are ordinarily protected by the "work product" privilege (covered in Chapter 7). This means that you will not have to turn your notes over to the deposing party. If, however, you bring your notes with you and use them to refresh your memory while testifying during your deposition, you may then have to show the notes to the other side. So if you plan on using notes at your deposition, make sure they do not contain information damaging to your case. Your notes should not, for example, have a section entitled, "The most glaring weaknesses in my case."

4. Deciding If You Want to Volunteer Additional Information

While preparing for your deposition, you should also think about a key strategic decision: Should you reveal information at your deposition even if your opponent's lawyer does not specifically ask you about it? The conventional "lawyer wisdom" is that volunteering information is a no-no. As a result, during predeposition planning meetings, attorneys often instruct their clients, "Do not volunteer information that you are not asked about." In large part, this advice is sound and reflects attorneys' general world view: the less you say, the less danger of getting into trouble.

But it is also true that volunteering information that strengthens your case can often improve your settlement position. This makes sense when you realize that much of the information your adversary will have concerning your version of events is likely to come from your deposition. In short, if you want to strengthen your settlement position by impressing the other side with just how compelling your case is (and what a strong and convincing advocate you are), you may want to make sure that highly favorable evidence makes its way into the deposition transcript.

If you decide that you want information that favors your case to come out at deposition, list that information on a piece of paper and bring it with you to the deposition for easy reference. You can put the helpful information on the record during your deposition in one of the following two ways:

- Mention the helpful information in the course of answering a related question.

Example 1

You are a plaintiff representing yourself in an auto accident case. You contend that the defendant's careless lane change caused your two cars to collide on Delta Street, resulting in your suffering a painful injury. But the defendant claims that your speeding was the cause of the collision. You are absolutely sure that you weren't speeding, in part because you slowed down after your passenger told you, "Be really careful when you get to Delta Street—the cops are ticketing people for speeding on that stretch of road like crazy." You want to make your adversary aware of what your passenger told you, because it suggests that you had a very good reason not to speed.

At your deposition, you are asked, "What were you doing just prior to the accident?" In response, you might say, "I was paying careful attention to the road, because my passenger had just told me to be really careful when I got to Delta Street because the cops were ticketing people for speeding on that stretch of road like crazy."

- If you don't have a chance to mention the helpful information during the questioning, wait until your adversary's lawyer concludes questioning you. Then say something like, "I have some additional information that I'd like to put on the record." You have a right to do this, as long as the facts you present are relevant to the case. Then simply state the additional information that you think helps your case.

Example 2

In the traffic accident case above, assume that you didn't mention the passenger's statement in the course of answering questions. When the opposing lawyer says, "I have no more questions," indicate your desire to testify to additional information, and then state what your passenger told you and how it affected your driving.

Volunteering information has potential downsides. For one thing, it's possible that information you think is helpful to your case may turn out to be helpful to your opponent. For another, you lose the opportunity to surprise your opponent with the information at trial. However, because most cases settle rather than go to trial, the surprise aspect of trial is mostly a fiction. Volunteering evidence you are pretty sure will prove helpful can be an effective way of securing a favorable case outcome.

C. Nonparty Witnesses

Few nonparty witnesses are represented by attorneys at depositions. (If you are a nonparty witness represented by an attorney, follow the advice in Section A, above, for represented parties.) The simple reason is that most witnesses are understandably reluctant to pay for a lawyer when they have nothing to gain or lose from a lawsuit's outcome.

However, not all nonparty witnesses are created alike—they typically vary in their willingness to prepare for a deposition. For instance, as a nonparty witness you may be:

- totally disinterested in a case's outcome (for example, you saw only a portion of an event, have no allegiance to either party, and want no more involvement than absolutely necessary)

- interested in helping one of the parties (for example, you believe that one party is "in the right," and want to prepare for a deposition in order to help that party by testifying completely and accurately), or

- fearful of being named as a party in a future civil or criminal case growing out of the incidents you will be asked about at the deposition.

This section looks briefly at how you might prepare for a deposition from each of these perspectives.

1. Responding to a Subpoena Duces Tecum

No matter how interested you are in a case's outcome, you may be served with a "Subpoena Duces Tecum re Deposition," which requires you to bring the documents specified in the subpoena to the deposition. Despite your nonparty witness status, the deposing party has a right to ask you to locate documents and bring them to the deposition. However, as discussed in Section B1, above, the subpoena may be improper (for example, because it is too vague or too broad), may ask for documents not within your possession or control, or may seek privileged documents. Before producing any documents in response to a subpoena, refer to Section B for information on how to proceed.

You have largely the same rights and alternatives as a party when it comes to withholding and revealing documents. However, a Subpoena Duces Tecum is a court order. Unreasonable failure to comply with it could result in your being held in contempt of court and having to pay the deposing party's expenses for going to court to obtain an order requiring you to comply with the subpoena. Before refusing to produce documents called for by a Subpoena Duces Tecum, therefore, you may want to seek legal advice.

2. Totally Disinterested Nonparty Witnesses

You may have no interest in a case's outcome. That is, perhaps neither you nor anyone close to you has anything to gain from a case's outcome, nor do you feel a psychological affinity for either of the parties. If so, you can keep pre-deposition involvement to an absolute minimum. All you have to do is gather whatever documents you've been asked to bring, and show up at the time and place indicated on the subpoena. You needn't refresh your memory or talk to either of the parties or to their attorneys.

Example

Mort and Bella Adella are in a court battle concerning the custody of their daughter. Mort's attorney subpoenas Pastor Present, the daughter's religious-school teacher, to testify at deposition to the daughter's behavior in Sunday school classes. If Pastor Present has no allegiance to either mother or father, the Pastor needn't look at school records, talk to either party or their attorneys, or do anything else to prepare for the deposition.

3. Interested Nonparty Witnesses

In contrast, you may approach a deposition with an economic or psychological interest in providing one of the parties with as much helpful evidence as you can (consistent with your obligation to testify truthfully) for a variety of reasons. For example:

- Your spouse may be a plaintiff in the case in which you're to be deposed. If so, you'll share in any financial gains your spouse receives through the lawsuit.

• One of the parties might be your friendly next-door neighbor.

• Though you know neither of the parties, what you do know about the case may lead you to believe that one of them is in the right. For example, you may have observed an arrest made by a police officer who has later been sued by the person arrested for using excessive force to make the arrest. Depending on who you think was in the right, you may be interested in seeing either the officer or the arrested person prevail.

If you are for any such reason an "interested" nonparty witness, you may want to thoroughly prepare to be deposed. Section B3, above, describes the steps you might take to refresh your recollection about the facts of the case. For example, you can visit the scene of important events, talk to other witnesses, and review documents. You can also talk informally to the attorney for the party whose position you support and refuse to talk informally to the other party's lawyer.

Though the attorney for the party you support does not represent you, it is proper to meet with him or her and even participate in a mock (practice) deposition. The attorney may also be willing to offer helpful suggestions at no cost to you if you need help understanding or complying with an order to bring documents to the deposition or if you want to reschedule the deposition. However, your conversations with the attorney would not be privileged (shielded from disclosure) because the attorney does not represent you. This means that you can be required to answer questions about these discussions at your deposition.

Nonparty Witnesses Can Meet With the Parties' Attorneys

There is no legal or ethical problem with a nonparty witness meeting with or talking to the lawyer for one or both parties, or talking to an unrepresented party. Unfortunately, nonparty witnesses sometimes create problems for themselves by trying to conceal meetings that are perfectly legitimate but that they mistakenly think are improper.

For example, assume that Vincent, a witness who wants to help one of the parties, meets with that party's attorney to prepare for a deposition. During a practice session, the lawyer conducts a mock deposition in which Vincent answers likely deposition questions. Vincent, however, mistakenly thinks that he shouldn't reveal the practice session to the other side. Thus, when during the deposition, the lawyer for the deposing party asks Vincent, "Did you discuss your deposition or the facts of this case with anyone prior to today?" Vincent nervously and falsely testifies, "No, I didn't." If the predeposition meeting later comes to light, Vincent's credibility may be impaired, to the detriment of the party Vincent wanted to help. Vincent did nothing wrong and should willingly disclose what happened and what was discussed when he met with the party's lawyer.

4. Nonparty Witnesses Who Might Become Parties

When, as a nonparty witness, you think there is a possibility that, as a result of information revealed at your deposition, you might later become a party to a civil lawsuit or be charged with a crime, you may want to hire a lawyer before your deposition. (For further discussion of situations in which you might want to hire a lawyer, see Chapter 1.) You should then handle deposition preparation just as though you were a party. (See Section A, above.) For example, communicate with the deposing party only through your attorney and review what you plan to say during a predeposition meeting with your attorney. If you decide not to involve an attorney, at least prepare for your deposition according to the suggestions in Section B, above.

Example

Dee Minimis is a supervisor on a construction project. Dee was on the job site at the time of an accident in which a bulldozer driver was killed. The driver's family has sued the construction company, and the local prosecutor is investigating to ascertain if any criminal laws were broken. Dee has been subpoenaed to give a deposition.

Dee should consider hiring a lawyer, even if the lawyer for the construction company is willing to advise her. Given the seriousness of the prosecutor's investigation and the fact that Dee was in charge of the project, it's reasonable for Dee to fear that she might eventually be named as a defendant in the civil lawsuit and that criminal charges might even be filed against her. And it's also possible that the construction company Dee works for might try to shift blame for the driver's death to Dee and other employees. If so, the presence of the company's lawyer at Dee's deposition might not adequately protect Dee's interests: That lawyer is there to watch out for the company, not for Dee. ■

Chapter 4

Responding to Questions

Depositions are often stressful. You will be questioned under oath about events that may have happened months ago by a lawyer who may be trying to intimidate you or influence your answers. Factor in that everything you say is being written down (and perhaps videotaped), and you have a recipe for an unpleasant day. This chapter is designed to help you give your best testimony, reduce the stress of testifying, and generally improve your day by:

- offering concrete suggestions about how to respond to deposition questions, and

- previewing questioning techniques that lawyers commonly use at depositions.

A. The Golden Rules for Responding to Questions

You may be represented at your deposition by an attorney, or you may be representing yourself. You may be a party to a lawsuit or a nonparty witness. No matter what your status, however, your deposition testimony is likely to be most effective if you comply with the following three "Golden Rules" when responding to questions.

1. Golden Rule #1: Listen to the Entire Question Closely and Answer Only That Question

After years of ordinary social conversations with friends, most of us develop a habit of anticipat-ing questions. The habit can be so strong that we get impatient halfway through a question and start to answer before it's even completed. Not surprisingly, this means that we occasion-ally answer a different question than the one we were about to be asked.

Example

Q: *What time did you…*

A: *Get to the party? I'd say it was after 9:00.*

Q: *Actually, I was wondering what time you left the party.*

This habit is tolerable (if a bit frustrating!) in social settings. Friends don't hold us to exacting standards; they are not going to later scrutinize everything we say to figure out how to attack it. But at your deposition, you must try to leave this habit at the door. Unless you wait for the questioner to finish a question and limit your answer to that question, you may unwittingly:

- testify inaccurately because you answered the question you thought would be asked rather than the one that was actually asked, or

- volunteer damaging information (or evi-dence that leads to damaging information) that the questioner would otherwise never have uncovered.

Example

Plaintiff Len Scap sued his former employer for "wrongful discharge," claiming that the employer fired him for discriminatory reasons. The employer claims that he fired Len because of problems Len had handling the Shutter account. When he is deposed by the employer, Len's deposition testimony goes, in part, as follows:

Q: *Mr. Scap, did your supervisor Millie Meeter offer to provide you with some help on the Shutter account so that you could make the January deadline?*

A: *Yes. She said that she could assign Matt Finish to work on the account with me.*

Q: *What did you say in response to that suggestion?*

A: *I told Millie that I didn't need Matt's help, that I could handle it myself and get the report done on time.*

Q: *And why did you...*

A: *Actually, I was so far behind on the report that I knew I would never make the January deadline. But I didn't want to work with Matt because we'd had a lot of personal problems in the past.*

Q: *I see. I'll want to know about those personal problems. But the question I was going to ask you was why you told Millie that you didn't need Matt's help in a written note, rather than to her face.*

In this example, Len assumes that the questioner wants to know why he told Millie that he didn't need Matt's help. As a result, Len volunteers that he'd had problems working with Matt in the past, a topic the questioner may never have thought to ask about. By pursuing the topic, the employer's lawyer might learn of additional problems Len had getting along with co-workers. Had Len waited to answer until the question was finished, he probably would have said nothing about past problems with Matt, and the employer's lawyer might never have gotten into this potentially damaging area.

2. Golden Rule #2: Answer Truthfully and Completely

The oath that you take at your deposition is the same as the one you will take in the courtroom, and your obligation to tell the truth at your deposition is also the same as in court. You should testify truthfully for at least three reasons:

- Our country's system of justice is based on honesty.

- If you are a party and your opponent is able to convince a judge or jury that you lied at your deposition, your credibility will be severely damaged, and you may lose the case as a result. Even if your case doesn't go to trial, if your opponent believes he or she can show that you lied at your deposition, he or she knows that you will not make a believable witness and will offer much less in any settlement negotiations.

- Whether you are a party or a nonparty witness, testifying falsely at a deposition could subject you to a criminal charge of perjury. (Realistically this risk is low, but you should be aware of it.)

Stating a conscious falsehood, such as testifying that "the light was red" when you know very well that it was green, obviously violates your oath to tell the truth. But you can also violate the oath in more subtle ways. For example, you violate the oath by claiming memory loss where none really exists. For example, you have testified falsely if you know that the light was red but testify "I don't recall the color of the light." The reverse is also true: If you can't remember the color of the light but you say it was green, that is also false testimony.

Example 1

Bill Clintoff is asked, "Were you ever alone in a room in the Green House with Monica Lupinsky?" If Clintoff does recall being alone with that person, Clintoff violates the oath by answering, "I can't remember."

Example 2

Mike Rohard, who runs a small business, has sued a computer manufacturer for breach of contract for failing to deliver a computer system by the date it promised to do so. Assume that Mike remembers that during a May 4th meeting, the computer company's sales representative told Mike, "We can have your system
installed by September 17th if we can get the hard drives from our overseas supplier before the first of September. If we can't, we may not be able to deliver the system until the beginning of December." The computer manufacturer deposes Mike, and a portion of the deposition goes as follows:

> Q: *Okay, now let's turn to the May 4th meeting. Please tell me what the company representative said at that meeting about when the computer system would be ready?*
>
> A: *Sure. The rep said that the company could have my system installed by September 17th.*

Mike's testimony is an improper half-truth. He testifies to only a portion of the rep's statement, omitting an important qualification—that installation by September 17th was contingent on the manufacturer receiving hard drives by September 1st.

If you're a party, you may be tempted to resort to a half-truth as a clever way of withholding damaging information without literally committing perjury. But the seeming advantages are often illusory. If exposed, a misleading deposition answer is likely to badly damage your credibility with a judge or jury. For example, when Mike Rohard's adversary calls Rohard's deposition half-truth to the judge's attention in a pretrial motion, a settlement conference, or at trial, the judge may conclude that Mike is not trustworthy. And even if misleading deposition testimony isn't brought to a judge or jury's attention, when deciding whether to make or accept a settlement offer, your opponent is likely to consider the effect your incomplete deposition answers will have on your credibility. Consequently, you should follow the golden rule and provide complete answers to deposition questions.

 Conflicting views on giving a "complete" answer.

Some lawyers—at least in some situations—disagree with our advice that you should give "complete" answers. They would advise you to give the shortest possible answer that is technically true. Lawyers who subscribe to this view believe that the risk that a deponent's credibility will be damaged by providing misleading answers (even if technically true) is outweighed by the danger that a deponent will volunteer harmful information in an effort to answer completely. If you are represented by an attorney, discuss this issue with him or her. By and large, we believe that a policy of giving complete and honest answers is the best approach. Put another way, as the whole country saw when President Clinton attempted to seek shelter in technical, strained interpretations of everyday terms, trying to torture the truth often backfires.

How to Correct Inaccurate Testimony Mid-Deposition

At some point during your deposition (whether at a lunch recess or even while you're testifying), you may realize that a previous answer you gave is inaccurate. For example, perhaps you've testified earlier that only Moe and Curly were with you at a particular meeting, and later in the day remember that Larry was also there. You should correct the inaccuracy as soon as possible. (In fact, at the beginning of the deposition, you likely promised to do so, in response to a common "admonition" [warning]. See Chapter 5.) For example, in this situation you might say something like, "I want to correct an earlier answer. Before lunch, I testified that only Moe and Curly were with me at the June 6th meet-ing. I now remember that Larry was also there." If you're represented by an attorney at your deposition, you may want to first tell your attorney that you want to correct earlier testimony. Your attorney may prefer to bring out the correction by questioning you at the end of the deposing party's questioning.

3. Golden Rule #3: If You Don't Understand a Question, Don't Answer It

A common "admonition" (warning) given at the beginning of most depositions reminds you not to guess at the meaning of questions you don't understand. (Admonitions are covered in Chapter 5.) Nevertheless, people routinely disregard this principle. Perhaps conditioned by schoolteachers to believe that if they can't understand a question, it's their fault, some deponents attempt to hide their confusion by guessing at the meaning of a question. As a result, they may unwittingly volunteer information the questioner wouldn't have thought to ask about. Or, they could lay the groundwork for needless contradictions when they answer what sounds like the same question differently at trial. At the very least, incorrectly guessing what questions mean will probably make a deposition take longer.

Example

Gwen Dolen is being deposed in a breach of contract case. The deposing party has been asking her about what took place during a June 6 meeting. Gwen is then asked, "Was anything ever said about hardware requirements?" Guessing that the questioner is still referring to the June 6 meeting, Gwen answers, "No."

At trial, Gwen testifies that hardware requirements were discussed in later meetings. Gwen thereby creates an apparent conflict with her deposition testimony, which may undermine the credibility of her truthful answers to other questions. Gwen would have been better off if

she had asked the questioner to clarify the question. For instance, at her deposition, Gwen might have proceeded as follows:

Q: *Ms. Dolen, was anything ever said about hardware requirements?*

A: *I'm not sure I understand the question. Are you still referring only to the meeting of June 6?*

Q: *Excuse me. I'm referring to the June 6 meeting as well as at any other time.*

A: *We didn't talk about hardware requirements at the June 6 meeting, but we did talk about hardware requirements in later meetings.*

By asking for clarification, Gwen could have avoided creating a possible conflict with later testimony.

 Don't make "off the record" comments.

As a rule, everything you say during your deposition is taken down word for word by the court reporter, including any offhand remarks you may make. For example, assume that you answer a question about what Joe did on a particular occasion and then add a remark such as, "Off the record, the guy was always being a jerk." Sorry, but this remark will appear in the transcript. Only the deposing party can instruct the court reporter to go "off the record," meaning that the reporter will stop transcribing what is being said. When the deposing party says, "Let's go back on the record," transcription will resume.

Also, if you engage in small talk while you're off the record (for example, before the deposition begins or during a break), be aware that when the deposition resumes you can be asked about what you said while off the record. Because of this, don't make small talk about any case-related matters while you're off the record.

The Golden Rule for Making a Good Impression

The impact of your deposition testimony will depend not only on what you say but also on how you say it—the impression you make on the lawyers and others. To be taken seriously, you need to treat the process seriously. For example, don't be flippant or try to make jokes in the middle of your testimony. And dress just as you would for a jury trial. Your clothes needn't be expensive or formal (no need for a pin-striped suit), but you should dress conservatively, as you would if you were going to attend an important business meeting or apply for a loan at the bank.

B. Responding to Common Questions

Though each case is factually unique, lawyers tend to ask certain questions in every deposition as a matter of routine. Often the purpose is to make you uncomfortable or cause you to give an evasive answer. Below is a list of routine ques-

tions which you may be asked and suggestions about how to respond to them.

1. "Did You Meet With the Other Lawyer?"

If you are a nonparty witness, you'll almost certainly be asked whether you met with the any of the other lawyers in the case prior to the deposition. Assuming you did have such a meeting, admit it right away: "Yes, I met with the plaintiff's attorney two days ago." You have nothing to hide; lawyers for all parties routinely hold pre-deposition meetings with witnesses. And during these meetings, it is perfectly proper for a lawyer to prepare you for your deposition. (See Chapter 3 for more on preparation.) The only mistake you can make here is to try to deny or conceal the purpose of the meeting.

Nevertheless, the deposing party may use your predeposition meeting with a lawyer for the other party to try to insinuate that the lawyer used the meeting to put words into your mouth. Your best defense against such tactics is to answer according to Golden Rule #2—answer truthfully and completely.

Example

Q: Mr. Kan, I'd like to return to your testimony that Mr. Dawson used profanity when he criticized Ms. Pines. Before testifying here today, did you meet with Ms. Stark, the lawyer for Ms. Pines?

A: Yes.

Q: That meeting took place in Ms. Stark's office, isn't that correct?

A: Yes.

Q: And during that meeting, Ms. Stark asked you questions of the type she thought you might be asked during the deposition, isn't that true?

A: Yes, Ms. Stark did ask me questions after explaining she thought similar questions might be asked by you today.

Q: And isn't it also true that at that meeting, Ms. Stark told you that she thought an important issue in this case was the extent to which Mr. Kan used foul language in criticizing Ms. Pine?

A: Yes.

Q: She also told you that you should emphasize that Mr. Dawson really did use foul language, isn't that true?

A: No. She told me to tell the truth as best I could. She didn't tell me to emphasize anything in particular.

Q: Well, Ms. Stark commented on your answers to the questions she asked you in her office, isn't that right?

A: Sometimes, yes.

Q: And today when you answered questions about the foul language you claim Mr. Dawson used, you knew from what Ms. Stark said to you earlier what kind of answers Ms. Stark was hoping you would give regarding foul language, didn't you?

A: Well, I knew what the lawsuit was about and who Ms. Stark represented. But I always planned to tell the truth and that is what I am doing.

Q: So when you testified here today, you were saying what Ms. Pine's lawyer wanted you to say, isn't that so?

A: No, that is not so. When I testified today, I was telling the truth as best I could. I believe that some of my answers will help Ms. Pine and Ms. Stark probably wanted to hear those answers. But I was just telling the truth.

In this example, the deponent openly admits to having met with the lawyer for the deposing party's opponent in advance of the deposition to prepare for the deposition. At the same time, the deponent denies that any words were put into his mouth or that he is testifying to anything other than the truth.

2. "Who Else Have You Discussed This Case With?"

Whether you are a party or a nonparty witness, the deposing lawyer is likely to ask you whether you discussed the case and your deposition testimony with anyone other than a lawyer. Again, you have nothing to hide. It is perfectly appropriate for you to talk to a friend or colleague about the facts of a case, including your concerns about being deposed.

Understand, however, that such conversations are not privileged (shielded from disclosure) unless you are talking to your spouse. (See

Chapter 7, Section A, for more on privileged conversations.) Even if you tell a friend something like, "What I'm saying to you is absolutely confidential," the deposing party can require you to testify to what you then said. Likewise, whoever you talked to can be deposed and asked to testify about your conversation. Consequently, especially if you are a party, it's a good idea not to say anything to a friend or colleague that you do not want revealed at a deposition or at trial.

3. "What Documents Did You Review in Preparation for This Deposition?"

The deposing party is very likely to ask you whether you reviewed any documents to refresh your recollection about the facts of the case in preparation for the deposition. It is perfectly okay to do this and does not subtract from your credibility. But if you answer "yes," realize that you will almost always be asked to identify the documents you looked at and to provide copies of these documents to the deposing party.

 Don't review documents you don't want to reveal.

If you are aware of documents that you don't want to reveal and that you think the deposing party doesn't already know about, do not review those documents when you prepare for your deposition. (See Chapter 3 for more on preparing for your deposition.)

C. Responding to Trick Questions

You are the author of your deposition story. This means your testimony should truly reflect your observations, your recollections, your impressions, and your characterizations—in your own words.

Whoever is deposing you, however, may try to become your coauthor by wording questions in a way that gets you to adopt or agree with the deposing party's spin on your story. As you'll see, some of these questioning tricks are legally objectionable. If the opposing party objects to a question, the deposing party probably won't be able to use the answer later in the case anyway. But other questioning tricks are legally proper, which means you'll want to be prepared to avoid the trap. The following sections identify common trick questions and suggest how you might respond to them.

1. Questions That Contain Hidden Assertions

Perhaps the most common questioning trick is to preface a question with an inaccurate assertion. The tactic is legally objectionable. But if no one makes an objection, and you answer the question without stating for the record that you disagree with the questioner's assertion, you might be understood to have adopted the assertion.

For instance, assume that Fred and Ethel are battling for custody of their two-year-old daughter Lucy. When Fred's attorney deposes their next-door neighbor Ricky, the following occurs:

Q: *Do you recall the evening of April 3?*

A: *Yes. I believe that was the night that Ethel came home barefoot and the bottoms of her feet were purple.*

Q: *How did little Lucy react to Ethel's weird behavior?*

Here, the questioner asserts that Ethel's behavior was weird. The assertion is "hidden" because the question doesn't give Ricky a chance to testify to whether Ethel's behavior was weird; the question assumes that Ethel's behavior was weird and asks him to testify only about Lucy's reaction. Thus, if Ricky disputes the conclusion that Ethel's behavior was weird, he needs to voice his disagreement with the hidden assertion. To do so, Ricky might respond as follows:

A: *I didn't say that Ethel's behavior was weird. But if you want to know how Lucy reacted after Ethel came home, I can tell you.*

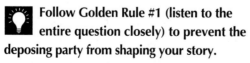 **Follow Golden Rule #1 (listen to the entire question closely) to prevent the deposing party from shaping your story.**

By listening carefully and waiting until questions are finished before you reply, you will be better able to spot hidden assertions and express your disagreement.

Avoid Letting Your Words Be Twisted

One way a deposing party may use a hidden assertion to try to change your story is to substitute the party's words for yours. For example, if you testify that Jones was "in a rage," the questioner may later ask you what happened after Jones became "irritated." Your best approach is to promptly correct the misleading assertion by repeating what you said. For example, you would say, "I didn't say Jones was irritated. What I said was that Jones was in a rage."

Of course, not every substitution of words constitutes a hidden assertion intended to change your meaning. For example, assume that you testify that Jones was "angry," and that the questioner later refers to Jones as "mad." Most people would understand these terms to mean substantially the same thing. Therefore, in this example you would not need to correct the record.

2. Questions Calling for "Yes" or "No" Answers

Many perfectly legitimate (not trick) questions call for "yes" or "no" answers. For example, you might be asked, "Was the light red when the blue car entered the intersection?" If you can fairly answer by saying "yes" or "no," you should do so.

However, the deposing attorney may use questions calling for "yes" or "no" answers in an attempt to unfairly shape your story. Or put another way, if you confine your answer to either "yes" or "no," the lawyer will have succeeded in altering your testimony if neither a "yes" nor a "no," standing alone, constitutes a fair or complete response to the question. If you believe that a completely honest and accurate answer requires you to elaborate on a "yes" or "no" response, you should do so. Following Golden Rule #2, give as complete an answer as you believe is necessary under the circumstances.

For example, assume that you're a nonparty witness in a wrongful employment termination case. Your former coworker has sued the company, and you've been asked the following series of questions by the attorney for the fired employee:

Q: *Had you sometimes disagreed with my client about various job procedures over the years?*

You: *Yes.*

Q: *And over the years, you told a number of your coworkers that you personally disliked my client, is that right?*

You: *Yes.*

Q: *So I take it that you were quite happy when my client was let go?*

You: *I can't really answer that "yes" or "no." We'd had our disagreements and I didn't consider him a friend, but I thought he was generally a good employee and I was sorry to see him lose a job he'd held for so long.*

Although the last question called for a "yes" or "no" answer, you did not confine the answer to one word. Instead, you elaborated in order to give an answer that was fair and complete. You should do the same whenever you believe that a question cannot be fairly and completely answered "yes" or "no."

3. Summary Questions

"Summary questions" typically recapitulate an event or series of events as part of asking you to agree to the summary's accuracy. These questions are perfectly legitimate if they accurately summarize or restate your testimony. However, because almost by definition summary questions tend to be complex, they may contain hidden assertions aimed at reshaping your story. Thus, you have to listen closely to the summary (Golden Rule #1, again) and be alert to inaccuracies. Never agree to a summary's accuracy if it is even partially wrong. Instead, make it clear that at least one element of the summary part of the question is not correct.

Example

You're being deposed by the defendant in an auto accident case, and you have described the events leading up to a car striking a pedestrian. Part of your testimony indicated that the pedestrian was in the crosswalk when struck by the defendant's car. The questioner then asks you the following summary question:

Q: *Let me see if I've got this straight. You were stopped at the intersection waiting for the light to turn green. You saw the defendant's car approach the intersection from your right and begin to make a left turn. At that point, you looked to your left and saw a pedestrian dart into the street, and then the defendant's car struck the pedestrian. Is that right?*

In the above example, the summary contains a hidden assertion that favors the deposing party—that the pedestrian "darted" into the street. Thus, the summary is inaccurate. If you recognize the change of story, you can point it out as follows:

A: *No, that's not correct. I didn't say that the pedestrian darted into the street. What I said was that the pedestrian was already in the crosswalk when struck by the defendant's car.*

But it can be tough to spot an inaccurate statement in a long summary question. (Did you spot it in the example before we pointed it out?) Especially when the deposing lawyer speaks fast, summaries are often too complicated to follow. Consequently, if you have any doubt as to a summary's accuracy, respond along these lines:

A: *I'm sorry, that's a long question and I'm not sure that everything you mentioned was accurate. Can you break it down into shorter questions that would be easier for me to follow?*

4. Argumentative Questions

Argumentative questions consist of the deposing party's argument or opinion about evidence put in the form of a question. A lawyer may ask argumentative questions in an attempt to get you to lose your cool and engage in a war of words that the lawyer expects to win. Alternatively, the lawyer may hope that argumentative questions will intimidate you into agreeing with the lawyer's characterization of the evidence.

Example

Q: *Your recollection, Ms. Smith, is that the light was green for the Ford when it entered the intersection?*

A: *Yes, that's right.*

Q: *Are you aware that Mr. Gillig testified under oath that he was standing only a few feet from the intersection when the accident occurred and that the Ford entered the intersection against the red light?*

A: *I don't know anything about what Mr. Gillig said.*

Q: *Now you admit that you were at least ten yards from the intersection when the accident occurred, correct?*

A: *Yes.*

Q: *Well, I represent to you that Mr. Gillig testified under oath that he was standing only a few feet from the intersection when the accident occurred. Don't you think that means that Mr. Gillig's testimony is probably correct and that you are probably mistaken about who had the green light?*

A: *I don't know anything about Mr. Gillig.*

All I can tell you is, as I said earlier, I clearly saw that the Ford had the green light when it entered the intersection.

Q: *Well surely you will admit that Mr. Gillig had a better opportunity to observe the light than you did?*

A: *I don't know anything about Mr. Gillig or what he had an opportunity to see or not see. I only know what I clearly saw.*

The last two questions in this example are argumentative. The questioner isn't asking the deponent—Ms. Smith—for information. Instead, the questioner is trying to intimidate the deponent into admitting that Gillig had a better opportunity to observe the color of the light than she. Ms. Smith, the deponent in this example, refuses to be swayed. She simply reiterates her previous testimony and refuses to speculate on what Gillig saw. In short, she follows Golden Rule #2 by sticking with the truth.

You may be especially tempted to rise to the bait and argue with the questioner who asks argumentative questions in a snide and aggressive manner. However, the best approach is to respond to the question, not to the questioner. If you lose your cool and respond with argumentative answers, you'll violate all three golden rules and probably wind up hurting your credibility. Moreover, the best way to stop a questioner from asking argumentative questions is to calmly stick to what you know to be the truth.

Responding to Verbally Abusive Questioning

In very rare instances, an attorney's improper behavior may go beyond argumentative questions to verbal abuse. For example, verbal abuse might occur if an attorney repeatedly pounds the table while shouting questions, perhaps laced with profanity and mischaracterizations of your testimony.

You need not put up with verbal abuse. In extreme cases such as these, advise the attorney on the record (meaning that the court reporter takes down what you say) that you will end the deposition unless the abuse stops. For example, you could say something like the following:

"You've been swearing and shouting questions at me repeatedly, pounding the table, and not even giving me a chance to finish my answers. I'm not going to put up with it. If you don't stop immediately I'm going to leave the deposition and I won't return unless a judge orders me to do so. And if you do go to court, I'll show up and tell the judge exactly why I left, because of your abuse."

If you do terminate a deposition based on an attorney's verbal abuse, be aware that the attorney may well seek a court order requiring you to return. If the judge concludes that you terminated the deposition unreasonably, you will probably be ordered to return to the deposition and you may have to pay whatever expenses and fees the attorney incurred in going to court. Consequently, while you should feel free to call what strikes you as verbal abuse to a lawyer's attention, do not walk out unless the attorney's behavior is extreme and repeated.

5. "Is That All?" Questions

Before leaving one topic and moving on to another, a questioner is likely to ask one or more "is that all" questions. For example:

- If you've just identified a number of people who were present at a meeting, the questioner may ask, "Are those all the people who were present at the meeting?"

- If you've just identified the misrepresentations made to you by a salesperson concerning a car's mechanical condition, the questioner may ask, "Is that everything that the salesperson said to you about the car's mechanical condition?"

- If you've just mentioned a number of factors that went into your company's decision to purchase a new computer system, the questioner may ask, "Are those all the factors that went into the decision to purchase the new computer system?"

The usual purpose of an "is that all" question is to prevent you from adding to your testimony at trial. It works like this: Assume that you answer "yes" to an "is that all" question, but at trial you later add information (for example, another misrepresentation about the car or another factor that led to the decision to buy the new computer system). You thereby create a conflict that the opposing party can point out to undermine your credibility.

As a result, if you are not absolutely sure that you have been able to recall all the information about a particular topic, you should respond to "is that all" types of questions by honestly replying that your testimony is your best recollection at present. Your response might go as follows:

> Q: *Is that everything that the salesperson said to you about the car's mechanical condition?*
>
> A: *That's everything I can recall at this time.*

By agreeing only that you can recall nothing further "at this time," you leave the door open for further recollection. Of course, if you really are sure that your testimony is complete and accurate, you should respond to an "is that all" question by answering "yes."

6. "Follow My Lead" Questioning

A questioner adopts what's called a "follow my lead" questioning pattern to try to encourage you to provide the questioner's desired answer. The pattern usually goes as follows:

- **Step 1:** The questioner seeks preliminary information that is consistent with the ultimate answer she wants.

- **Step 2:** The questioner seeks to elicit the desired answer. The questioner hopes that since you've already committed to the preliminary information, you'll take the final step and supply the desired ultimate answer.

Unlike some of the other questioning tricks, a "follow my lead" questioning pattern is perfectly proper—and not legally objectionable. Fortunately, if you simply follow Golden Rule #2—answer truthfully and completely—"follow my lead" questioning will have no effect on your testimony. But tread carefully: Problems can arise when you let the questioner lead you down the path towards providing a false answer. This can sometimes happen if you become so intent on keeping your answers consistent that you agree to something that is not true.

To understand how "follow my lead" questioning may occur, consider the following example.

Example

Mike Asimow is a nonparty witness in an auto accident case. Asimow is being deposed by the defendant, Eric Zolt. The plaintiff is Asimow's business associate, Eileen Johnson, who claims that Zolt's careless driving was the cause of the accident. Zolt hopes that Asimow will testify that when Johnson left the office to go to an important business meeting, she said she was worried about being late. Such testimony would bolster Zolt's argument that Johnson was speeding at the time of the accident, which caused the accident.

To try to elicit this response, Zolt might simply ask a straightforward question such as:

Q: *When she left the office, did Ms. Johnson indicate to you that she was worried*

about being late for an important meeting?

But for fear that this direct question wouldn't produce the desired answer, Zolt might adopt a more indirect strategy by asking "follow my lead" questions in an effort to coax the deponent into providing a different response. To do that, Zolt would ask Asimow to admit preliminary facts that are consistent with Johnson being worried (Step 1). Only after the preliminary facts are on the table would Zolt ask the key question as to whether Johnson really was in a dither about being late (Step 2). The "follow my lead" questioning might go as follows:

Q: *Mr. Asimow, when Ms. Johnson left the office just prior to the accident, where was she headed?*

A: *She was on her way to meet Mr. Trimble.*

Q: *Was Mr. Trimble a potential new customer for your business?*

A: *Yes.*

Q: *Before this, you and Ms. Johnson had tried to set up some other meetings with Mr. Trimble, correct?*

A: *Yes.*

Q: *But was the day of the accident the first time that Ms. Johnson succeeded in arranging a meeting with Mr. Trimble?*

A: *Yes.*

Q: Is it fair to say that this meeting with Mr. Trimble might have been important to your business?

A: I suppose so.

Q: Well, as you just testified, you had tried several times previously to set up a meeting with Mr. Trimble, right?

A: That's true.

Q: And would you agree that to the extent she could, Ms. Johnson wanted to impress Mr. Trimble?

A: Of course.

Q: Ms. Johnson was scheduled to meet Mr. Trimble at 3:00 p.m. on the day of the accident, correct?

A: Yes.

Q: Where was the meeting supposed to take place?

A: In Mr. Trimble's office.

Q: By car, how long would you normally expect it to take to get from your office to Mr. Trimble's office in mid-afternoon?

A: Probably about 20 minutes.

Q: And what time did Ms. Johnson leave the office to go to the meeting?

A: It was nearly 3:00 when she left.

Q: So at the time Ms. Johnson left the office, she was definitely going to be late for the meeting with Mr. Trimble?

A: Yes.

Q: Did Ms. Johnson talk to you just before she left the office to go to the meeting with Mr. Trimble?

A: Just briefly.

Q: And just before she left, didn't Ms. Johnson tell you that she was worried about being late for the meeting with Mr. Trimble?

A: No, not that I recall.

In the above example, Zolt tries to put Asimow between a rock and a hard place. Zolt's series of preliminary questions require Asimow to admit to circumstances suggesting that Johnson would have been worried about being late to the meeting with Trimble. Zolt would hope that the preliminary questions will encourage Asimow to give Zolt's desired final answer, that Johnson stated that she was worried about being late for the meeting.

However, as you can see, Asimow here refuses to be influenced by how his testimony might appear. Instead he follows Golden Rule #2 and tells the truth. Or, put another way, Asimow was not be taken in by the questioner's questions, carefully designed to make the truth seem inconsistent with common experience. Don't be worried if it seems that the deposing party is trying to lead you down the garden path. If you answer each question honestly and don't worry about appearances, you can't go wrong.

In response to a "follow my lead" questioning pattern, some deponents are tempted to argue with the deposing party or volunteer information rather than simply to respond to the question. For example, if Asimow realizes that Zolt wants him to admit that Johnson stated that she was worried about being late for the meeting, Asimow might respond to one of Zolt's questions as follows:

Q: *By car, how long would you normally expect it to take to get from your office to Mr. Trimble's office in mid-afternoon?*

A: *Probably about 20 minutes. But if you're suggesting that Johnson was worried about being late, you're off base. She's always rushing off to meetings at the last minute and it never seems to bother her.*

Here, Asimow does more than answer the question. He also volunteers additional information. While Asimow may think he's helping Johnson, in fact he may be doing just the opposite. Asimow's testimony that Johnson is "always rushing off to meetings" may help to prove that she was in a hurry on this occasion and therefore speeding at the time of the accident.

7. "Don't Throw Me Into the Briar Patch" Questioning

You may be familiar with the story of B'rer Rabbit, who escapes from B'rer Fox's clutches by insisting that the worst harm the fox can visit on the rabbit is to throw the rabbit into a briar patch. Conned into believing this, the fox throws the rabbit into the briar patch, enabling the rabbit to get away.

The point of recalling this fable here is to alert you to another trick questioning pattern: A deposing party may act like B'rer Rabbit, asking questions in a way that makes a particular an-

swer seem harmful to the deposing party's case and helpful to yours. But just like B'rer Rabbit, the questioner may really have a different purpose in mind—the suggested answer, in fact, helps the questioner. The result is, if you answer according to your sense of what kind of answer the questioner wants, there is a good chance you'll violate Golden Rule #2 (answer truthfully), damage your legal position and, just like B'rer Fox, end up with nothing to show for it. Consider the following example.

Example

Dean Lynch has sued Easy Trade, a stockbroker, for improperly advising Lynch to invest in a high-risk investment—buying the stock of a company that makes marshmallows that don't melt in hot cocoa. Easy Trade deposes Lynch and hopes to coax Lynch into bragging about his success as an investor (something many of us have been known to do). Easy Trade hopes to later use Lynch's own words to argue that Lynch was such an experienced investor that he was fully capable of evaluating the soundness of investments on his own, and therefore wasn't talked into making a bad investment by Easy Trade.

Given that Easy Trade knows that Lynch is suspicious of his motives, he tries to carry out this strategy (to lead Lynch to the questioner's desired answers) by suggesting that the desired answers are, in fact, the last thing in the world the questioner wants to hear. This type of questioning by Easy Trade's lawyer might go something like this:

Q: Mr. Lynch, the stockbroker advised you to invest $80,000 in a company that made marshmallows that would keep their shape in hot cocoa, correct?

A: Yes.

Q: But you didn't have an adequate investment background or experience to think this was a reasonably prudent investment, did you?

A: Oh yes, I did. I've had quite a lot of investment experience.

Q: Perhaps. But does that include knowing how to read a prospectus?

A: Of course. I've probably read hundreds of them over the years. I took finance courses in college, and I regularly read various business magazines and papers like The Wall Street Journal.

Q: But can you clearly remember that you carefully read the prospectus for the investment involved in this case?

A: Yes, I read it thoroughly.

Q: Okay, granted you may have some experience with investing, but at the time you made this investment it's fair to say that you had no experience with high-risk investing?

A: To the contrary. I like to read up on "small cap" companies, and since I retired, I have the time to spend looking at Internet sites that have investment information.

Q: Really? Tell me about some of your favorite sites.

A: Well, three that I look at daily include...

In this example, the questioner tries to give Lynch the impression that the questioner wants Lynch to say that Lynch has very little investment experience. Perhaps thinking that he is damaging the stockbroker's case, Lynch gilds the lily and exaggerates his experience. Only later is Lynch likely to realize that by not sticking to telling the truth (Golden Rule #2) and by paying attention to what the questioner seems to want, he made a serious mistake.

8. Leapfrog Questioning

"Leapfrog questioning" consists of shifting from one topic to another, often without any regard to chronology. Leapfrogging can be a symptom of a questioner's disorganization—or it can reflect a questioner's conscious effort to keep you off guard and interrupt your paths of association. While not technically improper, leapfrogging can be confusing and fatiguing as you repeatedly shift your attention from one topic to another.

If your questioner engages in leapfrogging, and particularly if the shifts from one topic to another are so rapid that you can't think straight, attempt to slow the questioner down. One way to do this is simply not to answer a question until you've had a chance to think clearly. (Your delay won't show up in a written transcript anyway.) Another is to simply state that you're not really sure of what a question means or that you don't understand. In either case, follow up by asking that the question be rephrased. Finally, if you find trying to keep up with a questioner's frequent shifts to be fatiguing, ask to take a break or, if it is near the end of the day, to terminate that session of the deposition (see Section F, below).

9. Burying Important Inquiries in General Background Questions

As explained in Chapter 6, most depositions begin with routine background questions. Some attorneys are fond of disguising important issues in what appear to be routine background inquiries. While you may not always be able to spot what will turn out to be important, you should do fine as long as you follow Golden Rule #1—listen to the entire question closely— at every stage in the deposition, even during what seems to be only routine inquiries. Here, of course, the danger is that the seeming routineness of a question may cause you to be inattentive and answer it inaccurately. (Chapter 6 provides an illustrative example of how a lawyer may hide important questions in background questioning.)

D. Responding to Requests for Future Action

Not every key part of a deposition necessarily takes place in the deposition room. The deposing party may ask you to take some future action related to the deposition as well.

Example 1

You refer to a document in the course of answering questions. Your deposition will continue to another day, and the questioner asks you to bring the document to which you referred with you when you return.

Example 2

Just before concluding your deposition, the deposing party asks if you will allow the questioner's associate to inspect a machine located at your factory, to which you referred during your deposition.

Example 3

After you testify that your company's gross sales fell by 30% last year, the deposing party asks what that amounts to in dollar terms. You respond by saying, "I'm not sure, I'd have to check a few records." The deposing party then asks if it is okay with you for the court reporter to leave a blank space at that portion of the deposition for you to fill in after you've checked your records. If you agree, you'd fill in the blank space when you review and sign your deposition transcript.

Start by understanding that a deposing party cannot require you to take any action unless the party complies with formal discovery rules. For example, you can legally insist that a deposing party who wants you to bring a particular document to your deposition serve you with a subpoena or a request to produce documents.

Nevertheless, lawyers commonly agree to each other's informal requests for information. Voluntary compliance is common for several reasons:

- Assuming that the request is valid, the party can probably get the information by following formal discovery procedures. If so, all that a refusal accomplishes is to add to your opponent's burden and expense. And your opponent may respond in kind should you make an informal discovery request or ask for some other accommodation (for example, to change the time or date of a deposition).

- Voluntarily complying with the request may shorten your deposition. For example, you may not have to be deposed on a separate day if you turn over a readily available document at once.

- Complying with the request may make you seem confident in your case by communicating that you have nothing to hide. By contrast, fighting it may simply call attention to a weakness.

Example

Q: *Did you take any notes about what happened in these meetings between you and my client?*

A: *Yes.*

Q: *Do you have those notes with you today?*

A: *No, they are at my office.*

Q: *Could you bring those notes to your deposition tomorrow?*

A: *I thought you were supposed to send me a written discovery request if you wanted documents from me.*

Q: *Well, that's generally true. And if necessary I can send you a formal request for production of documents, which will require you to produce your notes. But then I will have to suspend your deposition until you produce the notes and we'll have to meet again so that I can examine you about the notes. If you produce the notes voluntarily tomorrow, we can finish up your deposition tomorrow and won't need an extra session for me to ask you additional questions about your notes.*

At this point in the deposition, you might well decide to produce the notes voluntarily for the next day's deposition session. This makes sense, particularly if you are confident in your case and have nothing to hide, since it may shorten the deposition.

On the other hand, if you think that the notes may be embarrassing, you may wish to politely refuse to produce them voluntarily. After all, the deposing party, who probably has loads of other things to do, may not want them badly enough to bother sending out a formal notice to produce. Or, the deposing party may simply forget to do so. If you decide not to comply voluntarily, you would respond to the last question by saying something like:

A: *To keep our legal relationship clear, I'd prefer that you send me a formal discovery request.*

E. Finishing Interrupted Answers

Once you have begun to answer a question, you are entitled to finish your answer as long as it is responsive to the question. Nevertheless, a questioner may interrupt and cut you off mid-answer. Often, such interruptions are inadvertent or simply the result of bad manners. However, some lawyers try to make strategic interruptions. For example, a lawyer may interrupt your answer because:

- you are giving—or are likely to give— damaging testimony that the lawyer doesn't want in the record, or

- the lawyer wants to upset you and render you a less effective deposition witness.

If you are interrupted and you want to finish your answer, politely inform the questioner that you have not finished your answer and that you wish to do so.

Example

Q: *What did you do after you called the police?*

A: *I went over to see if I could help any of the people who had been involved in the accident, and ...*

Q: *Did my client say anything about whether he was hurt?*

A: *I'm sorry, but I didn't get a chance to finish my answer to your previous question. As I was saying, I went over to see if I could help any of the people who had been involved in the accident, and I talked to two other women at the scene who said they had seen the accident happen.*

F. Handling Fatigue

If you've never experienced it, you probably don't realize how tiring even a few hours of deposition questioning can be. Paying close attention to a multitude of questions (Golden Rule #1), searching your memory for details, and deciding how best to word your answers can be mentally exhausting, especially if you didn't get a full night's sleep. On top of that, you may have to contend with a questioner whose manner of questioning is aggressive or even antagonistic.

Some lawyers consider fatigue to be an ally. As the session goes on and on, your concentration may wane and you are more likely to violate the Golden Rules. You might, for example, stop listening closely to questions, guess at the meaning of a question, or volunteer information in an attempt to get the deposition over with as quickly as possible. Experienced attorneys anticipate the fatigue phenomenon and often save questions on important topics for late in the day—or just before the lunch break.

While you cannot completely eliminate mental fatigue, you can minimize the likelihood that it will adversely effect your deposition testimony. Steps you can take include:

- **Take time-outs.** You will be more mentally alert if you take frequent breaks throughout the day. If you have been testifying for 45 minutes or so, tell the questioner that you need a five-minute break to stretch your legs. Many questioners will readily agree, as mental fatigue is also a problem for them. Even if the questioner doesn't agree gracefully, you are legally entitled to take reasonable breaks; you should feel perfectly comfortable in insisting on taking them at reasonable intervals. (But don't overdo it—for example, absent special medical conditions, requesting to take a five-minute break every 15 minutes would be unreasonable.)

- **Get enough to eat.** Although food may be the last thing on your mind during your deposition, be sure to eat enough to keep your brain and body adequately fueled. It is much easier to think and remember clearly when you aren't distracted or light-headed with hunger. Experienced lawyers know that a deponent who has gone many hours without food is more likely to give careless answers—hence the common practice of asking the $64,000 question just before a lunch break. Even if you feel nervous or have other things to attend to during breaks, be sure to eat enough to stay alert.

- **Call it a day.** Under FRCP 30(d)(2), a deposition is normally limited to one day of seven hours. However, if you are too mentally fatigued to testify for this length of time in one stretch, you can insist on calling it a day. This is your right—you are not in prison and no one can stop you from leaving. Of course, you will have to agree to finish the deposition the following day or at some later date. But it's far better to return another day than to try to tough it out when you are too tired.

Good Reasons to Insist on Short Deposition Sessions

If you have a reasonable justification for needing to end a deposition session before the end of the day, let the deposing lawyer know at the outset of the deposition when you will need to conclude that day's session. Reasonable justifications include:

- important business meetings or other important personal obligations (such as child care responsibilities)

- taking medication or having some other physical condition that renders you unable to concentrate for more than a few hours at a time, or

- your age (young or old), if it renders you unable to complete a full day of deposition testimony.

Of course, if you do conclude a deposition session before the attorney is done questioning you, you'll have to return for one or more additional sessions.

Example

Q: *Please tell me everything that your supervisor did during the three years you worked at the company that you believe was discriminatory.*

A: *You know, we've been going for about six hours today, and I'm really getting tired. I'd like to stop now. I'll be happy to come back tomorrow, and we can finish up then.*

Q: *Actually, I only have a few more questions and then your deposition will be complete. So if you can stay for a half hour more, we can finish up today.*

A: *I understand, but these are important questions and I'm having difficulty concentrating and remembering things right now, so I'd like to end for today.*

Q: *How about a compromise. We'll finish for the day after I ask a few more questions, and then we can resume tomorrow.*

A: *No, I don't mean to be impolite, but I won't be answering any more questions today. What time do you want me to show up tomorrow?*

In this example, the questioner pressures the deponent to complete the deposition or at least stay for the proverbial "few more questions" (which, of course, often turn into a few hundred more questions!). However, the deponent wisely insists on suspending the deposition for the day.

 Don't let your own desire to complete the deposition blind you to fatigue.

Chances are it will be inconvenient for you to return another day (and, of course, the questioner might think of a lot more questions overnight). However, if you know that you can no longer concentrate adequately, don't get talked into staying for "just a little while longer." The very fact that the questioner is insistent that you do so should be a good clue that it's time to pack your briefcase and head for the door.

G. Objections

During the deposition, you may hear one of the lawyers (or a self-represented party) object to a question. For example, the lawyer representing the person being deposed may react to a question by saying, "Objection: Hearsay." When attorneys object at deposition, the usual reason is to preserve their ability to object to the same evidence at trial. In short, the objections do not affect the deposition itself—you almost always have to answer objected-to questions. Consequently, as a deponent you can usually ignore a questioner's objections. (If you are representing yourself, see Chapters 10 and 12 for more information on how to make and respond to objections.)

When Your Lawyer Tells You Not to Answer a Question

If you're represented by an attorney at your deposition, he or she may follow an objection by instructing you not to answer a question. For example, your attorney might instruct you not to answer a question that asks you to reveal privileged information (such as a conversation you had with the lawyer). You should, of course, follow your attorney's instruction and not answer the question—just remain silent until the next question. If you're not represented by a lawyer and want information about the limited circumstances in which you can refuse to answer questions, see Chapter 7.

H. Reviewing and Signing Your Deposition

Current deposition rules in most courts (see, for example, FRCP 30(e)) allow you to request an opportunity to review a written transcript of your deposition (or to view your videotaped deposition). If you are a disinterested nonparty witness, you probably will not want to make this request and take the additional time and trouble to review your deposition testimony. If you're representing yourself, however, at the end of questioning, you should ask for an opportunity to review the transcript of your deposition testimony. Making this request does not commit you to actually reviewing your deposition, but, unless you have a very good reason not to (such as your case is about to settle), reviewing your deposition is a good way to make sure that the reporter's transcript is accurate.

If you request to review the transcript, within a few weeks after your deposition, the court reporter will notify you that your deposition is available for review at the court reporter's office. If you opt to review the transcript and you believe that any portion of your deposition testimony is inaccurate, you should change it. You must sign the deposition under penalty of perjury. Your signature indicates your belief that your testimony is accurate as of the time you sign the transcript. Therefore, you must change inaccurate testimony before you sign. If you decide not to review the transcript, you waive the right to change your deposition testimony.

Offer to stipulate to "any notary" if the location of the court reporter's office is inconvenient.

At the conclusion of your deposition, ask the deposing party if you can review and sign your deposition before "any notary public." If the deposing party agrees, the court reporter can mail the deposition transcript to a notary near where you live or work, and you can review and sign it before that notary. In the absence of an "any notary" agreement, you'll have to go to the court reporter's office for the review, even if the location is inconvenient for you.

Your deposition answers may be incorrect for any of the following reasons:

- the court reporter transcribed your deposition testimony erroneously

- you realize that you made a mistake during your deposition, or

- subsequent to your deposition, you've learned additional information that makes your deposition inaccurate.

No matter what the reason for a change, the easiest way to make it is to indicate your change or changes on a separate sheet of 8½-x-11-inch paper, including the reason for the change, and then give the paper to the court reporter. That piece of paper may read something like the following examples.

Example 1

Page 47, lines 16 through 17: The testimony "should have canceled the meeting" should read, "should have considered canceling the meeting." Reason for change: The court reporter transcribed my testimony incorrectly.

Example 2

Page 63, line 22: The testimony "Binder and Boland were at the meeting" should read, "Binder, Boland, and Trimble were at the meeting." Reason for change: After talking to Trimble, I now realize that he was at the meeting, too, but that I had forgotten this."

Example 3

Page 87, lines 6 through 7: The testimony "We didn't talk about a new computer system" should read, "We did talk about a new computer system." Reason for change: I misunderstood the question. I thought the question was asking me whether we talked about a new computer system during the March 7 meeting, and we didn't talk about that subject at that meeting. I now realize that the question asked whether we ever talked about a new computer system, and we did talk about that at other times.

Of course, any change you make in your deposition transcript will be apparent to all parties. At trial or during settlement negotiations, a party may argue that your testimony is not credible because you later made a significant change. A substantial number of significant changes of key testimony might even result in a judge ordering your deposition to be resumed so that the deposing party can ask about the reason for the changes. In short, do not view your right to make changes as an excuse for sloppy testimony. Again, it's best to follow the Golden Rules and give your best testimony the first time around.

■

Chapter 5

Beginning a Deposition: "The Usual Admonitions"

At last it's deposition day. You arrive at the law office of the attorney who scheduled your deposition. After a short wait in a reception area, during which you are offered coffee or a cold drink, you are shown into a small conference room. Waiting in the conference room are two attorneys. The deposing attorney, who represents the plaintiff, is a stranger to you. You'd met with the other attorney, representing the defendant, a couple of days earlier to discuss what would happen at the deposition. Also in the conference room are the plaintiff and a court reporter. After a few moments of small talk about the foul weather outside, everyone sits down and the plaintiff's attorney says something like, "Let's go on the record."

Relax. The beginning stages of most depositions are routine. Here is what you can expect to happen as soon as everyone is in place:

- The court reporter (acting as a court officer) will note a few details "for the record"—meaning to include in the transcript (and/or videotape) of the deposition. The court reporter is likely to mention his or her name and business address; the date, time, and place of the deposition; and your name as the deponent.

- The reporter will place you under oath (or affirmation, if your religious beliefs prohibit you from swearing an oath). The oath is the same one that witnesses take in court.

- The reporter will identify for the record all of the persons who are present.

With these technicalities out of the way, the court reporter will turn to the deposing lawyer (or the deposing self-represented party) and say something like, "You may begin the questioning." If an attorney is taking your deposition, the attorney will probably begin by reviewing what are often referred to in lawyer-speak as "the usual admonitions." The rest of this chapter discusses these "usual admonitions" and explains their purposes.

A. Admonitions Defined

"Admonitions" are the preliminary matters that attorneys usually review with deponents before getting into the substance of their testimony. Some admonitions explain deposition procedures. Others establish that a deponent understands the rules of the game and is in good physical and mental condition to participate in that game. For example, one routine admonition indicates that the court reporter will be taking down everything that is said during the deposition, and another asks if the deponent is taking any medication that could impair his or her ability to testify.

B. Purposes of Admonitions

Admonitions can serve as social icebreakers. Since a deposing attorney and a deponent are usually complete strangers to each other, the admonitions portion of a deposition allows for a comfortable few minutes of dialogue to get acquainted before the real questioning begins.

But admonitions can have other, less benign purposes as well. For one, the deposing lawyer may attempt to use admonitions to appear fair, nonpartisan, and solicitous of your welfare. Don't believe it. While it's all well and good for the deposing attorney to be polite, always remember that the lawyer has one set of interests and you have another. It's possible that at times these interests will be congruent, but it is at least as likely that they won't. Don't bend over backwards to please a lawyer just because the lawyer has a good bedside manner.

Admonitions can also be a tool the deposing attorney can use to attack your credibility if you contradict your deposition testimony later in the case. For example, assume that you're a nonparty witness in an auto accident case, and you testify at trial that "the BMW ran a red light." On cross examination, the lawyer representing the BMW's driver confronts you with your deposition testimony, which was that "the light was yellow when the BMW entered the intersection." To explain the contradiction, you say, "At the time of the deposition, I was taking medication that affected my concentration and memory." However, a routine admonition undermines this explanation: If you were asked at your deposition whether you were taking any medication that might affect your ability to give your best testimony that day, and you answered "no," a judge or jury is unlikely to accept your explanation for the contradiction. As a result, your trial testimony may not carry much credibility.

C. Admonitions: Examples and Explanations

Set out below are some typical deposition admonitions. The brief explanatory notes inserted into the dialogue should help you understand why an attorney might ask some of these questions. While the example admonitions represent what is likely to happen at your deposition, variations are common. You may well encounter different admonitions or admonitions that cover the same ground but are phrased differently.

Where Do Admonitions Come From?

The admonitions below are not legally required, nor are they simply meaningless creatures of legal custom. Rather, each represents past experience, most of it undoubtedly painful, for one attorney or another. Thus over the years, as attorneys were confronted by witnesses' clever explanations for changes in their testimony at trial ("I had taken so much Prozac before the deposition that I could hardly remember my name"), lawyers developed new admonitions for use in future depositions ("Are you taking any medication that might affect your memory?"). Thus, the admonitions you are given are likely to reflect both the received wisdom of the legal profession and the unique experiences of the lawyer who conducts your deposition.

Example 1

Q: *Ms. Varat, my name is Andrea Sherry, and I am the attorney for Mr. Flowers. Just so there won't be any misunderstanding, let me briefly describe what will happen. Jessie Flowers has filed a lawsuit concerning the loan secured by a deed of trust for the property at 1234 E. 88th Street. Today I will be asking you questions to learn information that might be relevant to that lawsuit. My questions and your answers will be taken down by the court reporter on this machine that you see in front of you. The court reporter can't take down nods or shakes of the head so it's necessary for you to answer my questions audibly, all right?*

A: *I'll try.*

Q: *When I begin a question, you may know what I'm going to ask before I finish my question, but it's easier for the court reporter to get everything down correctly if you let me finish my question before you start to answer. Will you try to do that?*

A: *Sure.*

Explanatory Note

The initial questions above endear the attorney to the court reporter and help to produce a more accurate transcript by reminding you that the reporter cannot take down two voices talking over each other.

Example 2

Q: *Have you ever been deposed before, Ms. Varat?*

A: *Yes, a couple of times.*

Explanatory Note

Your acknowledgment of prior deposition experience can undercut any possible claim later that you were confused about deposition procedures. Also, the deposing attorney may want this information to get an idea of how cagey you are likely to be when answering more important questions.

Example 3

Q: *Do you understand that you were administered an oath by the court reporter and are testifying today under penalty of perjury?*

A: *Yes, I do.*

Q: *And do you understand that your testimony has the same importance and significance it would have if you were testifying in court before a judge and a jury?*

A: *Yes.*

Q: *And you'll do your best to tell the complete truth at this deposition, won't you, Ms. Varat?*

A: I will.

Explanatory Note

Your acknowledgments that deposition testimony is as significant as courtroom testimony and that you are testifying under penalty of perjury undermines any possible explanation for a change of testimony later based on a claim that you didn't take the deposition seriously or didn't understand the oath. (Some lawyers like to get these facts on record so much that they repeat these questions after any significant break in the deposition.) And your agreement to tell the "complete" truth at the deposition makes it harder for you to add information when you testify at trial or swear to an affidavit or declaration (written statement signed under oath). Finally, some lawyers believe these admonitions intimidate a witness who might otherwise shade the truth, by reminding the witness that the proceeding is important—and will have consequences.

Example 4

Q: *Ms. Varat, if you don't understand a question I ask you, you shouldn't answer it. Instead of answering a question you don't understand, you should just tell me you don't understand the question. Will you agree to do that?*

A: *Sure.*

Q: *If you do answer a question, I will assume that you have understood the question*

and that you are giving me your best possible answer. Do you understand that?

A: *Yes.*

Explanatory Note

These admonitions undermine any claim later that you later changed your story only because you didn't understand a question at the deposition.

Example 5

Q: *Sometimes you will understand my question just fine, but you won't be sure you really know the answer because the answer that comes to mind is really a guess or an estimate. When your answer is a guess or an estimate, you should tell me that you're guessing or giving an estimate. Will you agree to tell me when your answer is a guess or an estimate?*

A: *Okay.*

Explanatory Note

This admonition makes it hard for you to justify a change of story later by claiming that when you gave what seemed to be a definitive deposition answer, you were only guessing. A variation on this admonition instructs deponents, "Do not guess at all. If you can answer a question only by guessing, please tell me that." This type of admonition also cuts off later explanations that your deposition testimony was only a guess.

However, this variation is given less often, since it tends to discourage deponents from making even the most conservative estimates, which may in turn prevent the deposing lawyer from uncovering a lead to helpful evidence.

Example 6

Q: *If you find yourself getting tired at any time during the deposition, please let me know and we'll talk about taking a break. Is that all right?*

A: *That's fine.*

Explanatory Note

As you have probably guessed, this admonition cuts off a potential explanation that a change of testimony later resulted from your being tired and not thinking clearly during your deposition. As you see, the admonition does not commit the attorney to agreeing to your request for a break. Indeed, if the deposing attorney believes that you are providing helpful information, the attorney may request that you delay taking a break until he or she has finished questioning you on the particular topic. As discussed in Chapter 4, however, you are entitled to take a break at reasonable intervals and can call it a day when you feel too tired to continue.

Example 7

Q: *After you've given your best complete answer to a question, you may remember additional information later in the deposition that responds to the question. If this happens, you should just tell me that you've remembered additional information that relates to an earlier question, and you can tell me about the additional information. Is that OK with you?*

A: *Sure.*

Explanatory Note

This admonition acknowledges a common occurrence—delayed recollection of important information. By inviting you to add to a previous answer at any point in the deposition, this admonition encourages you to provide complete information. In addition, it undermines another potential explanation for a change in testimony later, that you were aware of the additional information at the time of your deposition, but by the time you remembered it, the questioner had moved on to another topic.

Example 8

Q: *Sometimes when you are answering a question, you may realize that looking at some documents would help refresh your memory. When that happens, you may tell me that the documents would help you to answer my question better and we'll talk about what to do. Is that all right with you?*

A: *Okay.*

Explanatory Note

By inviting you to enhance your memory with a document, this admonition encourages you to testify as completely as possible. It can also undermine another potential explanation you may give for changed testimony—that since your deposition, you've had a chance to look at documents that you didn't have a chance to examine at the deposition. And, through this admonition, the deposing lawyer may find out about documents he or she may not have discovered otherwise.

Example 9

Q: *After the deposition is over, the court reporter will type up my questions and your answers into a transcript. If you request to do so, you can review the transcript for accuracy and sign it under penalty of perjury. When you review your transcript you may change answers that are inaccurate. You should know, however, that if you make changes to the sworn testimony in the transcript after you review it, I and other lawyers in the case will be entitled to point out to the judge or jury at trial that you made changes. So that's why I would like you to give me your most complete answers to my questions today. Do you understand that the lawyers may be able to comment on any changes you make in the transcript of your deposition testimony?*

A: *Yes.*

Q: *You should also know that if you testify at trial differently than you testify here today, the lawyers in this case may have an opportunity to ask you why you changed your sworn testimony. Do you understand that?*

A: *Yes.*

Explanatory Note

By warning you that changes to your answers can be called to the attention of a judge and jury, these admonitions encourage you to testify accurately and completely. They also undermine a potential claim later that you didn't realize the importance of giving complete and accurate testimony at deposition.

Example 10

Q: *I'm going to ask you a few questions about how you're feeling today. I am not trying to pry into your medical situation, but I need to make sure just for the record that you are feeling fine and are able to testify today. Are you ill today?*

A: *No.*

Q: *Do you feel fine physically?*

A: *Yes.*

Q: Are you on any medication?

A: Yes, I'm taking Relafen to reduce inflammation in my knees and ankles, and Lotensin for high blood pressure.

Q: Are you taking any other medications?

A: No.

Q: Do either of the medications that you are taking affect your ability to remember or to testify completely and accurately?

A: Sometimes the Relafen makes me tired and I have difficulty concentrating.

Q: Are you experiencing those symptoms now?

A: No, I'm feeling fine at the moment.

Q: So you feel that, at the moment, you are having no difficulties remembering and that you can testify accurately and completely?

A: Yes, I do.

Q: If that should change—if you develop problems concentrating or develop any other symptoms—will you let me know right away?

A: Yes.

Q: Are you currently under a doctor's care for any illness?

A: No.

Q: Have you had any alcohol today?

A: No.

Q: Is there anything at all preventing you in any way from giving accurate testimony today?

A: No.

Q: Is your memory working as well today as it usually does?

A: Yes.

Explanatory Note 1

All of these admonitions cut off potential explanations for changed testimony later—in this example, that a temporary mental or physical infirmity existed on the day of your deposition that caused your deposition testimony to be inaccurate or incomplete. If your answers make the deposing lawyer doubt your ability to testify fully and accurately, the lawyer may choose to recess the deposition until a later date. Of course, if you have a permanent memory impairment (for example, you testify, "I had a stroke several months ago and I don't remember things as well since then"), the lawyer will have no choice but to depose you in your present condition.

Explanatory Note 2

Sometimes, deponents are under medical treatment for conditions or illnesses that they do not want to reveal. For instance, a deponent may be taking medication to treat HIV, or may be receiving cancer treatments. If you do not want to reveal a medical condition or medications that you are taking, you might respond to questions concerning your physical condition as follows:

Q: Are you on any medication?

A: Yes, but I prefer not to disclose what it is.

Q: Well, I don't want to pry into personal medical matters unnecessarily. Let's try to deal with it this way. Do any of the medications you are taking affect your ability to remember or testify completely and accurately?

A: No.

Q: Are you experiencing any symptoms now?

A: No, I'm feeling fine.

Q: So you feel that, at the moment, you are having no difficulties remembering and that you can testify accurately and completely?

A: Yes, I do.

Q: If that should change—if you develop problems concentrating or develop any other symptoms—will you let me know right away?

A: Yes.

Q: Do you have any questions about what we've covered so far?

A: No.

Q: Okay, then let's turn to some general questions about your education and work experience …

After covering all admonitions, the deposing lawyer will turn to background questioning, which is the subject of the next chapter. ■

Chapter 6

Background Questions

After giving "the usual admonitions" (see Chapter 5), the deposing lawyer (or self-represented party) will usually continue the deposition by asking a series of questions about your personal background. This chapter describes the two most common subjects these questions cover: your education and your employment history.

When Lawyers Skip Detailed Background Questioning

Personal background questioning extends a deposition's length and, thus, makes a deposition more costly for the deposing party. As a result, especially when deposing nonparty witnesses, lawyers sometimes do only perfunctory background questioning—or even skip it entirely. For example, if you're a nonparty witness with no ties to either party who simply had the bad luck to observe an auto accident that gave rise to a lawsuit, the deposing lawyer may ask you very few personal background questions.

A. Hidden Agendas

You might think of personal background questions merely as a warm-up for later questioning, like stretching before a jog. However, just as is true with admonitions, savvy deposing lawyers are likely to have more subtle purposes in mind.

For example, the lawyer might pretend to be your friend. Since background questions seem nonthreatening, some lawyers think of them as a way to try to ingratiate themselves with you. The idea is that if you can be beguiled into thinking of the deposing lawyer as a congenial professional rather than as an adversary, perhaps you'll spill some beans you'd otherwise keep to yourself.

Or, the lawyer might attempt to hide questions about important topics in general background questioning. Again, some lawyers hope that your defenses will be down during these seemingly innocuous personal background inquiries. If the tactic causes you not to realize the significance of a question, you might disclose information that you would not reveal in response to pointed, case-related inquiries.

For example, assume that you are being deposed by the plaintiff, Ms. Smith, in a lawsuit against Mr. Jones for sexual harassment. The plaintiff claims that she was subjected to repeated verbal harassment by Jones, her supervisor. You are the plaintiff's coworker, and are prepared to testify that you never heard any harassment, even though your office is between the plaintiff's office and Jones's office. You don't believe the plaintiff was harassed.

Going into the deposition, the plaintiff's lawyer hopes to establish that a noisy copy machine located just outside your office prevented you from overhearing sexually harassing conversations that took place outside your office—especially since the copier noise frequently forces you to work with your office door closed. The lawyer might wait to ask about your ability to hear hallway conversations until the heart of your deposition. However, the lawyer may fear that asking you about copy machine noise when challenging your ability to hear what goes on in the hallway may lead you to deny that the copier affects your ability to hear hallway conversations. You will know, from the sequence of the questions, that admitting that the copier is noisy necessarily means admitting that you might not have heard everything that happened in the hall—and that the plaintiff could have been harassed without you noticing.

Note how the questioning pattern below clues you in to the purpose of the lawyer's inquiries, thereby offering you a chance to fit your testimony to your belief that the plaintiff was not harassed.

Q: *Did you ever hear Jones talk to the plaintiff?*

A: *Yes, all the time. They used to talk outside my office, which was between their offices.*

Q: *And you never heard Jones make rude comments to the plaintiff during those conversations?*

A: *No, Jones was always very polite to her.*

Q: *When Jones spoke with the plaintiff outside your office, were you ordinarily able to hear what they both were saying?*

A: *Yes.*

Q: *Isn't there a copy machine located just outside your office?*

A: *It's in the adjacent room.*

Q: *Was it noisy?*

A: *Not noisy enough to drown out a conversation taking place right outside my office.*

Contrast the above questions and answers with the following deposition excerpt. This time, the deposing lawyer slips questions about the noisy copy machine into general background questioning about your job.

Q: *I'd like you to describe the layout of your workplace as of the time the conversations which are the subject of this lawsuit allegedly took place. Did you have your own office?*

A: *Yes.*

Q: *Did your office have a door that opened and closed?*

A: *Yes.*

Q: *When you walked out of your office, what was directly in front of you?*

A: *The plaintiff's office.*

Q: *What was immediately to the right of your office?*

A: *Jones's office.*

Q: *What was immediately to the left of your office?*

A: *A small room with a water cooler and a copy machine.*

Q: *Was the door to the small room with the water cooler and copy machine normally kept open or closed?*

A: Open.

Q: I assume that when the copy machine was being used, you could hear it in your office?

A: Yes, unless I closed my door.

Q: Would you often close your door to block out the copy machine noise?

A: Quite often, when I needed to concentrate.

In this second excerpt, the lawyer asks about copy machine noise in the context of background information, "the general office layout." In that context, you may not be consciously thinking of your already formed conclusion that no harassment occurred. Perhaps as a result, you disclose that you often had to close your door because of copy machine noise.

The point of this example is not to urge you to skew testimony to fit preformed conclusions. Rather, the point is simply that you should answer as carefully and correctly during background questioning as during any other portion of a deposition. Do not adopt an attitude such as, "It's only background—I don't have to listen too closely to the questions or be too careful about what I say." You are under oath during an entire deposition, and any information may prove important to a case's outcome. Your legal obligation to provide accurate information applies to all stages of a deposition.

B. Legitimacy of Background Questions

Especially if you are a nonparty witness, you may believe that a deposing lawyer has no right to poke into your private life. However, discovery rules do allow questions about your general educational background and work experience. While most of the information would probably be irrelevant at trial, during discovery a party can inquire into any topic that "appears reasonably calculated to lead to the discovery of admissible evidence." (FRCP 26(b)(1).) General background questions are usually proper under this broad standard, because some part of your past may reveal a connection to one of the parties or special knowledge of the facts involved in a dispute.

Example

You are a nonparty witness whose deposition is being taken by a defendant in a personal injury case involving an automobile accident. You happened to be walking by the intersection when two cars collided. Probing your background, the defendant learns that you worked your way through college as a bartender. Since the plaintiff has alleged that the defendant was under the influence of alcohol at the time of the collision, your bartending experience may be relevant to your testimony.

The scope of discovery, however, is limited. FRCP 26(c) protects you from answering questions that cause "annoyance, embarrassment, oppression, or undue burden or expense." In general, this means that if a lawyer's questions concern private details of your life that have no bearing on a case, you can refuse to answer them. (See Chapter 7 for more information on refusing to answer questions.) The deposing lawyer then would have to go to court and ask a judge to order you to answer the questions. Rather than halting the deposition to try to convince a judge to order you to answer a bunch of irrelevant and personal questions, the lawyer is likely to move on to more relevant matters.

 Don't set your privacy threshold too low.

You run a risk when you refuse to answer personal questions. If a judge decides that the questions were proper, the judge may order you to reimburse the deposing party for expenses and attorney's fees spent going to court to secure an order that requires you to answer. (You may even have to reimburse the deposing party for air travel if the need to stop a deposition, seek a court order, and return forces a deposing party to travel a long distance.) Therefore, it makes sense to refuse to answer personal background questions only if they are genuinely invasive of your privacy and you are confident that they are improper. For more on how to respond to questions you believe improperly invade your privacy, see Chapter 7.

C. Your Employment History

The deposing lawyer may ask about your past and present employment in an effort to uncover information that is relevant to the facts of the case, or to build rapport and encourage you to relax. Just as likely, questions about your employment history are simply part of the lawyer's standard repertoire.

The subsections below explain two approaches that a deposing lawyer may follow when asking about your employment history. They are not mutually exclusive; the deposing lawyer may follow both tacks.

1. The "Timeline" Approach

The deposing lawyer may start background questioning by seeking a "timeline" of your employment history. A lawyer following this approach may either begin with your most recent employment and move backwards, or begin with your first "real" job (for example, not your high school part-time job delivering flowers) and continue to the present. Subjects you may legitimately be asked about include:

- the names of the companies for which you've worked

- your job titles and general responsibilities, and

- the circumstances under which you left each employer.

Acknowledge gaps in your employment history.

An employment timeline is not always an unbroken line. If background questioning reveals a gap or two in your employment history, the deposing lawyer may ask why you were unemployed. Such questions are probably legitimately within the broad scope of discovery. You should answer honestly and forthrightly, whether the reason is that you left work to care for a child or ailing relative or that you were fired and had trouble finding a new job. Similarly, if you're retired at the time of your deposition, the lawyer is likely to ask about what jobs you held for several years prior to your retirement.

As you might expect, employment-related questions will be more extensive if you're a party, or if background questioning reveals a link between your work history and the issues in a case. As in the example in Section B, above, of the nonparty witness to an auto accident who was a part-time bartender all through college, since alcohol use may have been involved in the accident, the deposing attorney may delve more deeply into the witness's bartending experiences.

The following examples further demonstrate how links between employment background and the issues in a case can extend the scope of background questioning.

Example 1

Party's employment history: Annette is a plaintiff in a sexual harassment lawsuit against her present employer. At Annette's deposition, the employer's lawyer will, of course, explore Annette's job performance with her present employer, her relationships with other employees, case-related conversations she's had with other employees, and so on. In addition, however, the employer's lawyer may well question Annette in detail about her previous jobs. For example, Annette will probably be asked about working conditions in those previous jobs and whether she filed sexual harassment claims against former employers.

Example 2

Party's employment history: Guillermo is a plaintiff in a personal injury case growing out of an automobile accident. Among other things, Guillermo is seeking damages for wages he has already lost due to his injuries and for wages he expects to lose in the future. The deposing lawyer will undoubtedly question Guillermo in detail about such matters as his salary history, the basis on which he is compensated, his work record (job descriptions for the positions he's held, absenteeism problems, performance evaluations, and so on), and skills that Guillermo has acquired while on the job.

Example 3

Nonparty witness's employment history: Sickel has sued Hammer, a police officer, for false arrest and for using excessive force when making the arrest. Bathke saw the arrest and is now being deposed. During background questioning, Bathke testifies that he has been a security guard for ten years. Because Bathke's work experience relates to the facts of the case, the deposing lawyer is likely to question Bathke in detail about his training and experience as a security guard. For instance, Bathke will probably be asked about any training courses he's taken, the situations in which he's worked, approximately how many arrests he's made, and any ties he has to law enforcement.

2. The "Hidden Bombshell" Approach

One of a deposing lawyer's worst nightmares is to be surprised at trial with important evidence that should have been gleaned at deposition. For example, if you have work experience that relates to issues in dispute, the lawyer wants to know about it at your deposition. While in theory such work experience would emerge during timeline questioning (see Section C1, above), the deposing lawyer may use "hidden bombshell" questioning as insurance. In other words, rather than relying on your recall of your work experience, the lawyer may ask proactively whether you've had particular case-related work experiences. For example, during your deposition you may be asked pointed questions of this sort:

- "This is a case in which the plaintiff claims to have been sexually harassed. Have you

ever personally been involved in a sexual harassment claim?"

- "This is a case in which the plaintiff claims that a police officer used excessive force when making an arrest. Do you have any background in police or security work?"

- "This case involves the alleged failure of a computer software program to comply with promised criteria. Do you have any background or experience in the design of computer software?"

If you answer "yes" to any such questions, the lawyer will undoubtedly follow up by probing your case-related experiences.

D. Your Educational Background

The deposing lawyer is also likely to elicit a timeline of your educational background. Typically, questions about your education start with your graduation from high school and continue through any college and post-graduate education. You may also be asked about job-related adult education, such as a course you took to qualify for a professional license or simply to improve your professional skills.

A deposing lawyer may ask about your educational background in order to size up your general level of intellectual achievement. Even if the attorney realizes that formal education is often a poor indicator of intellectual capacity, the lawyer will know that how judges and jurors evaluate credibility can be affected by your educational achievements. Thus, educational history is well within the scope of discovery and a topic that the deposing lawyer may explore.

A deposing attorney is likely to ask about your educational background for another reason, too. Just as your work experience may provide you with case-related expertise, so may your educational background. Thus, an attorney will want to know whether you have any formal schooling in case-related matters.

Example 1

Davies is a defendant who operates a small business that has been sued by a municipality for violating the Clean Water Act. The damages that Davies might have to pay if he violated the act depend in part on whether Davies acted "in good faith" (that is, with honest intentions). Davies's answer to the City's complaint claims that Davies was unaware of the environmental regulations that he allegedly violated. In addition to seeking a timeline of Davies's formal education, at deposition the City's lawyer will probably ask Davies about adult education courses he has taken, government- or industry-sponsored meetings he has attended, and literature he has received explaining provisions of the Clean Water Act.

Example 2

Kann is the plaintiff in a real estate fraud case. Kann's lawsuit claims that the defendant's false statements about the terms of the loan that she took out in order to finance home repairs induced her to make unnecessary repairs and lose her property to the defendant. To win the case, Kann has to prove "reasonable reliance" on the defendant's false statements. When deposed by the defendant, in addition to her formal education, Kann will likely be asked about whether she attended any language courses (if English is not Kann's first language), took real estate and other investment courses, and consulted any self-help real estate books prior to financing the home repairs.

E. Other Background Topics

Your educational and employment history are the most common topics likely to be covered in background questioning. But the deposing lawyer may also ask about any other aspects of your background that may be related to the case. For example, assume you witnessed an incident allegedly involving the use of excessive force by the police. At your deposition, the police department's lawyer may inquire into your experience with police officers (for example, during traffic stops) or your attitudes toward the police department or law enforcement issues generally. These are permissible topics of inquiry because they may reveal information about your attitude toward the parties and the issues in the case. ■

Chapter 7

Questions You Can
Legally Refuse to Answer

This chapter describes and illustrates the limited number of circumstances in which you can justifiably refuse to answer a deposing lawyer's questions. Because a central purpose of depositions is to allow broad investigation into all facts that underlie a lawsuit, only a few such circumstances exist.

Normally, under FRCP 30(c), even if deposition questions are objected to and would be improper at trial, you have to answer them. For example, if an attorney defending a deposition properly objects that a question you've been asked "calls for hearsay," you'll nonetheless have to answer it. The point of the objection is to prevent the answer from being used against the lawyer later in the case. (To understand why parties sometimes object to deposition questions that have to be answered anyway, see Chapter 10.)

Thus, the circumstances discussed in this chapter constitute exceptions to the general rule that objected-to questions must be answered at deposition. (Lawyers, who are usually delirious with joy when they have a good reason to instruct clients to keep their mouths shut, often call these circumstances "islands of sanctuary.")

A. Privileged Communications

One major category of questions that you can refuse to answer involves what lawyers call privileged (legally confidential) communications. These are private communications (written or oral) between people who are in a relationship that state or federal laws recognize as off limits or privileged. In other words, whether you're a party or a nonparty witness, if a communication is legally privileged, you have the right to keep it to yourself.

A communication is privileged only if it is made in a legally confidential relationship. For example, assume that a friend tells you something "in strictest confidence." At deposition, the deposing lawyer would be able to compel you to disclose what your friend told you because no court system has a legal rule recognizing a privilege for conversations between friends, no matter what their private intentions.

The sections below review common privileges recognized in practically all courts and identify some others that may be applicable to your case. The law of privilege, however, is very complex. The rules vary from one court system to another. In some court systems, privilege rules can be created only by statute. In others, judges can create privileges. Thus, if you anticipate being asked about something you've said or written that you want to keep private, be sure you understand (discuss with a lawyer or research independently) your court system's rules before you attend your deposition.

If you fail to claim a privilege to which you are entitled, or if you erroneously claim a privilege that does not apply, you run one of the following risks:

- If you testify at deposition to privileged information, you've waived (given up) the privilege and cannot reclaim it later in the case.

- If you erroneously claim a privilege that is inapplicable, the deposing lawyer may stop the deposition and seek a court order compelling you to reveal the information. If the judge agrees to make that order, the judge may also order you to pay any expenses the deposing lawyer incurs by having to seek the court order and reschedule the deposition.

If you're represented by an attorney, you should of course rely on your attorney's advice as to whether a communication is privileged. If you're not represented by a lawyer and are uncertain about whether an important communication you want to keep private is privileged, consider paying for an attorney's advice on the issue. Also, for a brief nontechnical discussion of privilege issues, see *Federal Rules of Evidence in a Nutshell*, by Michael Graham.

What Privilege Rules Apply to Your Case?

Since one court system's privilege rules can be different from another's, knowing which system's rules apply to your case can be important. Here are the general rules:

- If you're involved in a state court case, that state's privilege rules apply.
- If you're involved in a federal court case, but the legal claims will be decided under state law—the laws of the state in which the federal court is located—that state's privilege rules apply. *Example:* A California resident vacationing in New York is involved in an auto accident with a New York resident. The California resident sues the New York resident in a federal court in New York. (Under what is called "diversity" jurisdictions, federal courts have the power to decide civil cases involving residents of different states, so long as the amount in dispute is at least $75,000.) In this case, the New York federal court would decide the case under New York state rules, including New York's privilege rules.

- If you're involved in a federal court case, and the legal claims are based on federal law (these are called "federal question" cases), federal privilege law applies. *Example:* Crabapple Corp. sues Ibey Em Inc. in federal court for infringing Crabapple's patent rights. Patent cases are governed by federal law, so the federal law of privileges will apply. (You might expect that federal privilege laws would be listed in the Federal Rules of Evidence. They are not, however, due to political wrangling over scope. As a result, Federal Rule of Evidence 501 simply states that federal privilege issues are decided under "common law principles," meaning that you'll have to find federal privilege law in judicial opinions, not in statutes.)

⚠️ **Don't waive a privilege carelessly.**
Most privileges are subject to exceptions. If an
exception applies, a communication won't be
privileged even if it was made during a legally
protected relationship. (For examples of specific
exceptions, see the discussions of individual
privileges below.) In addition, you can waive
(give up) a privilege by not treating a communication as confidential—even unintentionally.
For example, assume that you have a case-
related discussion with an attorney. You'd waive
the privilege—and could be required to disclose
what you and the attorney talked about—if you
allowed other people to hear the information.
For example, if you:

- conduct the discussion in a crowded
  elevator or public bathroom, so that it
  might be overheard by others, or

- reveal what you and the attorney said to
  each other to a friend or next-door
  neighbor.

To maintain a privilege, hold confidential
discussions in private places and don't reveal
what you talked about to anyone outside the
privilege.

1. Attorney-Client Privilege

You have a privilege to refuse to answer questions concerning private communications between you and a lawyer from whom you've
sought legal advice. The privilege applies even if
you don't end up hiring the lawyer. (The lawyer,

by the way, has an obligation to refuse to disclose what you talked about unless you give the
lawyer permission to do so.) The following examples illustrate when communications are
protected by the attorney-client privilege.

Example 1

*You're a nonparty witness in a real estate fraud
case. Because you feared that you might
eventually be named a party to the suit, you
sought legal advice from an attorney after you
were subpoenaed to have your deposition taken.
Regardless of whether you hired the attorney,
and regardless of whether the attorney is
representing you at the deposition, your predeposition communications with the attorney
are privileged, and you do not have to reveal
them.*

Example 2

*You're a defendant representing yourself in a
breach of contract case and are being deposed
by the lawyer for the plaintiff. When the lawsuit
was filed, you sought legal advice from a lawyer,
Jerry Atric, but ended up representing yourself.
At the deposition, you're asked, "What did you
discuss with Jerry Atric when you consulted him
about this case?" You could refuse to answer the
question on the ground that it calls for privileged information.*

Example 3

*In the same case as the previous example,
assume that before you met with Jerry Atric,
Jerry asked you to write up a summary of the*

case and send it to him so that he could do some research before meeting with you. You did so. At the deposition, the plaintiff's lawyer tells you, "Please turn over the summary of the case that you mailed to Jerry Atric. I asked you to bring this summary with you in the Notice of Deposition." Again, you could refuse to bring the summary to the deposition or hand it to the lawyer even if you did bring it. Since the summary is a case-related communication between you and an attorney you asked for legal advice, the summary is privileged.

Example 4

You're one of three partners of a small business involved in a lawsuit against your insurance company. Prior to filing the lawsuit, one of your partners sought advice from an attorney. The attorney prepared and sent to each of you an analysis of your legal claims. At your deposition, the insurance company's attorney asks for the attorney's written analysis. You could refuse to turn it over on grounds of privilege, since the attorney-client relationship extended to each of the partners.

Example 5

You're a bystander who saw an automobile accident and is being deposed by the plaintiff's lawyer. Prior to your deposition, you met with the defendant's lawyer to review how to answer the questions you'd probably be asked. At the deposition, the plaintiff's lawyer asks you, "What did you and the defense lawyer say to each other during your predeposition meeting?" You would have to answer this question. Since

you and the defense attorney did not have an attorney-client relationship, your discussion was not privileged. (While you spoke with the attorney to prepare for the deposition, you were not seeking legal advice as a client or potential client.)

Like most privileges, the attorney-client privilege is subject to "exceptions." In other words, your conversation with a lawyer may not be privileged even if you do everything in your power to keep it confidential. Typical exceptions to the attorney-client privilege include:

- seeking legal advice in order to perpetrate a crime or fraud

Example

If a client asks an attorney for advice about how to cheat on the client's income taxes, the conversation will not be privileged.

- lawsuits between the client and the attorney

Example

If you sue an attorney for legal malpractice, the case-related conversations you had with the attorney are not privileged.

- lawsuits between joint clients

Example

If two people seek legal advice on a matter of common interest and end up suing each other, case-related conversations that either had with the attorney (whether or not both clients were present) are not privileged.

If you've talked with an attorney under any of these circumstances, you would have to answer deposition questions about what was discussed.

2. Spousal Privilege

Communications between spouses are privileged in all states and in federal lawsuits. At your deposition, you do not have to disclose any case-related communications you've had with your spouse. Here are some examples of privileged communication between spouses:

Example 1

You're a plaintiff representing yourself in an auto accident case. Your spouse came to the accident scene to pick you up. At your deposition, the defense attorney asks you, "What did you and your spouse talk about at the accident scene?" You can refuse to answer the question because your communications with your spouse are privileged.

Example 2

You're a plaintiff suing your former employer for wrongful termination and are represented by an attorney. Whenever you discussed the case with your attorney, you later described those conversations to your spouse. At your deposition, the defense attorney asks you to testify to your communications with your attorney and your spouse. You can refuse to answer the questions, since privileges exist for both relationships.

Example 3

In the same case as the previous example, assume that your three-year-old daughter was in the room when you discussed the case with your spouse. Ordinarily, the presence of another person outside the privilege during an otherwise confidential communication destroys a privilege. (See "Don't waive a privilege carelessly," above.) However, most court systems continue to recognize a privilege for spousal communications when a young child is present. However, if you talk over a case with your spouse in the presence of an older child (for example, a teenager) or a friend, you'll probably lose the privilege.

The privilege for communications between spouses is also subject to exceptions. Typical exceptions to this privilege include:

- planning a crime or fraud

  ### Example

  No privilege exists if a married couple discusses how to defraud an insurance company.

- lawsuits between spouses

  ### Example

  No privilege exists if you and your spouse are in court fighting over custody of your children.

3. Other Privileges

Other common privileges include:

- **Penitential communications.** This privilege covers private communications between lay members of religious organizations and religious officials such as priests, ministers, and rabbis, if their religious practices require them to maintain confidentiality. In order for states not to interfere with religious practices, the privilege for penitential communications is typically not subject to any exceptions. *Example:* In a conversation that Church doctrine requires him to keep private, a Catholic priest hears a congregant's confession that "I ran a red light and hit another car." The congregant has a privilege to refuse to answer questions about the confession.

- **Physician-patient communications.** This privilege covers private communications between patients and doctors, nurses, or other medical personnel relating to the patients' physical or mental conditions. The most common exception to this privilege arises when a patient makes his or her physical condition an issue in a court case. *Example 1:* You consult a doctor about a psoriasis condition and, before your appointment, fill out a written questionnaire concerning your health history. Both the questionnaire and your health-related communications with the doctor are privileged. *Example 2:* You're hit by a bus, sue the bus company, and ask for damages to compensate you for your injuries. Conversations you've had with medical personnel relating to your injuries will not be privileged because you've made those injuries an issue in your case.

- **Psychotherapist-patient communications.** This privilege is nearly identical to the physician-patient privilege, but extends to mental health professionals, rape crisis counselors, domestic violence victim counselors, and the like.

Finally, privileged relationships which only a very few court systems presently recognize include:

- parent-child communications

- accountant-client communications, and

- in business or other institutional settings, communications between an ombudsperson and a grievant concerning working conditions and similar matters.

4. Claiming a Privilege

If you believe that a question asks for privileged information, first decide whether you want to refuse to answer it. As the "holder" of the privilege (for example, the client who consulted the lawyer, the patient who consulted the doctor), it's up to you to decide whether you want to claim it. But remember, if you decide to reveal privileged information at your deposition, you waive the privilege and cannot reclaim it later in the case. If you want to keep the information private, politely indicate that you refuse to answer the question and identify the privilege on which you are relying.

Example

You are a plaintiff representing yourself, being deposed by the defendant. At one time you consulted with a lawyer to plan strategy on your case, but that lawyer no longer represents you. During your deposition, the following occurs:

Q: *Prior to filing the lawsuit, did you discuss what happened with anyone?*

You: *Yes.*

Q: *Did you consult with a lawyer?*

You: *Yes.*

Q: *Please describe as best you can recall what you and your lawyer talked about during the first meeting in which you discussed this case.*

You: *I'm sorry, I will not answer that question, based on the attorney-client privilege.*

No matter how insistent the deposing party becomes, you should continue to refuse to answer. Do not be cowed by the deposing lawyer's threat to "take your refusal to court." A judge cannot order you to reveal privileged information. And even if the deposing lawyer does take you to court and a judge decides that your claim of privilege was reasonable yet erroneous, the judge is highly unlikely to do anything more than order you to answer the question.

Example

In the same case, following your refusal to answer based on the attorney-client privilege, the deposing lawyer responds by arguing that the privilege does not apply. For example, the lawyer says something like, "My information is that the conversation you had with the lawyer took place on a subway train at rush hour, within the hearing of numerous other passengers. Under these circumstances, the privilege doesn't exist." If you continue to refuse to answer, and the deposing lawyer goes to court and proves that the supposedly privileged conversation did take place in a public space like a subway train car, the judge might consider your refusal to answer unreasonable and sanction you for the refusal. The sanctions could consist of your having to pay the deposing lawyer's expenses for going to court.

5. Refusing to Answer

At depositions, attorneys normally instruct the deponents they represent to refuse to answer questions calling for privileged information. Thus, if you're represented by an attorney and are asked to disclose privileged information, your attorney will probably object and instruct you not to answer the question. You should, of course, follow your attorney's advice.

If you're not represented by an attorney, you'll have to make up your own mind about whether to answer a question calling for privileged information based on the circumstances.

B. The Work Product Privilege

The "work product" privilege was created to protect attorneys from having to turn over their thoughts and the fruits of their labors to free-loading adversaries. For example, if attorney Sue Asponte interviews ten eyewitnesses and prepares summaries of their statements, it would be very unfair to force Sue to turn over the summaries to her opposing counsel, Jess Gimmey.

FRCP 26(b)(3) is a typical work product rule. It provides that "documents and tangible things … prepared in anticipation of litigation or for trial" must be disclosed to an adversary only under the terms of a court order, and only if the adversary can show that it would cause "undue hardship" if disclosure weren't granted. Even if a judge does order an attorney to disclose some trial preparation materials, the adversary can't have access to materials that would disclose an attorney's "mental impressions, conclusions, opinions, or legal theories."

Under this definition, only an attorney or a self-represented party can claim the work product privilege; a nonparty witness cannot. If you're representing yourself, here's how the work product issue may arise at your deposition: Your adversary may ask you to disclose your legal theories or ask you to turn over a document that you've prepared in anticipation of litigation or trial. If so, you could respond that the requested information is protected by the work product privilege and refuse to provide it.

Example 1

You're a defendant representing yourself in an auto accident case, being deposed by the plain-tiff. As required by "voluntary disclosure" rules (see Chapter 9), you've disclosed to the plaintiff the name, address, and phone number of a potential witness named Marsha Mallow, who was a passenger in your car at the time of the collision. You have in your file your notes from your conversations with Marsha about the accident, which you wrote down to use in case you got sued. At the deposition, the plaintiff's lawyer asks you to turn over the notes. You could refuse to do so based on the work product privilege, as you prepared the notes "in anticipation of litigation." If the plaintiff wants the notes, the plaintiff will have to go to court and convince the court that it would be an undue hardship for the plaintiff not to have them. (If the plaintiff can readily depose Marsha, a judge is unlikely to allow the plaintiff to have your notes.)

Example 2

In the same case as the example above, before the deposition, you did some legal research and developed the arguments you will make if the case goes to trial. At your deposition, the plaintiff's lawyer asks you, "What legal strategies will you rely on if the case goes to trial?" You can refuse to answer, saying that the information is your work product.

Example 3

You're a defendant representing yourself in a patent infringement case. You're being deposed by the plaintiff, who is also self-represented. Before the deposition, you did some research into patent law, including finding out the definition of the term "infringement." During the deposition, the plaintiff asks you, "Based on your legal research, as used in patent law, what does the term infringement mean?" You can refuse to answer, saying that the information is your work product.

C. Evidence of Criminal Activity

Under the Fifth Amendment to the U.S. Constitution, everyone has a "privilege against self-incrimination," in every type of legal proceeding and in every state and federal court. What this means is that you can refuse to answer a deposition question if you reasonably believe that the answer might help to establish that you have engaged in criminal activity. Or to put it bluntly, if a truthful answer might assist the authorities in investigating or prosecuting a criminal case against you, you should refuse to answer regardless of whether:

- you are a party or a nonparty witness
- the question is asked at a deposition, rather than in a courtroom, or
- you are being deposed in a civil rather than in a criminal case.

It is the use to which your testimony might be put, rather than the type of case in which you testify, that determines whether you have a right against self-incrimination.

It's very unlikely that you will be in a position to refuse to answer on the ground of self-incrimination. Few civil lawsuits involve behavior that might expose you to criminal punishment. And even when they do, criminal cases usually move through court much quicker than civil cases, so they are likely to conclude one way or the other by the time your deposition is taken. If a criminal case has ended or if a criminal statute of limitations has expired (meaning that you can no longer be prosecuted), you would no longer have a Fifth Amendment privilege not to testify.

Example 1

At deposition, Mort Gage is asked about how he acquired ownership of a parcel of land four years earlier. Mort actually acquired title to the land through means that were illegal. However, Mort was never prosecuted. Mort's state has a three-year statute of limitations for the crime that Mort committed, meaning Mort could have been prosecuted only within three years of committing the illegal act. Since Mort is no longer subject to prosecution for acquiring title illegally, Mort cannot "claim the Fifth" and would have to answer the questions at deposition.

Example 2

Pop Sailerman has civilly sued Bluto for damages for injuries that Bluto allegedly inflicted on Sailerman as the aggressor in a barroom brawl. Bluto was charged criminally with assault and battery. Before being deposed by Sailerman in the civil case, Bluto pleaded guilty in the criminal case, was put on probation, and paid a fine. Because the criminal case has already concluded at the time Sailerman takes Bluto's deposition, Bluto's deposition testimony cannot expose him to criminal punishment. Bluto has no Fifth Amendment right to refuse to answer Sailerman's questions.

On some occasions, criminal charges might still be in the offing at the time of a deposition. For example, assume that Batten is a police chief who has been named (along with a police officer) as a defendant in a civil suit. The plaintiff, an arrestee, claims that policy guidelines Batten issued resulted in the officer's use of excessive force when making an arrest. Batten is aware that based on this and other complaints of excessive force, a federal prosecutor is looking into the possibility of bringing criminal charges against him. In this situation, the federal prosecutor's investigation may be ongoing when Batten's deposition is taken in the civil lawsuit. If so, Batten may want to refuse to answer questions on self-incrimination grounds. A portion of Batten's deposition testimony may go as follows:

Q: Chief Batten, are you familiar with Exhibit 3, the "Police Procedures Policy Manual?"

A: Yes, I am.

Q: Are you also familiar with Section 3 of that manual, "Use of force when making arrests?"

A: I am.

Q: Please describe the role that you personally played in developing the procedures described in Section 3 of that manual.

A: I refuse to answer that question on the grounds that the answer may tend to incriminate me.

 It pays to exercise legitimate Fifth Amendment rights.

Just because the average person on the street probably considers someone who claims the privilege against self-incrimination to be guilty, you should never be afraid to exercise it in appropriate situations. The truth is, many people who are not guilty of any wrongdoing find it necessary to exercise their privilege (constitutional right) against self-incrimination. Or put another way, criminal charges are frequently filed against innocent people. And of course, even guilty people are perfectly justified in claiming the Fifth—in the American system of justice, people cannot be compelled to provide testimony to support their own conviction.

If in doubt, seek legal advice.
If you're testifying at a deposition and fear that
the answers to some questions might provide
even a little evidence of your criminal activity,
you should consult with a lawyer before your
deposition takes place. If that's not possible, or
if you're not sure whether criminal prosecution
is a realistic possibility, better that you assert the
privilege. That at least puts the burden on the
deposing lawyer to go to court and seek a court
order that you answer. In court, a judge will
have the chance to evaluate your Fifth Amendment privilege not to testify.

D. Private Information

Under FRCP 26(b)(1), questions must be "reasonably calculated to lead to the discovery of
admissible evidence." The key word here is "reasonable." It limits questioning to topics that
have at least some connection to the case. This
makes sense; otherwise, depositions would give
the deposing party license to rummage around
at will in deponents' private affairs.

The deposing party should not ask you
questions seeking private information that is either totally unrelated to a case or is so marginally related that its disclosure is not "reasonably"
calculated to lead to admissible evidence. Such
questions would subject you to "annoyance, embarrassment, oppression, or undue burden or
expense," in violation of FRCP 26(c).

At the same time, however, it's important to
remember that the term "reasonable" is elastic.
If questions seek information related to the case,
they are proper—even though they may seek information about highly private matters.

Example 1

*You are the plaintiff in a personal injury case
and have asked for damages for (among other
things) "loss of consortium" between you and
your spouse (meaning diminished enjoyment of
your spouse's companionship, including
interference with sexual relations). In this
context, the deposing lawyer could properly ask
you a question such as, "How has the sexual
relationship between you and your spouse
changed since your injury?" Even though most
people would consider the details of a married
couple's sexual relationship to be private, the
question is legitimate because harm to a sexual
relationship is part of a "loss of consortium"
claim.*

Example 2

*You are a nonparty witness, a bystander who
happened to observe an auto accident. After you
testify to your educational background, the
deposing lawyer asks, "What was your grade-
point average in college?" After you testify to
your current employment, the lawyer asks,
"What is your current salary?" and "Have you
ever been the subject of a sexual harassment
claim?" In the context of the facts of this case,
all of these questions are clearly improper. Since
they pertain to private matters that are of no
possible relevance to the purpose of your
deposition, you can refuse to answer.*

If you're represented by a lawyer at your deposition, the lawyer is likely to object to a question asking for personal or private information that does not appear related to the case. And if your lawyer is daydreaming and does not object, you should indicate to your lawyer that you do not want to answer the question on invasion of privacy grounds.

In either case, your lawyer may then ask the deposing lawyer to explain how the question is reasonably calculated to lead to admissible evidence. If the deposing lawyer cannot give a satisfactory answer, your lawyer should advise you, "You need not answer the question." You may, in turn, either remain silent or say something like, "I will not answer that question." A deposing lawyer who doesn't agree that a claim of privacy is legitimate can stop the deposition and request a court to order you to answer the question.

If you are not represented by a lawyer and do not want to answer a deposition question that seeks irrelevant private information that you do not want to disclose, you may say something like, "I will not answer that question. The information is private and has nothing to do with this case. I may reconsider and answer the question if you can explain why the information would have some bearing on this case."

Although the deposing lawyer is not required to explain to you why the question is proper, the lawyer may try to convince you of the topic's relevance. If so, consider carefully what the lawyer says before persisting in your refusal. Topics that initially appear to you to be totally unrelated to the issues in the lawsuit may in fact have some bearing on them. If the lawyer's comments satisfy you that an answer to the question might have some rational connection to the case, you can simply answer and continue with the deposition.

If you persist in refusing to answer, and the deposing lawyer believes that a topic is proper, the lawyer can ask a judge to order you to answer (as mentioned above). As a preliminary step, the lawyer may ask you a number of questions all related to the same topic, to put on the record your refusal to answer any of them. If the lawyer files a motion in court, and the judge decides that the questions were proper, you will then have to answer them. It's also possible that the judge will order you to pay the lawyer's motion-related expenses and legal fees. Thus, you should refuse to answer only if you do not want to reveal the private information and you are confident that the information has no bearing on the case.

 Answer questions when a judge orders you to do so.

Ignoring a judge's order to answer questions carries serious consequences. You would be in contempt of court (violation of a judge's order), and the judge could order you to pay a fine or even serve time in jail. If you are a party, your refusal to answer might cause a judge to enter judgment against you. Make sure that you consult with a lawyer before willfully disobeying a judge's order to answer questions. ■

Chapter 8

Expert Witness Deponents

This chapter provides information for expert witnesses. The chapter begins by explaining the unique rules that govern expert witness testimony. The chapter then discusses experts' disclosure requirements before a deposition, the topics deposing lawyers typically address during expert depositions, and (most importantly) how experts can prepare to testify effectively at deposition.

If a party to a lawsuit has retained (hired) you to provide expert testimony, you're not alone. In an age when people know more and more about less and less, expert witnesses have become ubiquitous in civil lawsuits. Even routine cases can have more experts than politicians have fundraisers.

Since only a small percentage of cases actually goes to trial, the deposition is likely to be your only opportunity to testify. Therefore, the value of your expert services to the party who retained you (and your potential future employment as an expert) is likely to depend on your performance at the deposition.

⚠ **Always remember the three Golden Rules for responding to deposition questions.**

See Chapter 4 for a discussion of lawyers' typical deposition questioning techniques. And pay particular attention to the three Golden Rules that all deponents—including experts—should follow when testifying (covered in Chapter 4, Section A).

A. The Difference Between Expert and Nonexpert Witnesses

As an expert, you can use "specialized knowledge" to "assist" a judge or juror to understand the evidence in a case (Federal Rule of Evidence 702). That is, you interpret the meaning of unfamiliar evidence for nonexperts. At your deposition, you'll typically explain the significance of evidence in the form of opinions, and also explain what information you relied on in arriving at those opinions.

Experts who testify in court are often referred to as "forensic experts." ("Forensic" simply means "of, or used in, court.") Thus, a doctor who testifies as an expert in medical malpractice cases regularly might be said to practice forensic medicine.

Example 1

A purchaser of a new home sues the developer for damages when the homeowner finds out that the home was built on improperly compacted landfill. The purchaser hires Bonnie Prince, a soil engineer, as an expert witness. After reviewing records and examining the property, Bonnie's opinions are that the soil was improperly compacted and that the cost to repair it is $100,000. If the developer's lawyer took Bonnie's deposition, Bonnie would undoubtedly be asked to explain the data that she used and the tests that she ran to arrive at these opinions.

Example 2

A pedestrian struck by a car sues the car's driver for personal injuries. Jane Quinn is a physician hired by the pedestrian. After reviewing the pedestrian's medical records, physically examining the pedestrian, and running various tests, Quinn concludes that the pedestrian's injuries are permanent. If Quinn is deposed by the driver's lawyer, Quinn will undoubtedly be asked to explain what injuries the pedestrian suffered and her bases for concluding that the injuries are permanent.

Example 3

A purchaser of an allegedly "flawless" diamond sues the seller after the purchaser finds out that the stone is not a diamond at all but rather a fake of relatively little value. Jim Ologist is a jeweler with many years of experience in the jewelry business. Retained by the purchaser, Jim examines the stone and concludes that it is a cubic zirconium worth little compared to the value of a flawless diamond. If deposed by the seller's lawyer, Jim would certainly be asked to explain how he determined that the stone was cubic zirconium rather than a diamond and how he calculated the fair market value of each.

In each of these situations, nonexperts (such as judges and jurors) would lack the training and experience to reach these conclusions on their own. For example, few untrained people could look at a shiny jewel and be confident of whether it was a diamond or a cubic zirconium. Even judges and jurors who might be able to do so would lack an expert jeweler's

knowledge of their relative market values. Thus, the expert's role is to use specialized knowledge to interpret information for nonexperts.

Sources of Specialized Knowledge

Your specialized knowledge can come from any of a number of sources, including experience, training, and education. (See Federal Rule of Evidence 702.) You need not, however, have an advanced academic degree to qualify as an expert. For example, if a key issue in dispute involves the market value of a failed rutabaga crop, an academic with an advanced degree in agrarian economy could qualify as an expert witness, but so too could an experienced rutabaga farmer. Of course, titles and degrees such as Dr., Ph.D. and M.F.C.C. may have as much of an impact on judges and juries as anyone else, so if you can't back your expertise with academic credentials, you'll have to stress the value and extent of your experience.

Expert witnesses are forbidden from testifying on topics that are fully within the scope of the average judge's and juror's training and experience. For example, experts would not be allowed to testify in the following areas:

- In an ordinary negligence suit against the driver of a car involved in an accident, an expert witness generally could not testify to an opinion that the driver was "careless." That's a judgment that the average judge or juror can make after hearing the evidence. (On the other hand, an expert could testify to some of the data on which judges and jurors could rely on when making that judgment. For example, an expert in automobile accident reconstruction could testify to her opinion that "My analysis of the length of the skidmarks and the condition of the pavement indicates that the driver of the blue car was traveling at least 60 m.p.h. before applying the brakes.")

• Experts cannot testify to which party's witnesses are telling the truth. Judges and jurors are supposed to make credibility judgments based on their own experience and common sense.

• In a fraud case against a car seller, an expert could not testify that the purchaser acted "reasonably" in believing the seller's allegedly false remarks. Whether the purchaser's behavior was reasonable is a decision that ordinary people can make. (By contrast, an automotive expert would be allowed to testify to what was wrong with the car.)

In fields such as these, an expert's opinion would not "assist" judges or jurors because they have sufficient background to understand the significance of evidence on their own.

Does Our Legal System Place Too Much Reliance on Experts for Hire?

The system of using expert witnesses is often challenged by critics who claim that lawyers can find an expert to say almost anything for money. Some of these critics have suggested that the legal system could greatly reduce the reliance on experts by trying cases before judges and jurors who are themselves experts.

However, these suggestions have not gotten very far, in large part because of the ingrained tradition of our legal system that judges and juries speak for the community as a whole. Or put another way, under the Anglo-American legal tradition, it's considered to be important that litigants are judged by their peers, not by a small band of technocrats.

In addition, the premise that experts would render perfect justice is subject to serious question, since expert judges and jurors would inevitably bring their personal biases with them into courtrooms. (So do nonexpert judges and jurors, of course, but parties can challenge and excuse those whose biases would prevent a fair trial.) Finally, even if "judgment by experts" might make sense in some instances, the legal system simply lacks the resources to staff courtrooms with bevies of experts who have all the specialized knowledge needed in modern litigation.

In the meantime, we continue to muddle through with the present system in place. Remarkably, assuming that both sides can afford to hire experts, the present system, which allows each party to try to persuade a judge or jury that its position is meritorious, works pretty well.

Expert Testimony Must Be "Reliable"

As the influence of experts on modern litigation has grown, courts have become increasingly concerned that jurors could be easily misled by experts peddling unreliable opinions dressed up as scientific facts. Before the last decade, courts were required to apply the "*Frye* test" (named after a 1923 U.S. Supreme Court case) in deciding whether to allow an expert to testify. Under the *Frye* test, an expert could testify only if the theories underlying the expert's opinion were generally accepted within the expert's field.

In two recent cases, the U.S. Supreme Court has abandoned the *Frye* test. Instead, the Court decided that judges can admit expert testimony as long as the expert can prove to the judge's satisfaction that the testimony is "reliable"—even if the expert's theories are not generally accepted by others in the expert's field.

This change in the rules will probably have little practical effect on deposition questioning of experts. Before these cases were decided, lawyers would typically ask an expert deposition questions designed to expose weaknesses in the expert's testimony— weaknesses that could be used later to attack the expert's credibility in front of a jury. Now, lawyers can use these weaknesses to argue not only that the expert is not credible, but also that the expert is unreliable—and should be prevented from testifying at all.

These Supreme Court cases apply only in federal court. However, evidence rules in many states closely mimic the Federal Rules of Evidence (just as civil procedure rules in many states mimic the FRPC). Many of these states have already adopted the new "reliability" standard the Supreme Court has set forth, and more are likely to follow.

1. Personal Knowledge Unnecessary

Another important difference between experts and nonexpert (or "lay") witnesses involves their sources of information. Nonexperts can testify only on the basis of personal knowledge. That is, they can testify only to what they have personally seen, heard, smelled, touched, or otherwise directly experienced. Or, as lawyers say, they have to be "percipient" witnesses. While deposition evidence rules are not quite so strict as at trial, the bulk of a nonexpert's deposition testimony ordinarily consists of information within the nonexpert's personal knowledge.

In contrast, as an expert, you are not limited by the "personal knowledge" rule, either during a deposition or at trial. So long as information on which you rely is "of a type reasonably relied upon by experts in the particular field" (Federal Rule of Evidence 703), you may properly use it to arrive at an opinion.

Example

In a negligence lawsuit, an attorney asks an expert in automobile accident reconstruction for an opinion regarding the locations and relative positions of two cars in an intersection at the moment of impact. The expert can testify to such an opinion even though the expert has no actual personal knowledge of what happened. The expert will base the opinion on information such as photographs of the collision site, inspection of the cars following the collision, police reports, witness statements, depositions of percipient witnesses, and maintenance records for the automobiles. The expert may consult other records and reference sources as well. The point is that the expert is able to give an opinion even though the expert didn't see—and therefore has no personal knowledge of—the collision.

2. Expert Witness Fees

As an expert, you can charge the party who retains you for all of your services on a case. For example, you can charge for such tasks as reviewing files, speaking with attorneys, conducting tests, doing research, and attending and testifying at your deposition and at trial.

You can charge for your services in a number of ways. Some experts charge by the hour and, depending on the expert's field, charges of hundreds of dollars per hour are common. Other experts charge flat fees—for example, "$10,000 to consult and testify at trial if necessary." Experts who charge flat fees usually ap-

pear repeatedly in similar cases and so have a reasonable basis for estimating how much time a case will require. (If the party who hired you wins the case, that party will ask the judge to order the adversary to pay your fee.)

Many experts also accept court appointments. For example, in a civil commitment proceeding involving Ann Teek's capacity to manage her own affairs, a psychiatrist may agree to evaluate Ann and prepare a report concerning her mental condition. Experts who accept court appointments usually agree to accept lower fees than they would charge private clients. Whatever your compensation arrangement, make sure that it's reflected in a written contract with the party who retained you.

 Don't tie your fee to litigation results.

Steer clear of attorneys who offer to pay you on a contingency basis—for example, "$5,000 now, and another $5,000 if we win the case." It's unethical for attorneys to pay experts on a contingency basis, because it gives an expert too much of an incentive to slant testimony to earn an extra fee. An attorney who tries to flout this rule may well cut other corners in a way that could embarrass you. For example, the attorney may give you incomplete information, leaving you looking foolish at deposition when the adversary confronts you with facts that were withheld from you.

Ordinarily, the party who retains you must pay you for all of your efforts in connection with a case, including testifying at a deposition. However, there is a big exception to this rule: The adverse party is legally responsible to pay for the time you spend testifying at a deposition. (See FRCP 26(b)(4)(C).) As a result, the party who retained you generally pays for your preparation time; the deposing party normally pays for the time you spend testifying. The rule requires that your fee be "reasonable," in order to prevent you from charging an exorbitant fee calculated to discourage the adversary from deposing you.

Just in case the deposing party fails to pony up, your contract with the party who retains you should specify that you will be compensated for all the time you spend working on the case—and that it is not your responsibility to make sure that the deposing party pays up. That way if the deposing party stiffs you, the retaining party has the legal obligation to pay your fee. (This situation probably won't arise. In most cases, if the deposing party hasn't paid your deposition fee when you arrive at the deposition, the party who retained you will simply refuse to allow you to be deposed.) In many locales, the custom is for the deposing party to pay your fee to the party who retained you, not to you directly.

Compensation of Experts Not Retained

In some situations, whether you're paid as an expert or treated as an ordinary nonparty witness (covered in Chapter 1) may depend on whether you're asked to give an expert opinion at the deposition. For example, doctors and other professionals are entitled to their "usual professional fees" for the time spent at a deposition if they provide expert opinions, but not if they simply testify to their observations or to the content of their records.

Assume the defendant in a personal injury case deposes Dr. Liz Ishen, the emergency room physician who treated the plaintiff following a slip and fall. If Dr. Ishen is asked at deposition only to describe the injuries she observed and the treatment she prescribed, Dr. Ishen will probably be treated as an ordinary nonparty witness and receive only a nominal witness fee. However, if Dr. Ishen is asked to testify to expert opinions (such as "What was the likely cause of the injury?"), Dr. Ishen may be able to refuse to answer unless the defendant tenders Dr. Ishen's "usual professional fee" for her time spent at the deposition. (See FRCP 45(c)(3)(B).)

B. Predeposition Disclosures

If the party who retained you expects to call you as an expert witness at trial, FRCP 26 imposes a number of requirements both on you and on the party who retained you. These requirements seek to eliminate the possibility that one party can surprise the other at trial with secret expert testimony. Under Rule 26, the retaining party must:

- voluntarily disclose an expert's identity to its adversary, even if the adversary neglects to make a formal request for such a disclosure, and

- send the adversary a written "disclosure report" prepared by the expert, probably in consultation with the attorney for the retaining party.

Under Rule 26(a)(2), as an expert, your disclosure report should contain:

- your opinions

- your reasons for arriving at those opinions

- information you considered before arriving at your opinions

- any exhibits you will use at trial to summarize or support your opinions

- your qualifications to give expert testimony and your recent publications, if any

- your fees, and

- a list of any other cases in which you have testified as an expert (either in a deposition or at trial) during the preceding four years.

The retaining party has to submit all this information to the adversary at least 90 days before the date a case is scheduled for trial. (An advance warning of only 30 days is necessary if you have been hired solely to rebut [contradict] an adversary's expert.)

Because you can hold off on making these disclosures until 90 days before trial, you and the party who retained you will have time to gather information, conduct any necessary tests, and prepare the written report. After you hand over the report, the adverse party still has time before trial to study your disclosure report and decide whether to depose you.

Deposing Physicians and Mental Health Professionals Not Expected to Testify

Health care experts are often hired to examine patients and prepare reports, with no expectation that they will testify at trial. For example, if you're a physician, a party considering filing a personal injury lawsuit may hire you to conduct an examination and advise on the seriousness of the injury. Under FRCP 35, the adversary can depose you even if you're not expected to testify at trial. However, unlike with testifying experts, the adversary has to first obtain a court order requiring you to appear for a deposition. If the court orders your deposition, you will also have to furnish the adversary with a detailed written report.

You may be wondering why an adversary might go to the expense of taking your deposition when you've already handed over a disclosure statement setting out your opinions and your bases for reaching them. The answer is that your disclosure statement—which is most likely a joint product of you and the attorney for the party who retained you—is likely to be written in general terms. This gives away as little information as possible and leaves you with considerable wiggle room to change or supplement your opinions based on new information. Thus, by deposing you after you've submitted your disclosure report, the adversary can delve into the details of your written material and try to smoke out vagueness and generalities in your deposition testimony—thereby making it more difficult for you to change your opinions at trial.

C. Typical Predeposition Involvement

In complex cases involving large sums of money, your deposition may be but one of many pretrial activities you perform on behalf of the party who retained you.

For example, assume that an estate planning lawyer has been sued for legal malpractice. The plaintiff in this lawsuit claims that the defendant lawyer made a serious mistake in drafting a will for his mother, as a result of which $500,000 that the plaintiff was supposed to receive under the will went to someone else. The cast of characters is:

- Noah Dinero—the plaintiff, who believes he was ripped off.

- Sue Meal—the litigation lawyer hired by Noah to sue the lawyer who drafted the will (Anna Turnery).

- Will Drafter—the expert witness hired by Sue and Noah. Will is an estate planning lawyer with many years of experience who has testified as an expert witness in a number of other lawsuits.

- Anna Turnery—the lawyer whose mistake Noah claims cost him big time.

- Foggy & Foggy—the law firm hired by Anna Turnery's malpractice insurance company to defend her against the lawsuit filed by Sue and Noah.

Will's involvement as an expert witness in this lawsuit may unfold something like this:

1. An unhappy Noah meets with attorney Sue, shows her the will drafted by Turnery, and explains what happened. Sue, an experienced litigator but not an expert in estate planning, says that before she can recommend going ahead with the case, she will have to ask an expert whether Turnery really screwed up. At Sue's suggestion Noah agrees to hire Will Drafter, a veteran and highly regarded estate planner who has testified previously as an expert witness in legal malpractice cases involving estate planning. Will's normal fee is $250 per hour. At this initial stage, Will is to be paid for four hours of preliminary work to advise Sue and Noah as to whether Noah has a good case.

2. Sue prepares a summary of the case and sends the summary, the allegedly improperly drafted will, and a few other papers to Will. After reviewing the material, Will advises Sue that Noah does have a good claim for legal malpractice. Sue then begins a lawsuit by filing a "Complaint" alleging that Turnery's legal malpractice caused Noah to lose thousands of dollars. At this point, Noah might authorize Sue to retain Will for additional expert services, including testifying. However, Noah and Sue might decide to retain a different expert instead (perhaps one who charges less).

Question

If Noah and Sue decide to retain an expert other than Will, could Foggy & Foggy (Turnery's lawyers) hire Will as their expert witness?

Answer

No. Even if Will has nothing more to do with the lawsuit, once Noah employs Will to review Noah's case, conflict of interest rules would prevent Will from working for Noah's adversary. (Vengeful parties with "deep pockets" [a lot of money] occasionally try to take advantage of this conflict of interest rule when involved in a big-money case in a field where only a few reputable experts exist. The modus operandi is to attempt to "buy up" [retain] all the best experts by hiring them for preliminary consultations. The experts are then unavailable to the adversary.)

3. After Sue files the complaint, Foggy & Foggy files an "Answer" denying that Turnery made a mistake when drafting the will.

4. During the discovery process before trial, both sides send out written interrogatories and take the depositions of people expected to testify for the other side. (See Chapter 9 for an overview of written interrogatories.) During this time, Will acts as a consultant to Sue (still charging $250 per hour), advising her as to the questions she should ask in written interrogatories and other discovery in order to bring out the information necessary to put together a convincing case. Will also agrees to testify as an expert witness at the same fee on Noah's behalf if the case goes to trial. At trial, Will's role would be to describe what Turnery did wrong and explain why the mistake constituted a "failure to use at least ordinary skills." (This is what Sue has to prove if Noah is to prevail in the malpractice lawsuit.)

5. At least 90 days before the trial date, Sue must voluntarily disclose to Foggy & Foggy that she plans to call Will as an expert witness at trial. (See FRCP 26, discussed in Section B, above.) Along with the disclosure, Sue must send Foggy & Foggy a written report that sets forth Will's expert opinions, Will's reasoning for arriving at those opinions, the information that Will considered to arrive at those opinions, any visual aids or other materials (called "exhibits") that Will plans to use at trial to summarize or support his opinions, Will's qualifications as an expert (including a list of his recent publications

in the estate planning field), Will's fee, and a list of other cases in which Will has testified (either in a deposition or at trial) during the preceding four years.

6. After receiving the report, Foggy & Foggy is likely to send Will a Subpoena re Deposition, notifying Will of the time and date that Foggy & Foggy plans to take his deposition. (Foggy & Foggy, not Noah, will have to pay Will $250 per hour for Will's time to attend the deposition. However, if Turnery wins the lawsuit, Foggy & Foggy can ask the judge to order Noah to reimburse Foggy & Foggy for the cost of taking Will's deposition.)

7. Before the deposition, Will and Sue meet to discuss the questions that the lawyer from Foggy & Foggy is likely to ask at the deposition and how Will should answer those questions. Sue will probably also ask Will to review the depositions of other witnesses that have already been taken. (Some attorneys would allow Noah to attend the deposition preparation meeting. Others would not want their client present, on the theory that they can be more candid in the client's absence.)

8. Ole Foggy III, a lawyer with Foggy & Foggy, deposes Will. Before deposing Will, Ole would have read Will's disclosure report. And, like Noah and Sue, Ole may also have hired an estate planning expert to consult with and to testify at trial if necessary.

9. In consultation with their clients (Noah and Turnery), Sue and Ole will probably discuss possible settlement of the case. Will's deposition

testimony is likely to strongly affect whether the case is settled, and, if so, on what terms. For example, Ole may be very reluctant to go to trial if Will's deposition testimony clearly explains how Turnery goofed, and if Will's manner of testifying is clear and persuasive.

10. If the case doesn't settle, Will will testify on Noah's behalf at trial. Before Will testifies, Will and Sue will probably get together again to prepare for Will's testimony. Noah will pay for Will's time to prepare and testify at trial, but will ask the judge to order Turnery to pay these costs if Noah wins the lawsuit.

In this example, Will (the expert witness) played no part in the case until after the events giving rise to the lawsuit had taken place. This is a scenario common to many types of cases. For example, an expert in soil engineering might not be retained until after a house slips from its foundation, and an accident reconstruction expert might not be retained until long after a collision occurs.

It's possible, however, that an expert will have played an active role in the events leading up to a lawsuit. For example, assume that a pedestrian is injured when struck by a car and taken to a hospital. The pedestrian is treated by Dr. Aichemo. The pedestrian later sues the driver of the car. Dr. Aichemo may serve as an expert witness for the plaintiff and be deposed and testify at trial because of her involvement in the underlying events resulting in the lawsuit. (For more on this, see "Compensation of Experts Not Retained," in Section A2, above.

D. The Importance of Thorough Deposition Preparation

At the deposition, your only immediate audience is the adversary's deposing attorney, not a judge or a jury. Nevertheless, for the reasons set forth below, you want to demonstrate to the adversary both that you have mastery of the relevant subject matter and that you can explain what you know in a clear and credible fashion. Thus, you should prepare for your deposition as carefully as you would for a trial.

A big reason to prepare thoroughly for your deposition is that most cases settle; they never go to trial. Along with the documents produced during discovery, the deposition testimony of each party's witnesses are the primary factors that shape settlements. As an expert, you may well be the most important of these witnesses.

Example

Wood B. Widower sues a life insurance company seeking to collect the proceeds of a policy on the life of his wife Wendy. Wood claims that Wendy hasn't been heard from in over five years, and therefore under his state's law is presumed to be legally dead. The life insurance company refuses to pay, claiming that Wendy is alive, as evidenced by a message allegedly recently left by Wendy on Wood's telephone answering machine. The life insurance company bases its claim that the voice on the machine is Wendy's on the opinion of its expert in voice identification, Dr. Otto Cochlea.

Wood deposes Dr. Cochlea, who describes his credentials and then explains how he compared the voice on the answering machine with a known sample of Wendy's voice to conclude that the voice on the answering machine was indeed Wendy's. Especially if Wood cannot respond with equally impressive expert testimony, Dr. Cochlea's deposition testimony may cause Wood to drop the lawsuit or settle for a small sum.

A second reason to prepare thoroughly for your deposition is that if a case does go to trial, a judge may bar you from testifying to any opinions that you failed to identify either in your disclosure report or at your deposition. At the very least, the opposing party will be able to attack your credibility at trial by showing that your testimony has changed since your deposition.

Finally, thorough preparation is important because the deposing party will use your deposition not only to explore the substance of your opinions, but also to assess your personal qualities. Can you explain your opinions convincingly in a way that judges and jurors can understand? Do your demeanor and manner of testifying convey sincerity and credibility? In short, unless you have prepared well and testified authoritatively, the adversary may successfully disparage your testimony during settlement negotiations—in an effort to convince the party who hired you to accept a less advantageous settlement.

Will I definitely be deposed?

In a word, the answer is no. The fact that you've been retained as an expert witness doesn't necessarily mean that you will be deposed. Expert depositions tend to be costly—the adverse party has to pay for both your time and it's own attorney's time. As a result the party may decide not to depose you, especially if you are but one of a number of experts appearing for the same party.

Length of Notice Before a Deposition

Like nonexpert deponents, you're entitled to "reasonable" advance warning that your deposition is to be taken. (FRCP 30(b)(1).) It's very likely that the deposing lawyer will contact the lawyer for the party who retained you to clear a date before noticing your deposition. If this hasn't happened, and you have a conflict on the chosen date, contact the lawyer who retained you at once. The lawyers should be able to work around your schedule. If not, discuss your alternatives with the lawyer who retained you, who may decide to go to court and seek a "protective order" rescheduling your deposition. The lawyer would argue that the notice did not give you "reasonable" advance warning. For ordinary deponents, ten days is usually sufficient advance warning. However, judges often provide experts with more leeway.

E. The Predeposition Planning Meeting

The attorney for the party who retained you (or the self-represented party who retained you) will undoubtedly want to meet with you shortly before your deposition. In many ways, the predeposition planning meeting is likely to closely resemble such meetings between lawyers and nonexpert witnesses. For example, the lawyer will probably conduct a mock (practice) deposition to ask you questions of the type you may be asked at the deposition.

That said, one predeposition issue may be of special concern to you as an expert witness: the subtle (or maybe not so subtle!) conflict that can arise between you and the attorney (or self-represented party) who retained you over how best to present your deposition testimony. As the expert, you may believe that you are best qualified to decide how to educate a nonexpert opposing party, judge, or juror to interpret unfamiliar evidence. Yet the retaining attorney may be quite knowledgeable in your field of expertise, too.

For instance, if you're a physician retained in a medical malpractice case, the retaining attorney may have attended medical school or may have worked on so many similar cases that the attorney is nearly as knowledgeable about medical matters as you are. As a result, the attorney may have equally strong (and conflicting) ideas about how you should testify.

These conflicts are apt to arise when the retaining attorney conducts a mock deposition in a predeposition planning meeting. During the mock deposition, the attorney will question you as the deposing attorney is likely to do, and will analyze your answers. The attorney's comments on your answers may sound like the attorney makes tailored suits, not lawsuits—"Take in a little bit here, let out a little bit there"—and you may disagree with the attorney's advice. For example, the attorney may want you to give a concise two-sentence answer to a question such as, "Why did you run Test A and not Test B?" Especially knowing that the deposition may be your only chance to impress the adversary, you may believe that a fuller explanation is warranted. If such conflicts do arise, you should feel welcome to state your views. The predeposition meeting gives you and the retaining attorney a chance to come to an agreement about how best to present your opinions.

⚠ Beware the lawyer who wants to put unpalatable words in your mouth.

Be wary of the retaining attorney who says, "Here's what I'd like you to say," or otherwise tries to pressure you into giving stronger opinions than you believe the facts warrant. For example, perhaps you're a voice identification expert whose opinion is that the voices on two tapes "probably" belong to the same person; the retaining attorney wants you to testify that you are "99% certain" that the two voices belong to the

same person. Or, you may be a physician whose opinion is that an injured patient is "unlikely" to ever walk again; the retaining attorney wants you to testify that it's a "medical certainty" that the patient will never walk again.

It should go without saying that you should refuse to testify to anything other than what you believe to be the truth—which is what you will swear to do under oath at your deposition. Besides, if you take a position that is more extreme than the facts warrant, you risk having your credibility undermined by cross-examination at the deposition and by an opposing expert.

F. Typical Deposition Questioning

The sections below describe the kinds of questions an expert witness will probably face at his or her deposition. Of course, these questions will vary depending on the attorney's style and the experts field of expertise. In general, however, depositions of experts tend to include the four questioning stages reviewed below (though they may not occur in precisely the order set forth here).

1. Stage 1: Beginning Your Deposition

The beginning stages of both expert and nonexpert depositions tend to be routine. Here's what you can expect.

a. Admonitions

As set forth in Chapter 5, admonitions are a series of preliminary questions largely aimed at locking you into your deposition testimony. If you've been deposed before, you may need to be reminded of the admonitions about as much as an arrested police officer needs to be reminded of the *Miranda* warnings. Nevertheless, the deposing attorney is likely to start off your deposition with the same admonitions the attorney would give to nonexpert deponents. The attorney will want the admonitions in the deposition transcript in case your testimony changes between the deposition and the trial.

b. Identifying Documents

After you've been given the admonitions, you may next be asked what documents you reviewed when preparing for your deposition. The deposing party will then ask you and the attorney who retained you to turn over all such documents immediately (unless the deposing party has already gotten them through the use of other discovery methods).

Evidence rules in most states (and Federal Rule of Evidence 612) allow the deposing party to request and examine any documents you looked at to refresh your recollection for the purpose of testifying at deposition. Therefore, you should be careful not to make any embarrassing or private notations on any documents that you review in the course of preparing to be deposed.

In addition, you may be asked to identify any documents you consulted or prepared (for example, X-rays you took or reports you made) in arriving at your opinions. The deposing party normally has a right to review these documents, regardless of whether you looked at them to refresh your memory. By examining such documents at the outset of your deposition, the deposing party has a chance to question you about their contents. Thus, you should bring your "case file" to the deposition in order to prevent delays that might occur if your deposition had to be continued to another day for you to locate and produce relevant documents.

Of course, you'll want to review the contents of your file with the retaining attorney before the deposition, because some of the documents may not be "discoverable"—that is, they may be withheld on the basis of one or more privileges. (See Chapter 7 for an overview of privileges.) Again, be careful not to make any embarrassing or private notations on any documents that you review in the course of reaching your opinion.

c. Background Questioning

Questioning focused on a nonexpert's employment and educational background is routine in depositions. (See Chapter 6 for more information.) But because a lay witness's background is often unrelated to the substance of the witness's testimony (for example, a computer programmer might observe a plane crash), background questioning of lay witnesses is often little more than a warm-up to questions about what they actually witnessed.

In contrast, an expert's specialized background is precisely what qualifies the expert to give testimony. As a result, you may be questioned extensively about your background in your deposition. You may be asked about any or all of the following:

- **Education and professional training.** This may include a detailed review of your formal post-high school education (graduate and undergraduate) as well as continuing education courses; technical training courses (for example, an employer-sponsored course covering a new computer programming language); and certificate programs (for example, an attorney assistant might receive a certificate for attending a series of classes on advanced estate planning).

- **Work experience.** Depending on your field of expertise, this may include inquires about job titles and responsibilities, reasons for changing jobs, and so on.

- **Professional activities.** For example, you might be asked whether you've received any awards or honors; whether you're a member of any professional boards, societies, or peer review organizations; whether you've written any books or articles; and whether you've taught in your field of expertise.

- **Prior experience as an expert.** For example, you may be asked about the types of cases

in which you've been previously retained, who retained you, and whether you testified at a deposition or at trial.

The opposing attorney is likely to explore your credentials—even if the opponent concedes that you are qualified as an expert—because the attorney might find a weakness that could detract from the force of your opinions. For example, the deposing attorney may try to develop evidence showing any of the following:

- You are a generalist (for example, a surgeon) in a field in which many people—including the deposing attorney's own expert—are specialists rather than generalists (for example, neurosurgeons).

- While you have adequate academic qualifications, you lack practical experience. For example, in a legal malpractice case, a law professor may qualify to give an opinion that a conflict of interest existed such that the defendant attorney should have advised the plaintiff to seek alternate legal counsel. However, the fact that the professor has never actually practiced law may detract from the professor's credibility as an expert witness on the issue.

- Your background does not precisely mesh with the facts of the case. For example, an expert appraiser may have a significant background in commercial real estate, but minimal experience with industrial real estate—the type of property involved in the lawsuit for which the expert was retained. Similarly, the appraiser's experience may be in County A whereas the dispute concerns property in County B.

- You spend a large portion of your professional life serving as an expert witness rather than pursuing the activities in which you're supposedly an expert.

- You're a fiddle that plays but one tune. That is, you always appear in lawsuits on behalf of the same side (for example, you always work for physicians accused of malpractice, never for injured patients). This fact suggests that you mold the facts of a case to fit your preexisting biases rather than genuinely analyzing what happened.

If any such shortcomings do exist, the deposing attorney may refer to them when challenging your opinions later in the deposition. (See Section F3, below.)

 ### Provide complete answers to background questions.

When you are asked deposition questions about your background, provide complete information about how closely your knowledge, education, training, skills, or experience qualify you as an expert on the important issues in the case. Because this point is so important, let's look at several examples of how an expert might give complete answers about relevant background.

- You're a gemologist whose opinion is that a jewel sold as a diamond is really a cubic zirconium. You will also testify to the huge difference between the market values of diamonds and cubic zirconiums. When asked about your background and experience, explain in some detail your long experience in the diamond business and experience tracking the market value of diamonds. Don't be content to say something like, "I have many years of experience in the jewelry business."

- You're a real estate appraiser whose opinion is that a particular industrial plant has a market value of $100,000. When asked about your background as an appraiser, give a complete answer that details your long and deep experience as an appraiser of industrial real estate (which is distinct from residential or commercial property), and mention any experience you have had in the locale in which the property is situated. Assuming it's an impressive total, be ready to say how many industrial sites you have appraised and how many dollars were involved. Don't simply say something like, "I've had loads of experience as an appraiser."

- You're the manager of a used car lot whose opinion is that a three-year-old Lexus has a market value of $35,000. Your background testimony should include your up-to-date familiarity with the value of Lexus automobiles—not just your general familiarity with the market for used cars.

2. Stage 2: Establishing a Chronology of Your Case-Related Activities

The deposing attorney may also seek to establish a chronology of your case-related activities. That is, the attorney may want to know everything you've done to arrive at your opinions between the date that you were first contacted by the attorney (or self-represented party) who retained you and the date of the deposition. The opposing lawyer may use this chronology for a number of purposes, including the following:

- The attorney may seek to show that you agreed to serve as an expert before reviewing all the pertinent information in the case, suggesting that you were less than objective in evaluating the facts and arriving at your opinions.

- The attorney may seek to show that the party who retained you furnished you with incomplete information, suggesting that your conclusions are based on a distorted picture of the evidence.

- By eliciting a full picture of what methodology you followed, what tests you conducted (or failed to conduct), what research you did (or failed to do), and which witnesses you spoke with and when, the attorney may seek to show that the methods you used to arrive at your opinions were flawed.

- The attorney will learn about any assistants or independent third parties who contributed to your opinions, leading to possible additional deponents.

- You will identify any exhibits that you have prepared for use at trial, and when the exhibits were prepared.

For an example of what a chronology of your activities may look like, assume that you are Lex Purt, an engineer who has been retained by the defendant in a product liability case involving the alleged substandard design of a bicycle helmet. The deposing attorney's questions might reveal the following chronology:

- 10 January: First contact from defendant's lawyer. Agreed that lawyer will send copy of file to Purt, Purt will send CV to lawyer and evaluate case.

- 12 January: Purt calls lawyer, agrees to testify, fee arrangements made.

- 22–24 January: Purt reviews previous depositions given in case. Purt also reviews authoritative treatise, "Bicycle Helmet Design in a Nutshell."

- 29 January: Purt consults with Jack Aranda, president of the National Association of Bicycle Helmet Manufacturers.

- 14 February: Purt makes trip to the defendant's factory, gets copies of design specifications, inspects defendant's quality control system.

- 29 February: Purt runs strength and torque tests on helmets identical to the one worn by the plaintiff in Purt's testing lab. Purt prepares illustrative exhibits for use at trial.

- 5–6 March: Purt examines data and test results, arrives at conclusion that helmet meets standards set by several respected national bicycle safety organizations for design safety.
- 10 July: Purt's deposition.

The attorney may end this phase of the deposition by asking whether you have concluded your investigation and, if not, what activities you expect to engage in after the deposition. If you indicate that additional work is necessary, the attorney can argue that your opinions are based on incomplete information. Alternatively, the attorney may seek to schedule an additional deposition after your work is completed. If it turns out that you did not do any further investigation, the attorney may again argue that your conclusions rest on incomplete information. Thus, you should testify that you plan to investigate further only if you really mean it.

⚠ Document the information you receive from the retaining attorney

Your opinions can be only as good as the information on which they're based. Thus, you must make sure that the attorney who retained you turns over all the information necessary for you to arrive at a reliable opinion. Also, make an inventory of the documents and records the retaining attorney gave you to review. An inventory can protect your professional reputation and your right to collect your fee. Consider what might happen if, in mid-deposition, the deposing lawyer shows you a document or reveals a piece of

information that causes you to change your opinion. The attorney who retained you may contest your fee, claiming that your work on the case was careless. But if, by referring to your inventory, you can show that the retaining attorney never showed you the document or mentioned the item of evidence that led to your change of opinion, you can respond effectively to the claim that your work was sloppy.

 Keep a "Chron File."

To enhance your ability to reconstruct case-related activities, it's often wise to keep a chronological file or log for every case in which you're retained as an expert. Enter each significant event in the "Chron File" (which can be on paper or computer) soon after it occurs. For example, a Chron File entry might read as follows:

"12 March 20xx: Ran Test A. Entered results in computer case file."

You may want to take your Chron File with you to your deposition and refer to it if necessary to refresh your memory. However, remember that the deposing attorney is entitled to examine any document that you use to refresh your recollection—whether before your deposition or during it. So make sure that your Chron File (or any other document you bring to the deposition) is "clean." That is, don't make any notations on it that might embarrass you or suggest the existence of private information to deposing counsel.

3. Stage 3: Exploring Your Opinions

As you might anticipate, the bulk of your deposition is likely to be devoted to the substance of your opinions. The deposing attorney is likely to ask you about the bases for those opinions in an effort to challenge their accuracy.

a. Exploring the Basis of Your Opinion

The questioner will probably try to get you to commit to the specific factors on which you based your opinion. This information will consist of:

- physical evidence—for example, a blood sample, an allegedly defective piece of machinery, or the damaged rear end of a car involved in a collision

- information you obtained from documents such as business records, depositions of other witnesses, witness statements, police reports, a patient's medical charts, and X-rays

- information that you generated personally by, for example, conducting tests, interviewing witnesses, or taking X-rays, and

- factual assumptions that underlie your opinion—for example, that the current rate of inflation will continue for at least five years or that a piece of equipment was working properly before it suffered damage.

Below is an example of how this type of questioning might proceed.

Example

Dr. Cochlea, the expert in voice identification, was retained to compare the voice of a known person on a tape to an unknown voice on a second tape. Dr. Cochlea's analysis consisted of repeated listening to portions of the tapes and comparing diagrams ("sound spectrograms") of the actual speech sounds. After completing his analysis, Dr. Cochlea formed the opinion that the two tapes were made by different people: The unknown person's voice does not match the known person's voice. After eliciting this opinion, the deposing attorney asks Dr. Cochlea about the bases of that opinion. A portion of that questioning goes as follows:

Q: *So Dr. Cochlea, if I understand your testimony, you listened to each tape at least ten times?*

A: *Yes. Well, at least specific segments of each tape, the segments that had words or phrases in common.*

Q: *And in concluding that the tapes were made by different people, you considered how the voices sounded when you listened to them?*

A: *Yes.*

Q: *Your opinion is also based on comparisons of sound spectrograms of common speech sounds?*

A: *Yes.*

Q: *Can you state in percentage terms the extent to which your opinion is based on what you heard when you listened to the* tapes as opposed to what you saw when you looked at the sound spectrograms?

A: I'm sorry, I can't do that. I can tell you that my opinion is based in part on having listened to a number of common words and phrases at least ten times each.

Q: Dr. Cochlea, I'd like to focus for a moment on your analysis of the speech sounds themselves. What was there about the sounds that supports your opinion that the tapes were made by different speakers?

A: For one thing, the pronunciation of the letter "s" when it was the first speech sound in a word. The known voice pronounced the "s" sound with a slight lisp; the unknown voice did not.

Q: Still with reference to the sounds themselves, what other factors support your view that the tapes were made by different speakers?

A: Another factor I considered was the variation of the "o" sound in the word "consider," a common word on both tapes. The known speaker pronounced the "o" sound as the short "u" sound, as though the first three letters of the word were "c-u-n." The unknown speaker made an "ah" sound, as in the word "con."

Q: Any other factors you can think of?

A: Yes, another factor was…

The questioning would probably continue until Dr. Cochlea had given all possible reasons for his conclusion that the tapes were made by different speakers. Probably, the deposing attorney would not leave the topic before getting Dr. Cochlea's negative answer to a question such as:

"Can you point to any other differences in the speech sounds themselves that support your opinion that the tapes were made by different speakers?"

Once Dr. Cochlea testifies that "I've given you all the reasons," Dr. Cochlea probably cannot credibly testify to an additional reason at trial. Therefore, if you're in Dr. Cochlea's position, at the deposition you'll want to refer to every basis for your opinion.

b. Challenging Your Opinion

Once all the bases for your opinion are on the table, the deposing attorney is likely to challenge their adequacy. Obviously, the factors that a deposing attorney might use to try to challenge the accuracy of your opinion will vary depending on your field of expertise and the factual disputes in the particular case. The following subsections illustrate examples of typical types of challenges.

i. "My information is different."

The deposing attorney might compare the factors upon which you rely with the contrasting views of other experts (possibly including the deposing attorney's own expert). For example, in the deposition excerpt above, Dr. Cochlea testified that he based his opinion in part on having listened to common speech sounds "at least ten times." The deposing attorney might challenge this opinion if the deposing attorney has information that you have to listen to common speech sounds at least 20 times each to arrive at a reliable opinion. In this event, a portion of Dr. Cochlea's deposition might go as follows:

Q: *You listened to the common speech sounds at least ten times?*

A: *Yes.*

Q: *Dr. Cochlea, wouldn't you agree that a reliable opinion requires that you listen to common speech sounds at least 20 times each?*

A: *No, I don't agree with that.*

Q: *Well, the National Sound Spectrogram Institute recommends that common speech sounds be listened to at least 20 times each, correct?*

A: *I'm familiar with that report. I'd point out that that's only a recommendation. Also, if I recall the report, that recommendation assumes that the speech sounds are of poor quality. The tapes here were in excellent condition.*

Q: *Are you also familiar with the work of Dr. Peter Laddy?*

A: *Yes of course, he's an internationally recognized expert on voice identification.*

Q: *And Dr. Laddy is of the opinion that common speech sounds should be listened to at least 20 times each, correct?*

A: *That's true. However, in this case I chose not to because …*

As Dr. Cochlea does here, you should stick to your guns if you disagree with the factors that the deposing attorney puts forward to challenge the accuracy of your opinion.

ii. "Your opinion is only as good as the information it's based on."

Your opinion is likely to rely, at least in part, on information that has been provided to you in reports, witness statements, and the like. If so, the deposing attorney may use a "garbage in, garbage out" questioning strategy—that is, the deposing attorney may ask questions suggesting that if some of the information in those reports or statements is wrong, your opinion might be inaccurate.

For example, assume that Flinta Fuego's expertise is in determining the origin of fires. Ms. Fuego has been retained by a fire insurance company to investigate the cause of a house fire. Based on witness statements, photos of the ruins, and fire department reports, Fuego concludes that the fire started in the house's library, and that the fire was intentionally set. In an effort to undermine Fuego's opinion, the deposing attorney might ask questions such as the the following:

Q: *Ms. Fuego, your opinion is that the fire was set intentionally, correct?*

A: *That's right.*

Q: *In arriving at this opinion, you relied heavily on information in Colonel Mustard's statement, didn't you?*

A: Well, that and lots of other information, as I've previously testified to.

Q: But Colonel Mustard's statement is a basis for your opinion, correct?

A: Yes, as I've already stated.

Q: Now, do you agree that if Colonel Mustard's information is erroneous, that might alter your opinion?

A: Not necessarily. I'd have to know in what way the Colonel is mistaken.

Q: Well, assume for a moment that the first flames that were observed were in the conservatory, not in the library as the Colonel reported. Might that affect your opinion?

A: If that were the case, I'd probably have to reassess my opinion.

Q: You certainly have no first-hand information as to where the flames were first seen, do you?

A: No.

Q: And you do not know of your own knowledge that Colonel Mustard's statement is accurate, correct?

A: That's true.

Q: And if Colonel Mustard is wrong about where the flames were first seen, your opinion may well be inaccurate?

A: That's true.

If you rely for your opinion on information supplied by others, you will be potentially susceptible to this questioning technique. Do not be embarrassed by such questions. Answer them directly. You are not a guarantor of the information provided to you. Again, however, do not concede more than you need to. For example, Ms. Fuego reminds the deposing attorney that she relied on a variety of sources and asserts that not every mistake would cause her to reconsider her opinions.

iii. "Why didn't you do more?"

Your opinion may rest at least in part on tests you've conducted, research you've done, or experiments you've performed. For example, if you're an engineering expert who's been asked to give an opinion about the quality of the suturing material used by a hospital physician to close a wound, you might conduct tensile strength tests on samples of the hospital's suturing material.

Since you don't have a infinite amount of time or an infinite amount of money to conduct tests or do other research, undoubtedly you will leave possible stones unturned in arriving at your opinion. As a result, the deposing attorney may try to challenge the accuracy of your opinion by asking you about additional research you chose not to do. An appropriate reply is that the research you did was sufficient to support your opinion and that additional tests would have been a waste of both time and money.

To understand how this type of challenge might proceed, examine this portion of the deposition of a forensic psychologist:

Q: Dr. Jungfreud, the NNPI is a standard psychological test used to diagnose mental disorders, correct?

A: Yes, that test is often administered.

Q: Yet you didn't administer the NNPI in this case, correct?

A: That's correct.

Q: Wouldn't the results of the NNPI have aided your ability to make an accurate diagnosis?

A: Not in this particular case. In this case, you had a patient who ...

No matter how extensively you explored the bases for an opinion, it's likely that you could have done something else such as:

• looked at authoritative treatises

• consulted other experts

• read additional reports

• spoken to witnesses instead of simply reading their statements, or

• made personal visits to the scenes of events.

As always, you should answer questions such as these in a direct and straightforward manner. You have nothing to hide—you are not required to turn over every possible stone in reaching your conclusions. As an expert, it is your right and responsibility to decide when you have made a sufficient investigation to formulate an accurate opinion. If the deposing attorney asks why you neglected to take a par-ticular investigatory step, be prepared to explain why you considered it unnecessary to do so.

4. Stage 4: Searching for Bias

A distinct method of challenging the accuracy of your opinion involves a search for possible bias. If the deposing attorney can elicit information suggesting that you have an ax to grind in favor of the party who retained you, your credibility at trial might be weakened. To get this information, the deposing attorney may probe for potential evidence of bias. Factors that suggest possible bias include:

• Your relationship with the attorney and party who retained you. For example, have you been employed before by the attorney? If so, how often and in which cases?

• The percentage of your time devoted to, and income derived from, working as an expert witness. Juries may distrust "professional witnesses" whose main occupation consists of hiring themselves out as experts.

• Positions you've taken when giving expert testimony in previous cases. If you invariably express the same opinion (for example, that doctors were not negligent), it suggests that your opinion reflects preexisting bias rather than the circumstances of a particular lawsuit.

• The amount of your compensation. You might be happy about a high retainer, but unusually generous compensation may suggest that your testimony is a product of bias.

- Prior statements you've made that conflict with your opinion. If you've published books or articles, expect that the deposing attorney will be familiar with them. If you've changed your position, the deposing attorney may point out the conflict. If so, be prepared to explain if possible either that no actual conflict exists or that your changed opinion reflects new learning or technology. ■

Part Two: Taking and Defending Depositions

Part Two (Chapters 9 through 14) provides additional information for parties who are representing themselves in civil cases. As a self-represented party, you may have to take and defend depositions. These chapters, combined with the advice for deponents presented in Part One, will help you carry out both tasks effectively. (For an overview of the topics addressed in Part Two, please see Section B of the introduction.)

Chapter 9

The Lay of the Discovery Landscape

This chapter describes commonly used methods of civil discovery other than depositions. "Discovery" means the various methods by which parties to lawsuits can require their opposing parties and nonparty witnesses to answer questions and turn over documents before trial. If you're representing yourself, familiarity with these other discovery methods can help you decide whether you can obtain the case-related information you need without engaging in the relatively difficult and expensive task of taking depositions.

In contrast to depositions, other discovery methods rely largely on an exchange of paper. When using these other methods, you'll send out written requests for information to your opponent, to which you will receive written responses. The written discovery methods you are most likely to use include:

- **interrogatories:** a set of written questions that your adversary must answer in writing, under oath

- **notices to produce documents:** written demands that your adversary make documents available to you for inspection and copying

- **subpoena:** a court order that you prepare requiring nonparty witnesses to make documents available to you for inspection and copying, and

- **requests for admissions:** demands that your adversary admit the accuracy of specific facts.

Of course, all discovery methods are interrelated. For example, you may use information gathered through a Notice to Produce Documents to decide which witnesses to depose. In turn, the information you gain from a deposition might spur further document requests. For this reason, familiarity with these other discovery methods will be helpful even if you have already decided to take a deposition or two.

A. The Purposes of Discovery

State and federal governments have enacted discovery procedures to enable opposing parties to gain access to each other's potential evidence prior to trial. The perceived benefits of discovery include:

- **Settlements more often and more fairly.** If both your adversary and you know before trial what evidence each of you plans to introduce, you'll both be better able to predict the outcome of the trial with reasonable accuracy—and reach a fair and reasonable settlement.

- **Cost savings.** Settlements remove cases from the court system, saving public funds and private legal expenses.

- **Fairer trial outcomes.** For cases that don't settle, trial outcomes will be fairer when each side has a chance to learn the key evidence the other will rely on and prepare to explain or contradict it. As a result, verdicts will not be a result of surprise evi-

dence that one party springs on an unpre-
pared opponent.

B. Impediments to Achieving Discovery Goals

Unfortunately, the discovery rules have only
partly accomplished their lofty purposes. Solutions often give rise to new problems—as is certainly true for the discovery rules. Some of the
rules governing discovery methods have become
so complex that they offer less-than-scrupulous
lawyers new arenas in which to create disputes,
delay cases, and run up legal fees. Indeed, some
have observed that the primary result of discovery has been to move the hardball games and
tricks to hide evidence that some lawyers like to
play from the trial to the pretrial phase of lawsuits.

What lawyers—especially those who represent affluent parties against less affluent or self-
represented parties—often hope to accomplish
with these unfair tactics is to make discovery so
lengthy, painful, or expensive that their oppo-
nents give up or settle cases on the cheap. Some
common discovery abuses include:

- taking advantage of the absence of judges at
  depositions to question deponents in a de-
  liberately belligerent and hostile manner

- trying to avoid answering their adversaries'
  legitimate discovery requests by citing
  bogus ambiguities in questions that a child
  could understand or by relying on minor
  legal technicalities, and

- intentionally withholding properly sought
  information, forcing their adversaries to
  choose between the unappealing alternatives of doing without the information or
  having to go to court for an order that the
  information be disclosed.

Most courts have amended their discovery
rules in an effort to curtail such abuses. One
common remedy is to adopt a "voluntary disclosure" rule, which compels parties to divulge key
information without the adversary having to ask
for it. (See Section C, below.) Other common efforts and restrictions include:

- limits on the number of depositions lawyers
  can take and interrogatories they can send
  out, as well as strict time periods during
  which discovery can occur

- requirements that lawyers for the opposing
  parties "meet and confer" before discovery
  starts to set up a discovery plan to which
  they both agree, jointly (see FRCP 26(f))

- procedures whereby judges or their assistants (sometimes called "magistrates," "referees," or "special masters") are available to
  resolve discovery disputes quickly and
  cheaply by telephone rather than requiring
  that they be litigated in person in expensive,
  time-consuming court procedures, and

- the increased willingness of judges to impose sanctions (penalties) on those who
  abuse discovery rules, ranging from monetary fines to dismissal of an entire claim or
  defense depending on the severity and
  frequency of the misconduct.

Judges and lawyers rarely cut self-represented parties slack.

The discovery process is extremely complex. The rules themselves are detailed and sometimes cryptic, and even lawyers often have trouble framing discovery requests in a way that gets them the information they want. As a self-represented party, you will be held to the same standards as lawyers. For example, don't expect a judge to excuse your failure to comply with a discovery time deadline because you're representing yourself and doing your best to obey the rules. Similarly, don't expect an adversary's lawyer to overlook a sloppily worded request for information because the lawyer knows what information you're really after. Once you enter the minefield of discovery, you'll have to tread as warily as any attorney.

C. Voluntary Disclosure

Nearly every court has broad "voluntary disclosure" rules that require each party to disclose key information relating to its claims or defenses without waiting for the other party to ask for it. (See FRCP 26(a).) Typically, you have to voluntarily disclose information within a few days of the "meet and confer" conference in which you and your adversary agree to a formal discovery plan. Information that you'll probably be required to disclose voluntarily includes:

- the names and phone numbers of potential witnesses, along with a brief indication of the information they might have about the dispute

- a list of case-related documents, records, and tangible case-related objects in your possession (for example, the failed piece of equipment in a faulty design case)

- if you are a party seeking damages (monetary compensation), a computation substantiating the amount of damages you're seeking

- if you are a party against whom damages are sought, a description of any insurance policy that might be available to cover some portion of a judgment, and

- the identity and opinions of any expert witness you've retained.

D. Informal Discovery

Informal interviews are the most ancient and, perhaps still, the most common method of pretrial case investigation. You have the right to seek information from any witness who is willing to cooperate with you. (Ethical rules prevent lawyers from seeking information directly from an opposing party who is represented by an attorney without the consent of both the party and the attorney. If you are representing yourself, however, you're not subject to lawyers' ethical duties and so can seek information directly from your adversary.) Informal discovery encompasses such activities as:

- conducting interviews with eyewitnesses or others with important information, either in person or over the phone

- collecting documents or examining public records, either in person or by written request

- taking photographs of damaged property or accident sites, and

- discussing the case with an expert whom you are considering retaining.

There are two main advantages to informal discovery. First, because your adversary has no right to be present at an informal interview, the information you uncover is strictly for your benefit. Second, informal discovery can save you both time and money. For example, you needn't involve your adversary in the interview arrangements, nor do you have to pay for someone to make an official record of an informal interview.

Of course, a chief disadvantage of informal discovery is that you must rely on witnesses' voluntary cooperation. If witnesses refuse to talk to you or turn over documents voluntarily, you may be unable to get the information you need to prove your case or disprove your opponent's claims.

Thus, you may have to rely on a combination of informal and formal discovery methods to get the information you need. For example, you might talk to friendly witnesses (witnesses whose testimony supports you and who want to be of assistance) and seek documents and records from government agencies and businesses informally. However, when seeking information from your adversary and hostile witnesses, you may have to rely on formal discovery methods.

Exclusive reliance on informal discovery is generally possible only when the amount in dispute in a lawsuit doesn't justify the added expenses of formal discovery, or most witnesses will cooperate with your requests for information voluntarily.

E. Discovery Plans

As mentioned above, FRCP 26(f) and most states' rules require your adversary and you to "meet and confer" and agree jointly to a plan for discovery. Discovery rules generally leave parties and their attorneys free to follow whatever discovery procedures they think best suit a particular case. (See FRCP 26(d).)

For example, if you're the plaintiff in a personal injury lawsuit growing out of an auto accident, you may meet and confer with the defendant on March 1 and agree to the following:

- You will send out written interrogatories to each other by April 1, and respond to the interrogatories no later than May 30.

- You will take no depositions until after each party has received the other's answers to the interrogatories.

- You will take depositions in the following order:

  - You will depose the defendant.

  - The defendant will then depose you.

  - Next you will depose Shot Gunn, who was a passenger in the front seat in the defendant's car at the time of the accident.

- The defendant will then depose Luke Sharp, who was waiting to cross a nearby intersection at the time of the accident.

- The defendant will then depose Dr. Lisa Onlife, the emergency room doctor who treated you following the accident.

• You will limit discovery to particular topics. For example, the defendant may agree to limit Dr. Onlife's deposition to the subject of "the extent and likely future prognosis of your hearing loss."

Though neither a Supreme Being nor statute commands a precise order of discovery, typical discovery patterns do exist based on common sense. For example:

• Send out interrogatories and document requests before taking depositions. One reason to use these discovery techniques first is that depositions are comparatively expensive. It'll probably cost you around $750 for a court reporter to transcribe a day of deposition testimony. (A videotaped deposition will cost even more.) The responses to interrogatories and document requests can help you identify which individuals really do have important information (and therefore should be deposed), and which can be eliminated as deponents.

• Send out requests for admissions at the tail end of discovery, after interrogatories have been asked and answered and depositions have been conducted. Waiting to use this discovery tool until just before trial makes sense because the facts you will want the other party to admit are usually drawn from the information you glean from responses to other types of discovery requests.

• Depose an expert witness last (if at all), after the expert has gathered the information he or she intends to rely on to reach an opinion. That way you don't go to the trouble of deposing someone who says, "I haven't finished my investigation yet."

F. General Rules of Discovery Questioning

The rules of evidence are much broader in discovery than at trial. The basic rule is FRCP 26(b)(1), which provides that the information sought "need not be admissible at the trial if the discovery appears reasonably calculated to lead to the discovery of admissible evidence." This language greatly opens up the scope of inquiry during discovery, allowing you to inquire about information that could not be brought out at trial. (For further discussion of the broad scope of discovery questioning, see Chapter 10.)

Example

In a lawsuit involving a traffic collision, you could properly ask about statements made by bystanders following the collision—even if those statements would constitute inadmissible hearsay at trial.

Nevertheless, there are some rules that prevent disclosure of information even during discovery. (For additional discussion of the limits on discovery, see Chapter 7.) Briefly stated, the limits are these:

- **Work product.** (See FRCP 26(a)(3).) Parties do not ordinarily have to answer questions seeking their own "work product" (also known as "trial preparation materials"). What this means is that unless a party can convince a judge that he or she needs the information, that party can't use discovery to force an adversary to turn over information the adversary gathered during the trial preparation process. The work product rule prevents lazy parties from sitting by idly, then collecting the results of their adversaries' investigation efforts, including the fruits of the adversary's legal research efforts. In addition, the work product rule prevents a party from compelling an opponent to disclose its trial strategies or legal conclusions. If a discovery request seeks your work product, you can refuse to answer on that basis.

- **Privileged communications.** Privileges protect communications made in confidential relationships, such as between spouses, lawyers and clients, doctors and patients, and psychotherapists and patients. Communications made in these types of relationships are generally protected from disclosure, both during discovery and at trial. Though protecting such communications may sometimes prevent the whole truth from emerging, the law places a higher value on preserving the confidentiality of these relationships. Thus, you or a witness may, in an appropriate situation, respond to a discovery request by saying something like, "I decline to answer on the ground that the question seeks privileged information."

- **Private information.** Discovery is not an excuse for parties to harass witnesses by probing into private and irrelevant areas of their past lives. To take an obvious example, a witness to an automobile accident cannot ordinarily be questioned about his or her sexual history, political or religious beliefs, or annual income. You or a witness may respond to irrelevant inquiries by saying something like, "I decline to answer on the ground that the information sought is not reasonably calculated to lead to the discovery of relevant evidence and is being sought to embarrass me."

G. Enforcing Discovery Rules

The discovery process was, in theory at least, designed to run by itself. That is, your adversary and you are supposed to carry out discovery on your own, without court supervision. If things don't work out this way in the real world, however, you can ask a judge to step in and order a recalcitrant adversary or witness to abide by the discovery rules. The orders that judges may make and the sanctions (penalties) that judges may mete out include:

- ordering a party or a witness to turn over documents or records in response to a discovery request that the party or witness claims is irrelevant or unduly burdensome

- ordering a subpoenaed witness to attend a deposition and/or answer questions (a judge may issue a "bench warrant" for a witness who fails to obey a subpoena, which authorizes a sheriff or other police official to arrest the witness), or

- sanctioning a party who unreasonably objects to an opponent's discovery requests. Sanctions usually consist of monetary fines that judges can impose on both parties and their lawyers. If a party's failure to cooperate with legitimate discovery requests is severe enough, a judge has the power to enter judgment in favor of the wronged party.

Despite their broad power, judges generally encourage parties to work out discovery disputes on their own. Judges' reluctance to become embroiled repeatedly in discovery disputes is reinforced by statutes in most states that require parties to "meet and confer" to attempt to resolve disputes on their own before going to court. (See, for example, FRCP 37(a)(2).)

H. An Overview of Formal Discovery Methods

This section briefly reviews formal discovery methods other than depositions.

1. Written Interrogatories

Parties can send written interrogatories (questions) to opposing parties but not to nonparty witnesses. (See FRCP 33.) The subsections below answer the most frequently asked questions about interrogatories.

a. What Is the Purpose of Interrogatories?

Even in courts that have rules requiring voluntary disclosure of key information between the parties (see Section C, above), you may want to send written interrogatories to your adversary to seek additional information. Your adversary must answer these questions in writing, under oath, generally within 30 days. By forcing your adversary to answer in writing, the facts you learn from the interrogatories may help you target your discovery later. For example, interrogatory answers may help you decide which witnesses (if any) to depose and may help you identify the documents you want to request to examine. Of course, interrogatories are an even more important precursor to the use of other formal discovery methods if your court does not have rules mandating voluntary disclosure.

b. Are Interrogatories Less Expensive Than Depositions?

Definitely. Your only "cost" in interrogatories is the time it takes you to prepare the questions. If your case is a routine one (for example, it's a traffic collision at an intersection case), you may even find a practice book for attorneys in a law library that contains pre-prepared "boilerplate" interrogatories, to which you can add just a few questions that are specific to your dispute. By contrast, if you take a deposition, you'll have to pay for a court reporter to take down and transcribe deposition testimony.

c. Are Interrogatories in Any Way Superior to Depositions As a Means of Unearthing Information?

Yes. Interrogatories better enable you to elicit organizational or "corporate knowledge." When your adversary is a corporation (or a similar multiperson organization), information may be spread among a number of employees and agents. Taking just one or even a few employees' depositions may not turn up the needed information. By contrast, interrogatories require your adversary to gather information from all employees and agents and include this "corporate knowledge" in its responses. Even your adversary's attorney may have to reveal information.

For example, assume that you're a plaintiff in an auto accident case, and you've sent out an interrogatory asking the defendant to identify "all facts that indicate the defendant failed to exercise reasonable care at the time of the acci-

dent." If the defendant's attorney has talked to a witness who claims to have seen the defendant consume three martinis in a bar a few minutes before an accident, the defendant would have to include that information in response to your interrogatory.

d. What Limits the Effectiveness of Interrogatories As a Means of Gaining Information?

Interrogatories carry a number of significant disadvantages. First, you can send interrogatories only to your adversary. If you want information from a nonparty witness who refuses to speak to you voluntarily (for example, a bystander who sees an auto accident), you'll have to take the witness's deposition.

A second disadvantage of interrogatories is that, reflecting the desire to curb discovery abuse, rules in most jurisdictions restrict the number of questions you can include in a set of interrogatories. For instance, FRCP 33(a) sets a limit of 25 questions (including a reasonable number of subquestions); few states allow more than 50. If you want to ask more questions than that, or if you want to send your adversary a second set of interrogatories, you'll need to go to court and secure a judge's permission.

A third disadvantage is that while deponents personally have to respond to deposition questions, lawyers typically strongly influence the wording of interrogatory answers. As you might imagine, lawyers often suggest the narrowest possible answers, trying to conceal rather than reveal damaging information. Attorneys may also seek to avoid answering some interrogatories entirely by claiming that questions are vague, ambiguous, unduly burdensome, seek legal conclusions rather than facts, seek the attorney's work product, or violate the attorney-client privilege. Even if such claims are specious, they put on you the burden of seeking to iron out the problems in a "meet and confer" session and preparing a motion and going to court if you can't resolve the conflict.

Finally, interrogatories are inflexible. You have to prepare an entire set of interrogatories in advance of any answers. Thus, you have no chance to adapt questions to earlier answers, or to follow up on responses that seem promising.

e. Do Interrogatories Have to Be Answered Under Oath?

Yes. Interrogatory answers must be signed under oath by the answering party. When answers represent the collective contributions of more than one person in an organization, typically an officer or director of the organization signs the answers.

f. If a Party Learns of Information That Makes an Earlier Answer to an Interrogatory (or Deposition Question) Incorrect or Incomplete, Must the Party Provide a Supplementary Answer?

Probably. Discovery rules in most courts impose continuing obligations on parties to supplement incorrect or incomplete interrogatory answers.

(See FRCP 26(e).) For instance, assume that you're a plaintiff in an auto accident case, and you receive a set of interrogatories from the defendant. In response to an interrogatory asking for the names of anyone known to you who witnessed the accident, you truthfully answer, "None." A few weeks later, you learn that Juan Looker claims to have witnessed the accident. Within a reasonable time after learning this new information (and whether Looker's information helps or hurts you), you must inform your adversary of Looker's identity.

g. Examples of Common Interrogatories

A few examples must suffice to suggest the sorts of information that you can use interrogatories to discover:

- In most courts, a plaintiff's "complaint" (the common term for the legal pleading that often initiates lawsuits) need not provide much factual information to the defendant. Thus, as a defendant, you may use an interrogatory to gain additional factual information about the plaintiff's claims. For example, if you're a defendant in an auto accident case, you may send out an interrogatory such as, "Please state the facts on which you base your claim that the defendant operated the vehicle negligently."

- In the same type of personal injury case, a defendant's "answer" may allege that the plaintiff was "contributorily negligent"—that is, that the plaintiff's own carelessness caused or at least contributed to the accident. If so, the plaintiff may send the defendant an interrogatory asking for "the facts on which you base your claim that the plaintiff was contributorily negligent."

- In many types of cases, you may seek to discover information about your adversary's past conduct that might be relevant to the legitimacy of the adversary's present claims. For example, assume that you are a defendant and the plaintiff is an ex-employee who claims to have been wrongfully terminated by you as a result of age discrimination. You claim that you had good cause to terminate the plaintiff because of the plaintiff's excessive tardiness. You may use interrogatories to seek out information about the plaintiff's employment history. For example, one interrogatory may ask the plaintiff to disclose the "Name and address of each place of employment during the last ten years; your job title; your job duties; and the reason why you left that employment."

 For further information about and examples of interrogatories, see:

- Bergman & Berman-Barrett, *Represent Yourself in Court* (Nolo). Chapter 4 has a short description of interrogatories.
- *Bender's Forms of Discovery* (Matthew-Bender; regularly updated). This is a ten-volume treatise with sample sets of interrogatories for many types of legal claims.

2. Subpoenas and Requests for Production of Documents

To fully develop the facts of your case, you will have to do more than get written answers from your opponent to a limited number of questions you ask. You'll also want to examine documents, records, reports, and the like. Formal discovery rules authorize you to:

- compel production of documents for inspection and copying
- compel production of tangible objects for inspection, copying, and testing (for example, compel production of an allegedly faulty machine part), and
- enter land for purposes of inspection and testing (for example, to inspect and test soil).

Of these three possible options, compelling the production of documents is by far the most common. You can use the following formal discovery methods to require your adversary to make documents available for you to inspect and copy:

- When arranging for your adversary's deposition, you can attach to the Notice of Deposition a Request for Production of Documents specifying documents that your adversary must bring to the deposition. (See FRCP 30(b)(5).) For further discussion of requiring production of documents at deposition and a sample form, see Chapter 1 and Sample Form #5 in Appendix 3.
- In a set of interrogatories, you can ask your adversary to identify the documents on

which its responses are based and to voluntarily attach copies of the documents to the responses.

- If no deposition or interrogatories are pending, you can simply send (mail) your adversary a Request to Produce Documents. (See FRCP 34.)

You can also compel the production of documents from nonparty witnesses. The formal discovery you can use to do this include:

- Serving the witness with a Subpoena Duces Tecum re Deposition, if you plan to take the witness's deposition. (See FRCP 45(a).) A Subpoena Duces Tecum is a fill-in-the-blanks court form with spaces in which you can list the documents the witness must produce at the deposition. (See Sample Form #2 in Appendix 3.)

- Without taking a deposition, in most localities you can compel anyone who possesses or controls case-related documents to make those documents available for inspection and copying by serving them with a subpoena. The subpoena must identify the documents you seek and indicate the time and place they are to be made available. You normally have to serve a copy of the subpoena on your adversary as well, thereby giving your adversary a chance to examine whatever documents are made available in response to your subpoena. (See FRCP 45.)

The subsections below address common questions relating to document production.

a. Requests for Production of Documents

i. Can I send a Request for Production of Documents to nonparty witnesses?

No. Like interrogatories, you can send a Request for Production of Documents only to your adversary.

ii. How can I use a Request for Production to get documents?

You prepare a Request for Production just as you would many other types of court documents. In the upper left-hand corner of the Request is your name, address, and other identifying information. Below this is the "case caption" that identifies the court in which the case is pending, the names of the parties, and the case number. You would title the document as a "Request for Production of Documents," and then identify the documents you want your adversary to produce. While you needn't provide an exact title or date for each document, your request should be sufficiently specific to enable your adversary to identify which documents you want.

Your Request for Production should also advise your adversary of where and when the documents are to be produced. You might use language such as the following:

> *Plaintiff requests that defendant Allayee produce the following documents for inspection and copying at plaintiff's office, located at 229 Litigation Road, Court City, PA, on August 26, 20xx.*

You then continue by identifying the documents you want. Examples of how you might phrase requests include:

- "Each document identified in defendant Allayee's Answer to Interrogatory No. 6." (This type of request is appropriate when your adversary refers to documents in a response to an interrogatory but doesn't attach the documents to the response.)

- "All documents in defendant Allayee's possession relating to the leasing of Unit Number 3 to plaintiff on March 12, 20xx." (This request might be appropriate in a case involving a breach of lease for an apartment or a store unit in a shopping center.)

- "All records, receipts, invoices, and delivery instructions relating to the shipment of widgets from defendant Allayee to plaintiff during the period January 1, 20xx, through December 31, 20xx." (This request might be used in a case involving a shipper's alleged failure to deliver goods on time or in the condition specified in a contract.)

These examples do not refer to documents by title, date, name of sender, or other specific parts. This is typical, because you might not know the specific names or contents of documents that you've never seen. The rules require only that your request be specific enough for your adversary to identify the documents you seek.

Of course, if you can identify a document you seek more precisely, your request can be more specific. For instance, in a breach of lease case, you might request "the lease agreement dated Nov. 2, 20xx, and signed by plaintiff Geisman and defendant Heuga."

By contrast, a request for "all documents in your possession related to this lawsuit" would be too vague. Your adversary would undoubtedly object and refuse to answer. A judge would not order your adversary to respond to such a vague request. Instead, a judge would compel you to ask a more precise question.

iii. Do I get to keep the documents that are produced as a result of my Request for Production?

Not usually. The discovery rules recognize that most individuals and businesses want to retain possession of original documents. Thus, the rules allow you only to inspect and copy the documents that are disclosed. The originals are returned to the source. As the requesting party, you normally bear the cost of making the copies.

iv. Are there any limits on my right as a party to demand documents?

As mentioned above, there are some limits on discovery. Involvement in a lawsuit does not give you carte blanche to raid an adversary's files. A person or organization from whom you demand documents can refuse to turn them over on grounds that the demand is too broad and burdensome, that the information in the documents is legally privileged or too private to reveal, or simply that the documents are unrelated to the lawsuit. The burden would then be on you to try to work out the dispute by "meeting and conferring" with your adversary (that is, discussing the issues in good faith either in person or over the telephone). If the dispute remains unresolved, you would then have to file a "Motion to Compel Production of Documents" in court and try to convince a judge that you have a right to inspect the documents. (See FRCP 34(b).)

v. How much time does my adversary have to respond to a Request for Production?

The time limit set by law is normally 30 days. However, parties often reach agreements between themselves to shorten or lengthen the statutory time limit.

vi. How do I respond to a Request for Production if I think it's improper or I don't have the requested documents?

If you don't have one or more requested documents, you would respond along these lines:

> There are no documents in my possession
> or control requested by defendant's Request
> No. 7.

In most jurisdictions, if you later do come to possess a document that was requested earlier, you would have to send an amended response to the adverse party.

If you think that a request is improper, identify the reason for your objection in your response. For example, you might word an objection as follows:

> Plaintiff Slaughter objects to defendant
> Cestero's Request No. 4 on the ground that
> it is oppressive, unduly burdensome, vague,
> and seeks information not calculated to
> lead to the discovery of admissible evi-
> dence, in that it requests "all documents,
> records, memoranda, letters, and notes of
> every kind and description written to
> plaintiff by each person who has been a
> tenant of 11359 Elm Drive for the last ten
> years, or written by plaintiff to each such
> person."

b. Subpoenas

i. Do I need a judge's approval to serve a subpoena?

No. Though subpoenas are court orders, they are normally issued "in blank" and prestamped by the clerk of the court in which a case is pending. You need only pick up a subpoena in the clerk's office in the courthouse where the case is pending, fill in information—such as the case name and number and the documents you want produced—and serve it on the person or organization from whom you're demanding documents.

ii. Can I serve a subpoena by mailing it to the person or organization from whom I'm requesting documents?

No. A subpoena requesting documents must ordinarily be personally served on a witness by an adult who has no relationship to the case. In most states, subpoenas can also be served by marshals and, in some areas, by private process servers.

iii. Are the rules for identifying documents in subpoenas the same as the rules for Requests for Production?

Yes. See Subsection a.ii, above.

iv. How do nonparty witnesses respond to subpoenas seeking production of documents?

In much the same way as parties respond to Requests for Production. That is, witnesses can agree to turn over the documents or object that the subpoena is oppressive, is unduly burdensome, seeks privileged information, and so on. However, a witness who simply refuses to respond to a subpoena is in contempt of court. A judge can order the witness to comply with a subpoena, and has the power to sanction (penalize) the disobedient witness with a fine and (in an extremely aggravated case) jail time.

3. Requests for Admissions

Procedures governing Requests for Admissions are set out in FRCP 36. Requests for Admissions are less a tool for discovering new information than a method for making it easier for parties to prove facts at trial. If your adversary admits that facts listed in its Requests for Admission are accurate, those facts are deemed conclusively established, and you need not prove them at trial. You'd simply read admitted facts into the trial record. Thus, the "discovery" aspect of Requests for Admissions is really the discovery of which aspects of your case your adversary intends to

dispute at trial. The questions below address common issues raised by Requests for Admissions.

a. What Can I Ask an Adverse Party to Admit in Requests for Admissions?

Requests for Admissions have a broad scope. You could ask your adversary to admit that:

- **A document you want to offer into evidence at trial is genuine.** For example, in a case involving the breach of a lease agreement, you might send out a request that states as follows:

Plaintiff Chang requests that defendant Lagstein admit within 30 days of the service of this request, for the purpose of this action only, that the following document is genuine: The lease agreement attached hereto as Exhibit A is a true and accurate copy of the lease agreement signed by plaintiff and defendant on March 31, 20xx.

If the defendant admits that the lease is genuine, you could offer the lease into evidence at trial without further proof of its authenticity.

- **Evidence that you want to offer at trial is accurate.** For instance, in a personal injury case growing out of a traffic accident, you might send out a request that reads as follows:

Defendant Kann requests that plaintiff Wetanson admit within 30 days of the service of this request, for the purpose of this action only, that the following statement is true: "Following an accident that occurred at the intersection of Beach and Desert Avenues at 2 p.m. on February 14, 20xx, plaintiff said to defendant, 'The sun was directly in my eyes just before the accident.'"

If the plaintiff admits that this fact is true, you could simply read the statement to the judge or jury at trial.

- **A relevant legal status exists.** For example, assume that you are suing defendant Bivin Co. based on damages caused by the allegedly negligent driving of Bivin's employee, Matt Nguyen. In order to conclusively establish that Nguyen was in fact employed by Bivin at the time of the accident, you might send out a request that reads:

Plaintiff requests that Defendant Bivin admit within 30 days of service of this request, for the purposes of this action only, that on March 31, 20xx, Matt Nguyen was an employee of Bivin.

b. Why Should I Help to Prove an Adversary's Case by Admitting That Facts Mentioned in a Request for Admissions Are Accurate?

Requests for Admissions must be answered under oath, so you're compelled to tell the truth

under penalty of perjury. Moreover, the discovery rules enforce this legal and moral duty by imposing a financial penalty on parties who unreasonably refuse to admit that a fact contained in a Request for Admissions is true. If a case goes to trial and your adversary proves that a fact listed in a Request for Admissions and unreasonably denied by you is true, you could be forced to pay whatever your adversary spent proving that fact at trial—even if you win the case. (See FRCP 37.)

Example

In the example above, assume that defendant Bivin denied that Matt Nguyen was its employee on the date listed. At trial, you offer into evidence Bivin's employee records proving that Nguyen was in fact its employee on that date. Even if you were to lose the case, the judge would probably order Bivin to pay you the costs you incurred to prove that Nguyen was Bivin's employee.

c. What Happens If I Simply Ignore a Request for Admissions?

This is not a good idea. Requests not specifically denied (in writing) are "deemed admitted." This means that failing to respond has the same legal effect as admitting every fact in the Request for Admissions. Therefore, if you take issue with any fact in the Request for Admissions, you must respond on time, in writing, or give up your right to contest the fact. ∎

Chapter 10

Defending a Deposition

This chapter describes how parties who represent themselves can effectively "defend" depositions—which means being present and representing your interests at a deposition taken by the opposing party. The role of defender can thrust you into the deposition process even if you have decided not to take any depositions yourself.

Example

You're a plaintiff representing yourself who is suing a restaurant in which you slipped and fell for negligently failing to clean up the spill that led to your fall. If the lawyer for the restaurant deposes the friend who was with you when you fell, your presence at the friend's deposition makes you the "defender" of the deposition.

When defending a deposition, you have the opportunity to be a lot more than merely an interested spectator. As this chapter explains, effectively defending a deposition often entails:

- listening carefully to your adversary's questions and the deponent's testimony (if you do nothing else to defend a deposition, you can learn important information simply by being a good listener)
- objecting to legally improper questions, and
- asking your own questions to elicit additional information from the deponent after your adversary has completed questioning.

As a self-represented party, you will receive notice of any and all depositions your adversary plans to take. You are not required to defend any of them; however, it's almost always a good idea to do so, even if you plan on doing nothing more than listening to the testimony. Unlike when you take a deposition and have to pay a court reporter, the costs of defending a deposition are minimal—little more than an expenditure of your personal time. An alternative would be to skip the deposition and buy a transcript from the court reporter, but a transcript will likely cost several hundred dollars.

(Of course, you could save time and money by skipping both the deposition and the transcript, perhaps figuring to debrief a friendly deponent afterwards. We don't recommend this approach. Not only do you give up the potential advantages of defending the deposition, but also you may end up with an incomplete and misleading account of the testimony.)

 You don't have to buy a copy of the deposition transcript.

At the conclusion of a deposition you're defending, the court reporter will probably ask if you want to purchase the deposition transcript—at a cost of several hundred dollars. As a defender, you have no obligation to purchase one. You might be especially reluctant to purchase a transcript if:

- The deposition has extended over many hours or even days. Court reporters charge by the page, so the longer the deposition, the more expensive the transcript. Ask the court reporter for a cost estimate before deciding whether to purchase a transcript—as a rough guide, a transcript of one day of deposition testimony is likely to cost around $750.

- You believe that the case is very likely to settle before trial. While transcripts are often used in connection with summary judgment motions (requests to decide cases prior to trial), the primary use for deposition transcripts is at trial, where you may be able to offer deposition testimony into evidence. (For more information on using depositions in summary judgment motions and at trial, see Chapter 2.)

- You've been able to take detailed notes of the important testimony.

If you decide later in the case that you want a copy of the transcript, you can always purchase one from the court reporter. To facilitate this, get the court reporter's business card at the deposition. Give the reporter as much advance notice of your desire to buy a transcript as you can: Transcripts are not like French fries in a fast food restaurant, sitting already prepared under hot lights waiting for you to place an order. It will take some time for the reporter to get you the transcript. If you need a transcript in a hurry, most reporters will expedite your request—for a fee.

Defending Your Own Deposition

If your adversary takes your deposition, you will be in the role of both deponent and deposition defender. In such a situation, you should concentrate on your role as a deponent. What you say and how you say it is likely to be far more important to the outcome of your case than any legal objections you might make to your adversary's questions. Part One of this book provides virtually all the information you will need to defend effectively when you are the deponent.

A. Preparing for the Deposition

Your first step in defending a deposition may take place at least a day or two before the deposition itself. Just as attorneys commonly do, you can meet with a deponent who is on your side of the case ahead of time to help prepare the deponent to testify completely and accurately.

Together, you and the deponent can prepare for the deposition by reviewing the suggestions in Chapter 3 for refreshing the deponent's recollection of past events. (If the deponent hasn't done so already, you might recommend that the deponent read not only Chapter 3 but all of Part One of this book prior to meeting with you.)

During the predeposition meeting, you and the deponent can:

- decide how the deponent will respond to the adversary's likely demand that certain documents be produced at the deposition

- review the deponent's story so that the information is fresh in the deponent's mind at the time of the deposition, and

- practice for the deposition itself, with you playing the role of the adversary and asking questions that the adversary is likely to ask.

These suggestions and the others in Chapter 3 will help the deponent provide testimony that will best support your legal claims to the extent that the deponent's obligation to tell the truth allows.

 Predeposition discussions are not privileged.

Despite the fact that you are acting as an attorney in representing yourself, you and a friendly deponent do not enjoy an attorney-client relationship. Thus, whatever you say to each other prior to a deposition is *not* subject to the attorney-client privilege (covered in Chapter 3). If asked, the deponent must answer questions about what you discussed, even if both of you think that what you say to each other is in strictest confidence. Or put another way, you must assume that anything you say to a deponent may come out during a deposition, and act accordingly.

B. Listening Carefully

Your most important task when defending a deposition is to listen carefully to the opposing lawyer's questions and the deponent's answers. By paying attention to the topics the lawyer emphasizes during the questioning, you'll pick up clues to the legal strategies the lawyer is likely to pursue and the factual arguments the lawyer will make, both during settlement negotiations and at trial.

You also need to pay attention to the deponent's answers so that you can evaluate how they support either your legal claims or those of your adversary. Careful listening is necessary even if you've met with the deponent ahead of time and feel confident that you know what the deponent will say. Once "on the record" and under oath, deponents sometimes vary from what they've said in previous informal conversations.

Moreover, only by listening carefully to testimony can you evaluate:

- whether you will need to question the deponent yourself after the adversary has concluded questioning (see Section C, below), and

- the deponent's demeanor and credibility—which can often be at least as important as what a deponent says.

You can usually reap the most important benefits of defending a deposition simply by using good listening skills.

C. Eliciting Additional Information After Your Opponent's Questioning

Sometimes, you know that a deponent can provide evidence that's helpful to your legal claims. If so, you must listen carefully when defending a deposition to determine whether that helpful evidence came out in response to your adversary's questioning. Even if the deponent did testify to the helpful evidence, perhaps it came out garbled. In either event, defending a deposition gives you a chance to put helpful evidence on the record by "piggybacking" on the adversary's deposition. That is, you can question the deponent yourself after the adversary concludes the questioning. (See FRCP 30(c).)

You may want to question the deponent in order to:

- clear up testimony that you believe came out muddled during the adversary's questioning

- "set the record straight" by giving the deponent a chance to correct inaccurate testimony, or

- bring out helpful evidence that the adversary neglected to elicit.

The following sections look briefly at how you may achieve your goals in each of these situations.

1. Clearing Up Muddled Testimony

Deposition testimony that supports your legal claims should be as clear as possible. If the deponent is unable to attend the trial (for example, the deponent dies, becomes seriously ill, or moves out of the area), you may end up reading the deposition testimony to a judge or jury—and you want it to be persuasive. Thus, if your adversary's questioning leaves helpful testimony muddled or unclear, you should follow up with clarifying questions.

For example, assume that you are the plaintiff in an auto accident case; the defendant is the other driver, Swen Golli. Golli's lawyer is deposing a bystander who you know from previous informal conversations is prepared to testify that Golli made a left turn at an unsafe speed of at least 25 m.p.h. When questioned by Golli's lawyer at deposition, the bystander testified as follows:

Q: *Where did you first see Mr. Golli's car?*

A: *I suppose about 50 feet before he started to make the left turn.*

Q: *And after Mr. Golli turned left, what happened?*

A: *He went south on Bolas and got about 25 feet before hitting the other car.*

Q: *Did you observe the speed of Mr. Golli's car at this time?*

A: *Yes.*

Q: *And what was that speed?*

A: *I'd say at least 25 m.p.h.*

Here, you want the record to be clear that Golli was driving at least 25 m.p.h. at the time he made the left turn. Yet, if you look back at the testimony you'll see that it's unclear as to whether Golli's car was traveling at least 25 m.p.h. at the time Golli turned left, or after Golli made the turn. Thus, you might want to clear up the confusion when you have the chance to question the deponent as follows:

> You: *I want to call your attention to the point at which you noticed Mr. Golli's car make the left turn to go left on Bolas. Do you recall how fast Mr. Golli was driving at that point?*
>
> A: *Yes, I do.*
>
> You: *And how fast was the car going when Mr. Golli made the left turn?*
>
> A: *I'd say at least 25 m.p.h.*

This clarification establishes that the deponent's testimony is that Golli was driving at least 25 m.p.h. at the time he was turning left. This could be a significant point in your favor in deciding who was at fault—and, therefore, of great importance in settlement negotiations or at trial (if the deponent gives this testimony in person).

2. Reviewing and Correcting Inaccurate Testimony

You may also want to elicit additional testimony to allow a deponent to correct what you believe to be an inaccurate answer. Your belief may be based on documents you've seen or predeposition conversations you've had with the deponent. Especially if an accurate answer would support your legal claims, you'll want to correct the record when it is your turn to ask questions. (In some situations, you may want to correct an inaccurate response even if it was more favorable to you than the accurate one. If the case goes to trial and your adversary can prove that some portion of a deponent's testimony was inaccurate, the deponent may lose credibility in the minds of a judge or jury. If the deponent is an important witness whose overall testimony supports your legal claims, better to ask the deponent to correct an inaccuracy as soon as possible at the deposition.)

A good way to correct inaccurate testimony is to follow these steps:

- have the deponent testify that the prior testimony was inaccurate

- ask questions that will elicit the accurate testimony, and

- if you think that the deponent has a good explanation for the inaccuracy (perhaps based on a short discussion you had with the deponent during lunch or a deposition recess), ask for the explanation.

For example, assume again that the deponent is testifying in the auto collision case involving Mr. Golli. When questioned by Golli's lawyer, the deponent testified that your car was moving very slowly forward when it was struck in the rear by Golli's car. You realize that this testimony was inaccurate. During predeposition conversations, the deponent had always told you that your car was standing still when it was struck by Golli's car. To rectify the inaccuracy when it is your turn to ask questions, you might question the deponent as follows:

You: *Do you remember testifying earlier that my car was moving forward very slowly when it was struck by Mr. Golli's car?*

A: *Yes, I do.*

You: *Was that testimony accurate?*

A: *No, I made a mistake.*

You: *What is the actual fact?*

A: *Your car was completely stopped when Mr. Golli's car rear-ended it.*

You: *You're sure of this?*

A: *Yes, absolutely.*

You: *Is there any reason why you testified inaccurately earlier?*

A: *I think I just got confused. Your car had been inching ahead before the collision, and I guess I had that in my mind when I was asked about whether it was moving when you were hit, which it wasn't.*

3. Producing Helpful Evidence

You can also question a deponent to bring out helpful information that didn't come out in response to your adversary's questions. Perhaps the adversary's questions didn't give the deponent a good opportunity to mention the information. Or, the deponent may simply have forgotten to mention the information when a question gave the deponent a chance to do so. Whatever the reason, you are generally better off bringing out helpful evidence during the deposition than squirreling it away to spring on your adversary at trial.

Because your case is far more likely to settle than go to trial, you generally want to improve your negotiating position by getting helpful evidence out on the table at deposition. To do so, use this approach:

* first, return the deponent's attention to the portion of the story to which the helpful evidence pertains, then
* elicit the helpful evidence.

For example, assume that Red Riding has filed suit against Brad Wolf for "intentional infliction of emotional distress." Red claims that Wolf jumped out from behind a tree and threatened to harm her. Grant Mutter saw what happened. During predeposition conversations with Red, Grant told Red that he heard Wolf yell, "You're never going to see your cottage again!" when Wolf jumped out from behind the tree. When deposing Grant, however, Wolf's attorney never asked Grant whether Wolf said anything when jumping out from behind the tree. As a result, Grant never testified to Wolf's threat. Because evidence of Wolf's threat helps Red's case, Red should elicit this information when it's her turn to question Grant. Red's questioning may go as follows:

Red: Do you recall testifying that Wolf jumped out at me from behind a tree?

A: Yes, I do.

Red: Did Wolf say anything when he jumped out from behind the tree?

A: He did.

Red: What is it that Wolf said?

A: He said, "You're never going to see your cottage again."

Red: What was Wolf's tone of voice when Wolf said this?

A: Wolf yelled it very loudly, like a scream. He sounded really mean and angry.

The helpful evidence is now officially in the record should Red need to refer to it during settlement negotiations or trial.

Make a list of key information helpful to your case before defending a deposition.

If you want to make sure that helpful evidence comes out at a deposition, list that information on a piece of paper and bring it with you to the deposition for easy reference. You can then check each piece of evidence off your list as it comes out in in response to your adversary's questions. If certain key evidence is never touched on, you'll know that you should ask about it when your opponent is done questioning the witness.

Deposition time limits may prevent you from eliciting additional information.

FRCP 30(d)(2) normally limits depositions to "one day of seven hours." If your adversary uses up all seven hours with his or her questioning, you will be unable to follow up with your own questions unless your adversary agrees to extend the deposition, or unless you get a court order to extend the time for questioning the witness.

D. Entering Into Stipulations

Stipulations are simply agreements between the parties that are placed on the record of a deposition. Most depositions are conducted without any stipulations. However, if you're defending a deposition, your adversary may ask you to agree to stipulate to things such as the following:

- "Will you stipulate that objections as to the form of questions are reserved until trial?"

- "Will you stipulate that the time limit of one day of seven hours does not apply to this deposition, and that this deposition may continue for as long as is reasonably necessary for both of us to question the deponent?"

- "Will you stipulate that all copies of documents can be used as though they are originals?"

- "Will you stipulate that our exhibits to the transcript of this deposition will be numbered 1 through 100 for identification and that your exhibits will start with the number 101?"

As a self-represented party, you'll have to decide whether to agree to your adversary's offers to stipulate. You do not have to agree to these or any other stipulations, and you should not do so if you do not know what a stipulation means or if you suspect that the adversary's attorney is trying to take unfair advantage of your inexperience.

On the other hand, some stipulations are simply for the convenience of both parties, so you may as well agree to them. For example, the stipulation relating to the numbering of exhibits falls into this category, as it simply makes it easier for both parties to mark and refer to exhibits. (See Chapter 11 for a discussion of how to mark exhibits at deposition.)

E. Making Objections

This section explores the complex topic of making objections at a deposition. Objecting to improper questions requires knowledge of often highly technical principles of legal evidence, which you as a self-represented party may well lack. Assuming that you are not going to invest the time to attend a law school course on evidence rules before defending a deposition, keep these three principles uppermost in your mind as you read through the sections below:

• Your most important task when defending a deposition is to pay careful attention to the substance of questions and answers. It is far better to overlook technically objectionable questions or answers than to lose track of what's being said because you're thinking about whether to object.

• If your case settles before trial (as about 90% of cases do), your failure to object to a deposition question is unlikely to have any effect whatsoever on the terms of the settlement.

• Even if your case doesn't settle, your failure to object to a deposition question is unlikely to influence the outcome of the case. Usually, you'll have a second chance to make your objection later in the case, if and when your adversary seeks to use the deposition testimony in court. And even if your failure to object at deposition waives (gives up) an objection (meaning that your adversary gets to use improper evidence), it's unlikely that a few items of improper evidence will significantly affect a trial's outcome. (Nevertheless, if you are going to represent yourself at trial and your adversary is likely to offer harmful deposition testimony into evidence against you, you should talk to an attorney or research evidence rules to find out if you can properly object to the use of the deposition testimony at trial if you didn't object at deposition.)

To learn more about evidence rules in preparation for deposition or trial, you may want to consult one of these books:

- *Emanuel's Law Outlines—Evidence* (5th ed., 2004; Aspen Publishers): One of a number of outlines on the market that lawyers and law students use for a quick refresher on evidence rules; short examples illustrate most of the rules.

- *Casenote Law Outlines—Evidence* (Casenotes Publishing Co.): Another outline widely used by lawyers and law students.

- Michael Graham, *Federal Rules of Evidence in a Nutshell* (6th ed., West Publishing Co., 2003): Provides brief rule-by-rule explanations of the Federal Rules of Evidence, which govern federal court trials and provide the model for most states' evidence rules.

- Paul Bergman, *Trial Advocacy in a Nutshell* (3d ed., West Publishing Co., 1997): A general guide to trial techniques; Chapter 11 reviews and illustrates common evidentiary issues.

1. Can an Objection Prevent a Deponent From Having to Answer a Question?

Generally speaking, no. Even if you object, and even if your objection is proper, the deponent will almost always have to answer the question anyway. As FRCP 30(c) provides, when objections are made at depositions, "the examination shall proceed, with the testimony being taken subject to the objections."

The following example demonstrates how testimony simply proceeds despite the making of an objection. Assume that Vy Agra is suing a car dealer for breach of warranty for selling Vy a car that needed many expensive repairs. Vy is defending the deposition of her friend, who was present when the car broke down. A portion of that deposition goes as follows:

Q: *What happened just before the car broke down?*

A: *I heard a loud pinging noise coming from the engine, and then we saw smoke coming from under the hood. That's when Vy pulled over and turned off the engine.*

Q: *Did you hear the pinging noise before Vy started speeding?*

Vy: *Objection, the question assumes facts not in evidence.*

Q: *Please answer the question.*

A: *I don't think Vy was speeding, but I did hear the pinging before I saw the smoke.*

The general rule that objectionable deposition questions must be answered is subject to two common exceptions:

- **Questions seeking privileged information.** A deponent need not (and should not) answer a question that asks for privileged information, as might be the case if a deponent is asked what he or she said to his or her attorney, priest, or spouse. (For further discussion of privileges, see Section 5, below, and Chapter 7.)

- **Questions seeking irrelevant private information.** Deponents needn't answer questions seeking private information that has no bearing on the case. These questions subject deponents to what FRCP 26(c) refers to as "annoyance, embarrassment, oppression, or undue burden or expense," and need not be answered. (For further discussion of private information, see Section 5, below, and Chapter 7.)

⚠ **You can object that a question calls for privileged or private information, but you can't instruct a deponent not to answer it.**

Only an attorney who represents a deponent (a witness who is being deposed) can instruct the deponent not to answer a question at a deposition. As a self-represented party, you have the right to object that a question asked of a nonparty deponent calls for the disclosure of privileged or private information. But because you are not the attorney for the nonparty deponent, you cannot instruct the deponent to refuse to answer the question. In fact, you can't even advise the deponent to refuse to answer the question. For example, you can't say something like, "My advice to you is not to answer that question because it

calls for privileged information." Even after you object that a question "calls for privileged information," it's entirely up to the deponent to decide whether to answer.

2. If Most Questions Must Be Answered Despite an Objection, What's the Point of Objecting?

Objecting to a deposition question may prevent your adversary from using the objected-to testimony later in the case. For example, assume that your adversary attaches a question and answer from a deposition transcript to a summary judgment motion (a motion asking a judge to decide on a case before it goes to trial; see Chapter 2), or asks to read a deposition question and answer out loud to a judge or jury during trial.

In either situation, if the question was improper and you objected to the question at the deposition, your adversary will not be able to use the answer. This means that the judge will not consider the answer when deciding the summary judgment motion, nor will the answer be admitted into evidence at trial.

For example, assume that Rick Shaw is a defendant representing himself in an auto accident case. Shaw is defending the deposition of a passenger in Shaw's car that is being taken by the plaintiff. During the deposition, the following testimony occurs:

Q: How fast would you say that Shaw was driving just prior to the collision?

A: *I'd say about 30 m.p.h.*

Q: *And how long prior to the collision had Shaw been speeding?*

A: *Oh, for a couple of blocks.*

Here, the second question is improper because it mischaracterizes the testimony. (The deponent testified that Shaw was driving about 30 m.p.h., not that Shaw was speeding.) However, Shaw fails to object to the question at the deposition.

At trial, Shaw does object when the plaintiff seeks to offer into evidence this bit of deposition testimony. Though the deposition question was improper, the trial judge is likely to respond as follows:

Judge: *Mr. Shaw, I'd be inclined to sustain that objection, because I agree with you that the deposition question mischaracterized the witness's testimony. But that's an objection that's waived if it's not made at deposition. Since you didn't object at the deposition, it's too late to object now. The objection is overruled; the plaintiff may read that question and answer into evidence.*

Here, the judge ruled against Shaw's objection and allowed the testimony in as evidence.

By contrast, assume that Shaw had objected to the question at the deposition:

Q: *How fast would you say that Shaw was driving just prior to the collision?*

A: *I'd say about 30 m.p.h.*

Q: *And how long prior to the collision had Shaw been speeding?*

Shaw: *Objection, the question mischaracterizes the deponent's testimony.*

A: *I'd say for a couple of blocks. (Remember, the deponent normally answers objected-to questions.)*

Again, at trial, Shaw objects when the plaintiff seeks to offer this bit of deposition testimony into evidence. Because Shaw objected at the deposition (or, as attorneys say, "preserved" his objection), the judge should uphold his objection at trial and exclude the deposition testimony from evidence.

3. What If I Make the Wrong Objection or Object to a Proper Question?

If you object improperly at deposition, a judge will later disregard your objection—you will be in the same situation as if you hadn't objected at all. Your adversary will be able to use the answer later in the case, just as though you hadn't objected in the first place. In general, then, you have nothing to lose by making an objection, even if you're just guessing.

Don't regard this as an invitation or carte blanche to object, however. If you constantly interrupt a deposition with improper objections, your adversary may stop the deposition temporarily, go to court, and ask a judge to sanction you for your improper behavior.

4. Does Failure to Object at Deposition Always Allow an Adversary to Use the Answers Later in the Case?

No. In many situations, you can object for the first time if and when your adversary seeks to use deposition testimony later. Or as attorneys might say, some types of objections are automatically "preserved" to later in the case (when a summary judgment motion is filed or at trial), even if you don't make them during a deposition.

5. Which Objections Are Preserved and Which Are Waived If They're Not Made During a Deposition?

Alas, this question goes right to the heart of the complexity that we warned you about at the beginning of this section. Rules governing which objections must be made at depositions in order to be preserved for later in a case vary from state to state. Often, even judges within the same state will interpret their own court's rules in varying ways.

The best we can do here is to identify common objections that, in most jurisdictions, you'll probably have to make at depositions in order to preserve them for later in the case (Subsection a, below) and common objections that, in most jurisdictions, will probably be preserved even if you fail to make them (Subsection b, below). If you're still not convinced that the subject of objections is complex, we'll also describe a few "wobblers" (Subsection c), common

objections that could go either way depending on your locality's evidence rules, a judge's predilections, and the precise circumstances of your case.

Why Must Some Objections Be Made During the Deposition?

As you can see, evidence rules require you to make certain objections during the deposition itself or lose the right to make them later. For the most part, objections to the form of the question—that is, objections that the questioner could fix by phrasing the question a different way or asking some background questions first—must be made during the deposition. If this were not the rule, a deposition defender could try to sandbag his or her opponent by remaining silent at the deposition, and then raise the objection only at trial or in a pretrial motion—when it's too late for the questioner to do anything to fix the problem.

On the other hand, objections that are preserved for trial even if they are not made during the deposition ordinarily involve evidentiary problems that can't be cured, even if an objection is made. These objections are generally to the substance of the testimony the question elicits—for example, that the question asks for irrelevant information or hearsay.

a. "Make Them or Waive Them" Objections That Usually Must Be Made at Deposition to Be Preserved

Most judges are likely to rule that the objections discussed in this subsection are waivable—meaning that if you don't make these objections at the deposition, you probably won't be able to make them later in the case.

i. Objection: Assumes facts not in evidence

A question assumes facts not in evidence when it includes matters to which a deponent has not previously testified.

Example

A deponent who has not testified to knowing or having met with a Ms. Anthrope is asked, "When you and Ms. Anthrope met before the termination meeting, what did you talk about?"

Your adversary may try to use this sort of objectionable question in an attempt to put words in the deponent's mouth. In the above example, the deponent may implicitly adopt your adversary's assertion that the deponent met with Ms. Anthrope before the termination meeting by testifying only to what took place at the meeting. If you fail to object, your adversary might be able to use the deposition as evidence later that Ms. Anthrope and the deponent met before the termination meeting. To prevent this, you should object that the question "assumes facts not in evidence." Once you object, your adversary can fix the problem by asking the deponent whether the assumed fact is accurate: "Did you and Ms. Anthrope meet before the termination meeting?"

ii. Objection: Misquotes or mischaracterizes the testimony

This objection arises when your adversary misstates what a deponent said earlier in a deposition.

Example

Earlier in a deposition, the deponent had testified that Johnson "raised her voice" during a performance review. Later your adversary asks, "When Johnson shouted during the performance review, what did she say?"

Here, the adversary's question converts the testimony "raised her voice" into "shouted." If you fail to object, and the deponent answers the question, the deponent in effect adopts your adversary's characterization. By objecting that the question mischaracterizes the evidence, you prevent the adversary from later using the testimony as evidence that Johnson "shouted."

In addition, your objection calls the deponent's attention to the subtle change in the prior testimony. As a result, the deponent may correct the problem when answering the question. In the above example, for instance, the deponent might follow your objection by testifying: "I didn't say Ms. Johnson shouted, I just said she raised her voice."

iii. Objection: Question calls for privileged information

A deponent (whether or not a party) has a right not to disclose privileged information. (See Chapter 7 for a discussion of privileges.) When defending a deposition, you can object if your adversary asks the deponent a question that calls for privileged information. If you fail to object and the deponent answers the question, you waive the objection.

Example

Your adversary asks a nonparty deponent about a case-related discussion that the deponent had with her attorney prior to the deposition.

Here, you can object on the ground that "the question calls for information protected by the attorney-client privilege." Remember, however, that although your objection can signal to a deponent that a question calls for privileged information, because you are not an attorney, you cannot instruct or even advise the deponent not to answer on the grounds of privilege—only an attorney representing the deponent can do that. As a result, if the deponent answers despite your objection, the privilege is waived and your adversary will be able to use the information later in the case.

iv. Objection: Counsel is trying to intimidate the deponent

You can object if your adversary tries to bully or intimidate the deponent into giving a particular answer.

Example

Your adversary wants to establish that the deponent attended a particular meeting. Though the deponent repeatedly denies having been present, your adversary continues to ask

questions such as, *"Why won't you admit under oath that you were at the meeting?"*

If you fail to object and the intimidated deponent decides that the easiest way out is to testify that he or she was at the meeting, your adversary will probably be able to use the answer later in the case. To preserve your objection, you may say something like, "I object; you are raising your voice and trying to intimidate the witness by repeatedly asking the same question." (Putting the attorney's tone of voice on the record can support your request to a judge for a protective order should you decide that the attorney's questioning is so improper that you must stop the deposition. See Section F2, below, for more information on protective orders.)

v. Objection: Compound question

A question is compound when it is essentially two questions phrased as one.

Examples

- *"Who was at the party and which of them had you met previously?"*
- *"Where did you go after you left the meeting and what did you do there?"*

You typically waive the objection if you fail to object that such questions are compound. However, you probably needn't bother to make this objection because in most cases, your adversary can easily elicit the same information by breaking the single compound question into two or more smaller ones: "Who was at the party?" and "Which of them had you met previously?"

vi. Objection: Vague

A question is vague when it does not make clear what information the questioner is seeking from the deponent.

Examples

- *"Up until things changed, what was going on between you and your supervisor?"*
- *"What was going on in the restaurant that night?"*

These questions are improperly vague because they don't allow you to anticipate the topic that the deponent is supposed to address in the answer. As a result, a deponent may testify to improper evidence before you have a chance to object to it. While you might object to the answer, an objection may do little good once the cat is out of the bag. To avoid this problem, object when you think a question is too unclear to direct the deponent's attention to a specific topic.

vii. Objection: Leading

A leading question is a question that, either through the way it is worded or the questioner's tone of voice, suggests the answer the deponent should give. (See Federal Rule of Evidence 611(c).)

Example

- *"Isn't it true that you personally met with Ms. Anthrope before you went to the meeting?"*

Leading questions are permissible when your opponent is deposing a witness who is adverse to

the opponent's side of the case, such as one of your employees. But you can object if your adversary asks leading questions of a neutral nonparty deponent, such as a bystander to an accident.

viii. Objection: Calls for a narrative answer

A question "calls for a narrative answer" when it is overly broad or when it asks a deponent to testify to a series of events that unfolded over time.

Examples

- *"Please describe everything that led up to the decision to purchase the new computer system."*
- *"Tell me everything that occurred from the time you got up on the morning of July 12 until the collision."*

As with improperly vague questions, the main risk of narrative questions is that they are so open-ended that you may not be able to anticipate what the deponent will say. After you object that the question calls for a narrative, your adversary may ask a narrower, more focused question, such as, "Please describe what took place during the first meeting in which you discussed the purchase of the new computer system." This question is proper, since you know what information is being requested.

ix. Objection: Argumentative

An argumentative question asks a deponent to respond to your adversary's argument rather than to a question.

Examples

- *"Doesn't the fact that you can't remember who was present prove that you never were at that meeting?"*

- *"Since Mrs. Green's report was written right after the meeting, why shouldn't we believe Mrs. Green's report rather than your testimony?"*

It is not a deponent's job to respond to your adversary's arguments. Struggling to respond to an argumentative question, a deponent may give an answer that is only a guess or is speculative. Your objection prevents your adversary from using the deponent's answer later in the case.

Stating objections properly

Evidence rules are a bit like rules of etiquette in that they prescribe not only what objections you can make, but also the proper way of phrasing them. To be sure that your deposition objection is preserved to later in the case, try to follow these rules for phrasing objections:

- Make your objection specific enough to identify the impropriety you're objecting to:

  Examples of improper, unspecific objections:

  - "I object to that question."

  - "Objection: That's not admissible."

  Examples of properly specific objections:

  - "Objection: Assumes facts not in evidence"

  - "Objection: Misstates the witness's testimony"

- State your objection "concisely and in a non-argumentative and non-suggestive manner." (FRCP 30(d)(1).) Judges and attorneys often refer to objections that violate this rule as "speaking objections." Speaking objections are improper because they often constitute attempts to "coach" a witness to give the objector's desired answer. Also,

they often turn into long-winded legal arguments that disrupt and prolong depositions. (For a discussion of how to respond to a lawyer's speaking objections when you're taking a deposition, see Chapter 12.)

Example

Q: After the chicken hurried across the road, what's the next thing that occurred?

Improper Speaking Objection: "Objection: *The question misstates the testimony. The deponent didn't say anything about the chicken hurrying across the road. Maybe all the deponent saw was the chicken on one side of the road, and then later on the other side. The deponent might not have actually seen the chicken crossing the road. If you want to know what happened, ask a question but please don't put words in the deponent's mouth."*

A judge may even decide that a "speaking objection" such as this fails to preserve the objection. To avoid such a possibility, phrase objections succinctly.

Proper Objection: *"Objection: The question misstates the witness's prior testimony."*

b. Objections Usually Preserved Even If You Don't Make Them at Deposition

Judges generally consider the following objections preserved even if they are not made at the time of a deposition. Consequently, if you don't assert these objections at deposition, you can probably still make them later, if and when your adversary tries to use the objectionable deposition testimony against you.

i. Objection: Irrelevant

This objection asserts that evidence has no bearing on the issues in dispute in your lawsuit. (See Federal Rule of Evidence 401.)

Example

In a breach of contract case, your adversary claims that the agreed-upon sale price of widgets was $2 each. During a deposition, your company's general manager is asked, "How has the company responded to employee complaints of age discrimination?" The question seeks irrelevant evidence, because no factual or legal relationship exists between alleged age discrimination and a breach of contract claim based on the sale price of widgets.

You might, of course, object to this question as irrelevant at the deposition. If you fail to do so, however, you'll probably be able to make the same objection later in the case, if and when your adversary seeks to use the answer.

ii. Objection: Probative (proof) value is outweighed by undue prejudice

This objection is similar to an objection that a question is irrelevant. The difference is that this objection concedes that evidence is of some relevance, but asserts that the relevance is outweighed by the potential for unfair prejudice. (See Federal Rule of Evidence 403.)

Example

You're a plaintiff representing yourself in an auto accident case. After the deponent testifies to being your personal friend, your adversary asks, "Do you and the plaintiff belong to the same antiabortion organization?" Your adversary might claim that the answer is relevant to show that the deponent might be biased in your favor by the existence of a personal friendship. But the relevance of the evidence is very minimal, since the deponent has already testified to being your personal friend. And on the "unfair prejudice" side, evidence of antiabortion activity might cause some people to disbelieve the deponent for political reasons. As a result, a judge might well decide that the evidence is improper because its potential for unfair prejudice outweighs its probative value.

Again, you might at a deposition object that "the probative valued is outweighed by undue prejudice." Should you fail to do so, however, you can almost surely raise the objection later in the case, if and when your adversary seeks to use the evidence.

iii. Objection: Improper opinion

This objection asserts that your adversary has asked a lay (nonexpert) witness to give an opinion on a matter that is beyond everyday experience. (See Chapter 8 and Federal Rule of Evidence 701.) You might make this same objection if a deponent is asked to give an opinion on a matter as to which the deponent lacks personal knowledge (see Subsection c, below).

Example (Opinion OK)

A lay deponent who saw you in a bar could probably be properly asked to give an opinion as to whether you appeared to be under the influence of alcohol. How people tend to behave when they're under the influence is a matter known to most people, and therefore a proper topic for testimony.

Example (Opinion OK)

A lay deponent who personally saw you leaving a meeting could probably be asked to give an opinion as to whether you appeared to be happy, because how people tend to behave and appear when they're happy is also a matter known to most people.

Example (Improper Opinion)

A lay deponent who came upon the scene of an auto accident in which your were involved is asked, "From looking at the damage to the cars, how fast do you think each was going just prior to the impact?" In response, the deponent answers, "I'd say at least 60 m.p.h." This question calls for an improper opinion. Lay witnesses are not qualified by training or experience to judge the speed of cars from looking at their conditions following an impact.

When appropriate, you can object that the question "calls for an improper opinion." Even if you neglect to make this objection during a deposition, however, you'll probably be able to make the objection later, if and when your adversary seeks to use the answer to a question that calls for an improper opinion.

c. "Wobbler" Objections That May Have to Be Made at Deposition to Be Preserved

The following objections are what we call "wobblers": In some jurisdictions, you need not raise these objections at deposition, to preserve them for use later in the case. California is one such jurisdiction (see Calif. Code of Civil Procedure Sec. 2025-m-3). But depending on the circumstances of the case, the law in your state, and the philosophy of the judge hearing your case, you may need to object during a deposition in order to preserve these objections. Under FRCP 32(d)(3)(B), for example, you must raise an objection whenever the circumstances would have allowed your adversary to cure the problem had you made an objection.

i. Objection: Lack of personal knowledge (or lack of foundation or calls for speculation)

This objection asserts that your adversary has failed to establish that a lay (nonexpert) witness has personal knowledge of whatever it is the witness is asked to testify about. (See Federal Rule of Evidence 602, requiring that nonexpert testimony be based on personal knowledge.)

Example

Q: *What time did your meeting with Ms. Julian break up?*

A: *About 10:00.*

Q: *And where did Ms. Julian go after she left the meeting?*

A: *She went to meet with the company vice president.*

You might object that the second question "calls for speculation" or "lacks foundation" because the questioner has not established that the deponent has personal knowledge of where Ms. Julian went after the 10:00 meeting. If you do object, your adversary probably won't be able to use the answer later in the case.

If you don't object, however, the answer is less clear. Some judges would say that your failure to object waives this objection. These judges would reason that your objection would have given your opponent a chance to fix the lack of foundation problem right there at the deposition. If you fail to object at deposition, your adversary has no such opportunity to fix the question. For instance, had you objected, your adversary might have asked additional questions showing that the deponent did in fact have personal knowledge of where Ms. Julian went (for example, maybe the deponent watched her walk into the vice president's office).

ii. Objection: Lack of authentication (or lack of foundation for a document)

This objection asserts that the questioner has failed to establish that a document shown to the deponent is "genuine"—that is, established on the record that it was written or produced by the person claimed to be the author. (See Federal Rule of Evidence 901.)

Example

Your adversary shows the deponent a letter signed by Kim and asks, "When did you receive Kim's letter?" The deponent answers, "On August 31."

If your opponent hasn't presented any evidence that Kim wrote the letter (and you haven't stipulated [agreed] that Kim wrote it), you may object based on "lack of authentication." If you fail to object, some judges would rule that your failure waives any later claim that Kim was not in fact the author of the letter. Again, their reasoning would be that had you objected, you would have given your adversary a chance to present evidence showing how the deponent knew that Kim wrote the letter (for example, maybe the deponent saw Kim write it, or is familiar with Kim's handwriting).

iii. Objection: Hearsay

This objection asserts that your adversary has asked the deponent to testify about a statement made previously (outside of the deposition) in order to prove that the statement is true. (See Federal Rule of Evidence 801.)

Example

In an auto accident case in which you drove a green car, your adversary asks the police officer who investigated the collision, "What did a bystander tell you after the accident?" In response, the officer testifies, "The bystander told me that the green car ran the stop sign." The bystander's statement is improper hearsay if your adversary wants to use the statement to prove that you ran the stop sign.

At the deposition, you might preserve the hearsay objection for later in the case by objecting that your opponent's question "calls for hearsay." If you fail to object, some judges would rule that your adversary could use the bystander's statement later as evidence that you ran the stop sign.

The hearsay rule is riddled with exceptions. Because of these exceptions, what seems on the surface to be improper hearsay may in fact be proper evidence, depending on the circumstances under which a statement was made. For example, the bystander's statement above might be proper if the bystander made the statement almost immediately after the accident. (See Federal Rule of Evidence 803(1), which provides a hearsay exception for "present sense impressions"—statements made during or right after the events to which they pertain.)

Judges who would rule that your failure to raise a hearsay objection at a deposition means that you've waived the objection would probably do so on the theory that had you objected, you would have given your opponent a chance to ask additional questions establishing the basis of a hearsay exception.

⚠ **Pay close attention to testimony rather than worrying about the hearsay rule.**

The hearsay rule is extremely complex. Judges, lawyers, and evidence scholars have debated its foundations for hundreds of years—and you won't be able to master all of its permutations before you defend a deposition. In this area especially, you're far better off listening carefully to the testimony than obsessing about when and how to make objections.

d. Objections to Improper Answers

The discussion above addressed evidentiary problems that arose in your opponent's questions. The same problems, however, can also turn up in a deponent's answer.

Example

Q: *What happened next?*

A: *I heard a bystander say that the green car ran a red light.*

Here, the deponent testifies to possibly improper hearsay in response to an entirely proper question.

Example

Q: *After Mr. Bradley came out of the meeting, what happened next?*

A: *Bradley went into Ms. Gardener's office and told her what happened at the meeting.*

Here again, in response to a proper question, the deponent testifies to a matter as to which the deponent may lack personal knowledge.

You can make most of the same objections, regardless of whether an evidentiary problem appears in a question or an answer. (Obviously, objections concerning the forms of questions—for example, "leading" or "compound"—don't arise with answers.) And the rules as to whether an objection must be made at a deposition to be preserved for use later are the same. A judge will decide the issue in the same way, whether it was the question or the answer that was objectionable. But to be especially safe, you should both state your objection and move to "strike" (remove) the objectionable testimony in the answer from the deposition record.

Example 1

Q: *What happened next?*

A: *I heard a bystander say that the green car ran a red light.*

You: *I object and move to strike that testimony as hearsay.*

Example 2

Q: *After Mr. Bradley came out of the meeting, what happened next?*

A: *Bradley went into Ms. Gardener's office and told her what happened at the meeting.*

You: *I object and move to strike that testimony on the grounds that it lacks foundation.*

F. Terminating a Deposition

There are two reasons why you might terminate a deposition before your opposing counsel has finished questioning the deponent. If your adversary exceeded the deposition time limit, you may want to cut off any further questions. And if your adversary persistently acts improperly—by asking intrusive questions, badgering the witness, or otherwise abusing the process—you might consider stopping the deposition to seek a court order prohibiting this conduct.

1. Enforcing the Time Limit

FRCP 30(d)(2) limits depositions to "one day of seven hours" unless you and your opponent agree to extend the time. This seven-hour limit does not include breaks for lunch or "time-outs" for people in attendance to stretch their legs and see to other personal needs. Once the opposing lawyer reaches the time limit, you have the right to declare the deposition at an end.

For example, you might say something like: "We began this deposition about eight hours ago. We took a half-hour break for lunch, and

we had a couple of short recesses. So your time for asking questions has expired. I'll permit another 15 minutes, then I'll declare the deposition terminated under FRCP 30(d)(2)." After the 15 additional minutes are up, the deponent and you may leave.

You have the power to agree to extend the time for a deposition, and sometimes it makes sense to do so. For example, you may want to question a deponent after your adversary concludes questioning. If so, you may say something like: "I'll agree that you may have up to another hour for questioning, on the condition that I'll also have an hour to ask questions when you're done." Also, if a case is complex and you think a judge is likely to allow additional questioning, you might as well agree to extend the time, rather than spending time and money to fight a losing battle in court.

2. Suspending a Deposition to Seek a Protective Order

You can usually protect your interests at a deposition simply by making the occasional objection and enforcing the time limit. However, you may run into an opponent who is truly obnoxious, obstructive, or obstreperous. If you find yourself in the thankfully rare situation in which the deposing lawyer abuses the right to take depositions, this section describes how you might respond.

FRCP 30(d)(3) gives you the right to suspend a deposition and seek a "protective order" if a lawyer conducts a deposition "in bad faith" or "in such manner as unreasonably to annoy, embarrass, or oppress" the deponent. If you think you can prove to a judge that your adversary's lawyer is engaging in this type of severe misconduct, take the following steps:

- First, try to resolve the problem. FRCP 26(c) requires you to make a good faith effort to resolve deposition disputes before going to court. Local rules in your court district may describe just what you have to do to make a "good faith effort." For example, a local rule may require you to contact a magistrate or referee by phone from the deposition. Be sure to check your local rules before the deposition so you'll know what to do if things fall apart.

- If you can't resolve the dispute, announce that you are suspending the deposition and that you intend to seek a protective order.

- Promptly file a written Motion for a Protective Order in the court where the case is pending. Your written motion should state how your adversary acted in bad faith or in an unreasonably annoying, embarrassing, or oppressive manner during the deposition.

- In the written motion, ask the court to make an order terminating the deposition or limiting the deposition's "scope and manner." Also, ask the judge to sanction (fine or otherwise penalize) your adversary, such as by ordering your adversary to pay

you for the time, trouble, and expense of going to court.

- Serve a copy of the motion on your adversary's lawyer.

⚠️ **Don't terminate a deposition unless the opposing lawyer's misconduct is severe.**

Judges have almost unlimited discretion to grant or deny protective orders. Judges also recognize that depositions can often be unpleasant—and that everyone involved must put up with a certain amount of posturing and arguing. Thus, you shouldn't run to court seeking a protective order just because your adversary is difficult, bumbling, or irritating. If you seek a protective order based on conduct that falls short of "bad faith," the judge may decide to sanction *you* for improperly suspending the deposition.

Because judges have almost unlimited discretion when deciding whether to issue a protective order, these cases can go either way. However, you might terminate a deposition and seek a protective order if:

- the questioner repeatedly pries into a deponent's private personal conduct, medical condition, or confidential business practices, even though those matters have no bearing on the case, despite your objections, or

- the questioner repeatedly uses oral bullying tactics, such as asking questions angrily, constantly interrupting a deponent's answers, or insulting the deponent's memory and integrity. (Because a judge can't determine unspoken behavior or tone of voice from a written transcript, you may have to describe some of a questioner's bullying behavior for the record. For example, you might say something like: "I want the record to indicate that the deposing attorney has banged the table after each of the last ten questions.")

If you seek a protective order because your adversary has repeatedly pried into a deponent's irrelevant private conduct, your motion for a Protective Order would probably look something like the sample provided below. However, most courts have rules that detail the form and length of pretrial motions (even down to the paper you have to use), as well as requirements for serving your papers on your adversary. Thus, before preparing a Motion for a Protective Order, you should check your local rules or consult a lawyer or paralegal to make sure your motion meets all the necessary requirements.

MOTION FOR PROTECTIVE ORDER

Plaintiff Binder respectfully requests that this Court enter a protective order pursuant to FRCP 26(c) and 30(d)(4) against defendant Mal Odorous. The facts on which this Motion is based are as follows:

1. This case involves a contract dispute, in which plaintiff Binder contends that defendant Odorous materially breached a contract for the manufacture and sale of golf clubs, thereby interfering with Binder's business as a retail seller of golf equipment.

2. On February 1, 20xx, defendant Odorous began taking the deposition of Ken Barbie, the supervisor of plaintiff's purchasing department. The deposition began at 9:00 a.m. and was adjourned for the day at 2:00 p.m.

3. Plaintiff Binder terminated the deposition of Barbie to move for this protective order. The reason for the termination was that counsel for defendant Odorous repeatedly asked the deponent questions concerning plaintiff's membership in a private country club, including the source of the funds plaintiff used to join the country club, the club's policies with respect to admitting members of ethnic minority groups, and the names of other members of the club with whom plaintiff tends to associate.

4. None of these questions is reasonably calculated to the discovery of admissible evidence, and these questions were asked in bad faith in an attempt to embarrass the deponent.

5. Despite plaintiff's repeated requests to counsel for Odorous to cease asking these questions, counsel persisted in doing so. Attached to this Motion are the pages of the Reporter's Transcript that set forth counsel's improper questions.

6. Plaintiff respectfully requests that this Court issue a Protective Order ordering that no further deposition questioning of Ken Barbie take place. Plaintiff also requests that this Court sanction the defendant in the amount it deems fit to compensate plaintiff for the time and expense of seeking this Protective Order.

Dated: _____   Respectfully submitted,

David Binder

David Binder
Plaintiff in Pro Se

Chapter 11

Taking a Deposition: Deposing a "Hostile" Witness

This chapter reviews techniques for deposing a "hostile" (unfriendly) witness. A hostile witness is your opposing party or any nonparty witness who won't talk to you informally, probably because that witness is employed by or closely aligned with your opponent. If you're taking a deposition, chances are that the deponent will be hostile. (For a discussion of the less common situation in which you might depose a "friendly" witness, see Chapter 13.)

A. Should You Take a Deposition?

As a party representing yourself, think carefully about whether you want to take a deposition. Though you may have the right to do so, there are very good reasons to forego a deposition, especially if your case involves a relatively modest amount of money (say, in the range of $25,000 or less). Reasons you might decide to forgo depositions include:

- **Hassle.** You have to make all the arrangements, including finding suitable dates and locations, arranging for a court reporter, serving the notice papers on the deponent, and notifying your adversary in writing.

- **Expense.** As the party noticing the deposition, you have to pay a court reporter to attend the deposition and transcribe the testimony. Expect to pay about six dollars per page of deposition transcript; a full day of testimony will almost certainly consume

at least 100 pages. You also have to pay a nonparty deponent to attend the deposition, although in most jurisdictions that will be a nominal sum (probably less than $50), but much more for experts (see below). For a further discussion of witness fees for nonparty deponents, see Chapter 1.

- **Effort.** Effective deposition-taking is a difficult skill, even for many experienced attorneys. You will have to spend some time preparing for—and taking—the deposition, and it will be a challenging task.

> ⚠ **Beware the hazards of deposing an opponent's expert witness.**
>
> If you're representing yourself, think especially carefully before deposing your adversary's expert witness. Deposing an expert greatly increases both the difficulty and the expense of the deposition. To effectively depose an expert, you'll need in-depth knowledge of the relevant field of expertise. And you will probably have to pay the expert's reasonable hourly fee for the time he or she spends at the deposition (which can be hundreds of dollars per hour). If you decide to depose an adversary's expert nevertheless, be sure to read Chapter 8 for suggestions on what topics to cover at the deposition.

Because of all of the considerations, do not assume that you are being sloppy if you decide not to depose your opposing party or its witnesses. Because depositions are expensive, it's not unusual for lawyers to settle small cases or take them to trial without having taken even a single deposition. Your best bet may be to follow these lawyers' leads. In lieu of depositions, try to rely on other methods of gathering information, such as:

- **Informal interviews.** Witnesses may agree to talk to you, especially if you tell them that you have the right to subpoena them to appear at a deposition.

- **Inexpensive formal discovery techniques, such as written interrogatories.** Written interrogatories (which you can send only to your adversary, not to nonparty witnesses) are especially useful when you are after very specific information. For a discussion of written interrogatories, see Chapter 9.

Despite the difficulties and expense of depositions, the amount in controversy or your desire to vindicate your rights may make it worthwhile for you to take one or more depositions. You may, for example, be a tenant who feels that a vengeful landlord has filed suit in an effort to wrongfully force you out of your apartment. Taking the landlord's deposition could be an effective way of improving your legal position and signaling your intent to fight the eviction vigorously. Whatever your reasons, if you do decide to take a deposition, the suggestion in this chapter should enhance the deposition's effectiveness.

B. Deciding Whom to Depose

Unless you have unlimited time and financial resources, you'll probably want to limit yourself to taking one or two depositions. If so, make sure that the person you depose is a key witness who is likely to have important information that you can't get through other means.

In many cases, identifying a key witness is not difficult. For example, if you're a party representing yourself in a personal injury case arising from a two-car collision, the obvious key witness is your opponent—the driver of the other car.

If you're uncertain about who to depose, refer to the initial voluntary disclosures that many jurisdictions require parties to make. For example, under FRCP 26(a)(1)(A), your adversary and you must voluntarily disclose to each other the name and (if known) the address and telephone number of "each individual likely to have discoverable information." The disclosure must also identify "the subjects of the information" each of these individuals knows. Since your adversary's initial disclosure will identify all witnesses known to your adversary and the subjects about which those witnesses would likely testify, the disclosure should help you identify whom to depose.

Example

You're a defendant representing yourself in an auto accident personal injury case. The plaintiff's initial disclosure identifies the following people who can provide information about how the accident occurred: (1) the plaintiff, (2) a passenger in the plaintiff's car, and (3) a bystander. According to the disclosure document, the plaintiff has information about how the plaintiff and you were driving just prior to the accident, the point of impact, and statements you allegedly made following the collision. The passenger and the bystander have information about one statement you admittedly made following the collision. Based on these disclosures, at most you'd probably depose the plaintiff. The other two witnesses do not seem to merit the time and expense of a deposition.

If your adversary is a business or similar entity with numerous employees, even an initial disclosure might not enable you to readily identify which employee is the key witness whom you should depose. Whichever employee you subpoena may know little about the actions of other employees. If it turns out that the employee you select to depose was only marginally involved in case-related events, the deposition may consist of little more than a series of "I don't know" responses.

Example

In a case in which you claim that you were wrongfully terminated from a job, you decide to depose your former employer's human resources manager. However, it turns out that the manager was new to the job at the time you were fired and knows little about your situation. The deposition will likely be filled with "I don't know anything about that" responses.

To avoid this problem, consider the following approaches when you plan to depose a representative of an organization:

- Wait to take a deposition until after you've gotten sufficient information to enable you to identify a key witness. For example, if you claim to have been fired illegally, you might delay taking a deposition until after you receive answers to written interrogatories asking your adversary to identify the names and positions of the people involved in the termination decision.

- Use a "designated deponent" procedure. FRCP 30(b)(6) allows you not to name a specific deponent in a Notice of Deposition or a Subpoena re Deposition, but instead to list the topics you intend to ask about during the deposition. It's then up to the organization to designate and send to the deposition the one or more representatives who are knowledgeable about those topics. A judge has the power to sanction (penalize) an organization that intentionally sends a representative who knows little or nothing about case-related events.

C. Preparing to Take a Deposition

Once you've identified a suitable deponent, you will have to prepare to take the deposition.

1. Making Deposition Arrangements

Setting up a deposition initially involves choosing a date and location. When arranging deposition dates, attorneys often consult with each other informally and jointly agree on a date that is acceptable to both attorneys and the deponent before sending out official notice as required by the courts. You should make every effort to extend this same courtesy to your adversary and the deponent. To do this, arrange two or three dates that are convenient for you and the court reporting service you hire to conduct the deposition. Then call or send a message asking your adversary and the deponent to choose one of the alternatives.

If for some reason you don't want to contact your adversary—or your adversary gives you the runaround—you'll have to consult your locale's deposition rules and select a date that allows you to give the deponent at least the advance notice required by those rules. For example, FRCP 30(b)(1) requires only that the advance notice be "reasonable." As a general rule, written notice ten or more days in advance of a deposition is considered reasonable.

Hiring a Court Reporter

You'll find court reporting services listed in the Yellow Pages of most telephone books and on the Internet. (To find postings from many court reporting services, simply point your search engine to the term "depositions.") If you live in an urban area, you'll have a choice of many reporting services. Unless you have or can borrow a convenient office with a quiet conference room, you'll want to select a court reporting service that can also provide you with a conference room. The service you hire will probably want to be paid "up front" for a day of reporting and transcription of testimony into a deposition booklet; expect to be charged at least $500. The court reporting service can probably also advise you about any special notice procedures you'll need to follow in your locality.

With the basic arrangements in hand, you'll "notice" the deposition in writing (formally notify the deponent and your adversary where and when the deposition will take place). To notice a deposition of your adversary, you can mail a Notice of Deposition to your adversary's attorney (or to the adversary personally, if your adversary is also self-represented). If you want the party-deponent to bring documents or other physical objects to the deposition, you can identify those documents in the Notice of Deposition or in a separate Request for Production of Documents. (See FRCP 30(b)(5) and FRCP 34. See Sample Form #5 in Appendix 3.)

To notice the deposition of a nonparty witness, you'll need to have that witness personally served with a court form called a "Subpoena re Deposition." (See Sample Form #1 in Appendix 3.) Alternatively, if you want the nonparty witness to bring documents or other tangible objects to the deposition, you'll have the witness personally served with a "Subpoena Duces Tecum re Deposition," identifying the material that the witness is to bring. (See Sample Form #2 in Appendix 3.) As a general rule, you cannot personally serve either type of subpoena. (FRCP 45(b)(1).) You can ask a friend to serve a subpoena, or you can hire a professional process server.

You must also promptly mail a copy of the notice or subpoena to your adversary, since the adversary has a right to receive advance notice of and attend any deposition you take. (For additional discussion of the contents of these notices and subpoenas, see Chapter 1.)

2. Deposition Questioning Goals

To take an effective deposition, you must first figure out what you're trying to accomplish. Your goals might include:

- **Finding out all case-related information known to the deponent, even if it is harmful to your case.** Knowing all the "bad stuff" as early as possible helps you evaluate your case for settlement or trial and gives you a chance to disprove it through further investigation. As lawyers say, you want to know exactly how a deponent can hurt you.

- **Understanding the deponent's chronology of events.** It's often best to try to elicit the deponent's testimony in such a way that you can easily organize it chronologically. That way, you will be less likely to miss something important. You should also be able to understand the witnesses' key points and evaluate their strengths and weaknesses more easily.

- **Searching for information that supports your own legal claims.** You should go into a deposition with a list of helpful information that the deponent realistically might be able to provide. By the end of the deposition you should have asked about all the information on your list.

- **Evaluating the deponent's credibility.** Here, you'll want to search for information that might lead a judge or jury to distrust the deponent's testimony. For example, does the deponent have a financial stake in your adversary's claims? Has the deponent ever said anything that conflicts with the deposition testimony? Is the deponent a close friend or relative of your adversary? At the same time, you'll want to observe the deponent's demeanor and manner of answering questions. Does the deponent seem nervous or hesitant? Does the deponent repeatedly look to the adversary's attorney for help before answering questions? Nonverbal factors such as these may cause a judge or jury to disbelieve the deponent's testimony. And even if your case does not go to trial, you may be able to obtain a better settlement if you can make a strong argument that your adversary's witnesses are not credible.

3. Preparing to Ask Questions

The final preparation step is to prepare carefully for the actual questioning process. As you prepare, remember that FRCP 30(d)(2) limits depositions to one day of seven hours. (See Chapter 1, Section F.)

a. Make a Topical Outline

You might be tempted to try to write out a list of all the questions you intend to ask the deponent. However, this is rarely an effective approach to questioning. One of the primary advantages of taking oral depositions over serving written interrogatories is that you can adjust your questions according to a deponent's answers. If you're locked into questions you've prepared in advance, you're likely to be so inflexible in your approach that you miss out on important information. Instead of creating a list of questions, you're better off with an outline of key topics and events (possibly with important subtopics) that you can quickly refer to during your questioning.

Example

Assume that you're a plaintiff representing yourself in a personal injury case, and that you're preparing to depose the defendant driver whose car collided with yours. You create an outline of topics that you want to question the defendant about, which might sensibly include the following:

1. **Background:** *Education, job history, current employment and duties, health history (major health problems) and present physical condition, previous driving record, insurance carried.*

2. **Vehicle:** *Make, model, repair records.*

3. **Documents:** *Documents or other objects deponent brought to the deposition in response to Notice or Subpoena Duces Tecum.* (For an explanation of how to complete the forms necessary to have the defendant bring documents, see Chapter 2.)

4. **Accident scene:** *Traffic markings, traffic controls, weather, traffic conditions.*

5. **Events preceding collision:** *Chronology of activities on day of collision, alcohol or drugs ingested.*

6. **Collision:** *Location and direction of vehicles, speed of vehicles, presence of passengers, physical condition at time of collision, time of day or night, distractions, steps taken to avoid collision, point of impact.*

7. **Events after collision:** *Statements made by or to police officers or bystanders, physical condition after collision, medical treatment received.*

b. Gather Exhibits You'll Want to Use When Questioning the Deponent

Second, gather any exhibits (such as documents, photographs, or diagrams) in your possession that you intend to show to the deponent as part of your questioning. If possible, put "tabs" on the edges of documents or use some other method of quickly identifying documents so you don't have to waste deposition time looking for a document. (For a discussion of how to use exhibits effectively during deposition questioning, see Section G, below.)

c. Make a List of Helpful Evidence

You should also make a list of helpful information that you hope the deponent will provide during the deposition. Using the questioning patterns described below, try to elicit the information on this list during the deposition.

Example 1

You bought a house and are suing the seller for failing to disclose that the roof needed replacing to the tune of $20,000. You are about to depose the seller. After moving in, you talked to a neighbor who told you that about six months before you bought the house, a roofer told the seller that the roof was shot and needed replacing. On your list of helpful evidence, you'd make a note such as, "Ask seller to admit that about six months before the sale, a roofer told the seller that the roof needed replacing."

Example 2

You're suing a jewelry store for fraudulently misrepresenting the quality and value of some expensive baubles that you purchased. You're about to depose Ruby Diamond, the salesperson from whom you bought the baubles. Prior to the deposition, a couple of "regular" customers told you that they heard that Ruby had been warned that she had to increase her sales to keep her job. As this suggests a possible motive for Ruby to inflate the value of the gems that you bought, you'd make a note such as, "Ask whether jewelry store owner or manager had told Ruby that she had to increase her sales. If so, find out whether written notice of the warning exists."

D. Beginning the Deposition: Preliminary Questioning

As lawyers commonly do, you may begin a deposition with a series of "admonitions" (see Chapter 5), and then ask background questions (see Chapter 6). If you are an inexperienced party representing yourself, you may want to skip these routine deposition phases and go right into case-related questioning. You will save time and, therefore, money. Also, you'll reduce the opportunity for an aggressive defending lawyer to try to wear you down by repeatedly objecting to what should be routine questioning.

E. The Two Basic Forms of Questions

As you seek to accomplish the deposition goals set forth above (in Section C2), you'll rely on two general types of questions: deponent-centered questions and questioner-centered questions.

Deponent-centered questions are open-ended, relying on a deponent's independent memory and encouraging the deponent to describe events in the deponent's own words. In response to deponent-centered questions, the deponent may mention information that you never would have thought to ask about directly.

Examples of deponent-centered questions include:

- *"What was discussed during the June 6 meeting?"*

- *"After the car made the left turn, what happened?"*

- *"How did the broken ankle affect Kristi's daily activities?"*

Questioner-centered questions, by contrast, are more narrow, seeking to elicit specific pieces of information. They are questioner-centered because most of the factual information is in your question rather than in the deponent's answer. The information in questioner-centered inquiries may stimulate a deponent to recall information that he or she would have omitted in response to an open-ended inquiry. Here are examples of three questioner-centered questions covering the same subjects in the same order as just set out in the deponent-centered questions above:

- *"Was the purchase of new computers discussed during the June 6 meeting?"*

- *"What color was the light for east-west traffic at the time that the car started to make the left turn?"*

- *"How many times per week did Kristi go to physical therapy?"*

The most narrow questioner-centered inquiry is a leading question. A leading question is one that, either by its wording or through the questioner's tone of voice, suggests the answer the deponent should give. (See Federal Rule of Evidence 611(c).) The following are examples of leading questions:

- *"The purchase of new computers was discussed during the June 6 meeting, isn't that true?"*

- *"The light was red for east-west traffic at the time that the car started to make the left turn, correct?"*

- *"Kristi went to physical therapy only once every two weeks, right?"*

Leading questions are perfectly proper when you question a "hostile" witness (witness for the other side), such as your adversary or a person employed by your adversary. Leading questions can also be an effective and efficient method for having a hostile deponent provide information on your list of helpful evidence (for example, "You never heard me mention Matt's name, did you?").

However, try to avoid leading questions when deposing a "friendly" witness (witness for your side). Leading questions are improper in this situation, and if the defending attorney objects, you won't be able to use a helpful answer later in the case. (See Chapter 12 for more details.)

F. Using the Two Basic Forms of Questions

The two basic forms of questions described above enable you to both elicit a deponent's independent recall and seek answers to specific questions. The subsections below demonstrate how you might combine these questioning forms to achieve the deposition goals set out in Section C2, above.

1. Uncovering All Case-Related Information Known to the Deponent

One of your goals when deposing a hostile witness is to find out whatever harmful information the witness has. To do that, try to bring out all case-related information known to the deponent.

To see how combining deponent-centered with questioner-centered inquiries can help you achieve this goal, focus for a moment on a small portion of a larger story. Assume that an important event in a case concerns a business meeting

that took place on June 6. You want to find out as much as you can about what happened during this meeting. You might start out with a series of open-ended, deponent-centered questions designed to see what the deponent recalls and is willing to say:

> *You: What was discussed during the June 6 meeting?*
>
> *A: I remember we talked about the new employee health plan and a new marketing report.*
>
> *You: Anything else that you can recall being discussed at the June 6 meeting?*
>
> *A: Not at the moment. Oh, wait—we also talked about an employee stock option plan.*
>
> *You: OK, you discussed a new employee health plan, a marketing report, and an employee stock option plan at the June 6 meeting. Can you recall anything else?*
>
> *A: Nope, that's about it.*

While these preliminary open-ended questions do little to stimulate the deponent's recall, they leave the deponent's memory associations intact, with the result that the deponent may mention information you might not have thought to ask about.

Once the deponent's independent recall has seemingly been exhausted, however, if a topic is important, you'll want to change gears and use more targeted questioner-centered questions. Here are examples of specific questions you might ask in an effort to elicit a complete picture of all subjects that were discussed during the June 6 meeting:

> Q: *Was the purchase of new computers discussed during the June 6 meeting?*
>
> Q: *Was there any discussion of an employee discipline manual at the June 6 meeting?*
>
> Q: *Was there any discussion about how other companies handle employee discipline at the June 6 meeting?*

As you can see, the questioner-centered questions may help to stimulate a deponent's recall by suggesting specific topics to the deponent.

It's often a good idea to continue to move back and forth between deponent-centered and questioner-centered questions throughout a deposition. For example, assume that in response to the questioner-centered question, "Was there any discussion of an employee discipline manual at the June 6 meeting?" the deponent answers, "Yes, that was discussed." If this is an important topic that you want to explore further, you can begin to do so by reverting to deponent-centered questions:

> • *"Please tell me as much as you can about what was said at the June 6 meeting concerning an employee discipline manual."*
>
> • *"Is there anything else you can recall being said at the June 6 meeting concerning an employee discipline manual?"*

After the deponent's independent memory of the employee discipline manual discussion seems to be exhausted, you might then return to narrower questioner-centered questions:

> • *"Did you talk about the possibility of consulting the affected employees about employee discipline procedures during the June 6 meeting?"*
>
> • *"Did you talk about checking into the disciplinary procedures followed by other companies in the software design field during the June 6 meeting?"*

Of course, this process of exploring an event through a combination of deponent-centered and questioner-centered questions can continue until you are sure you've gotten all possible information from the deponent. For instance, assume that the deponent answers the last deponent-centered inquiry by testifying, "Yes, we did talk about checking into disciplinary procedures followed by other companies in the software design field during the June 6 meeting." You might then switch back to a deponent-centered form of question:

> • *"Please tell me what was said in the June 6 meeting about checking into the disciplinary procedures followed by other companies in the software design field."*

Beyond Questions: Other Things You Can Ask a Deponent to Do

You can ask a deponent to identify documents, draw a diagram (for example, of a collision scene or a work site—it doesn't have to be to scale), or make a sketch (for example, of a room's interior—it doesn't have to be exact). In addition, you can ask a deponent to perform a physical demonstration. For example, if a deponent testifies that you raised your hand in a threatening manner, you may ask the deponent to demonstrate how you held your hand. If the deposition is being transcribed, be sure to make a verbal record of a physical, nonverbal demonstration. To do so, verbally describe what the deponent did in response to your request for a demonstration. For example, after the deponent demonstrates how you held your hand, you might say something like, "For the record, the deponent has raised her right arm, and it's bent at the elbow so that the elbow is facing forward, her right arm is parallel to the ground, and her right hand is behind her head."

2. Developing a Chronology of Events

To facilitate your understanding of a deponent's testimony and stimulate a deponent's recall, it's usually best to have the deponent talk about events in the approximate order of their occurrence. Both deponent-centered and questioner-centered questions can help you do this; neither is better than the other for doing so.

For example, you'd probably like to start a chronology with the earliest case-related event known to the deponent. A deponent-centered question can seek out this information:

- *"What's the first thing you can remember about the chicken's attempt to cross the road?"*

- *"Please tell me how you first learned of your company's plans to purchase a new computer system."*

More specific, questioner-centered questions can also help keep a deponent on chronological track:

- *"After the chicken began to cross the road, but before the chicken reached the other side, did anything else happen?"*

- *"After the June 6 meeting, what was the date of the next meeting in which the plan to purchase a new computer system was discussed?"*

Where to Begin a Chronology

Identifying a chronology's best starting point is often difficult, even for experienced lawyers. Start too late, and you may overlook important information. Start too early, and you're wasting time and money uncovering useless information. The following examples may help you to decide where to begin a chronology in your case:

- If you claim that a used car dealer sold you a lemon and then refused to repair it or return your money, you might begin the car dealer's chronology at the time when the dealer acquired the car: "I'd like to begin by asking you for the date that you acquired the car that you sold me."

- If you've sued a dog owner whose dog bit you, you'd want to show that the owner was aware that the dog might be dangerous. Thus, you might start the owner's chronology by seeking information about earlier incidents: "When was the first incident in which someone complained that your dog had bitten or threatened them?"

- If your ex-landlord sues you for back rent after you've moved out because the landlord didn't respond to your complaints that other tenants were too noisy, you might develop a chronology of such complaints with a question such as, "What's the first complaint you can recall receiving from me or any other tenant that the building was too noisy?"

- If you've sued your former employer for firing you because of your age, and the employer claims that you were fired due to poor performance, your chronology of your ex-supervisor's testimony might begin with a question such as, "What's the first problem that you can remember that you claim led to my being fired?"

3. Eliciting Helpful Evidence

As mentioned in Section C3, above, a key part of preparing for a successful deposition is making a list of helpful information that you hope even a hostile deponent may be able to provide. If you're lucky, the deponent may mention an item on your list in the course of responding to an open-ended deponent-centered question. But much of the time you'll probably have to ask questions designed to seek out each bit of desired information—which often requires that you ask questioner-centered questions.

For example, assume that you are the plaintiff in a personal injury case. You're deposing your adversary John L. Way, a building contractor whose alleged negligent left turn caused his car to collide with your car. Naturally, at the deposition you suspect that Way will deny that his driving was careless in any way. However, according to the police report prepared by the investigating police officer, a witness observed Way talking on his cellular telephone just before starting to make the left turn. Your helpful evidence list includes the item, "Ask Way about what was discussed in the cell phone conversation just before the accident." If the conversation pertained to a troublesome matter, that might suggest a reason for Way's failure to concentrate on the road and for his careless driving. Your questioning in pursuit of this helpful evidence may go as follows:

You: *Mr. Way, shortly before the collision, did you receive a call on your cell phone?* [questioner-centered inquiry]

Way: *I did.*

You: *Could you please tell me what you talked about in that conversation?* [deponent-centered inquiry]

Way: *It was just my secretary, telling me about something that had taken place on a job site.*

You: *Please tell me as much as you can recall about what your secretary told you in this phone call.* [deponent-centered inquiry]

Way: *He said something about having missed an inspection on one of our remodeling jobs.*

You: *Anything else you can remember about that phone call?* [deponent-centered inquiry]

Way: *That's about it.*

You: *Did your secretary tell you why the inspection had been missed?* [questioner-centered inquiry]

Way: *Oh, yes. He said the supervisor had forgotten about the inspection so never went over to the job site.*

You: *Did your secretary say anything about when the inspection might take place?* [questioner-centered inquiry]

Way: *I think so.*

You: *What did your secretary say about when the inspection might take place?* [deponent-centered inquiry]

Way: *He just said I'd have to call to reschedule the inspection.*

You: *I'd now like to ask you some questions about the consequences of missed inspections. First of all, you might incur additional expenses because of a missed inspection, right?* [questioner-centered, leading inquiry; permissible with a hostile witness]

Here, you combine the two basic forms of questions in an effort to find out as much as you can about an important topic, the cell phone call right before the collision. The more information you can elicit about what Way was told about the missed inspection and its effect on his business, the stronger your argument that the phone call distracted Way.

 Encourage a hostile deponent to "build up" any lies.

A hostile deponent may refuse to testify to what you know is the truth. In the situation above, for instance, Way might lie and say that he never got any call on his cell phone before the accident.

When you know that a deponent is lying about a significant matter, you may want to have the deponent "build up" the lie at deposition. To build up a lie, simply have a deponent repeat untrue testimony.

For example, assume that at deposition Way says, "I didn't get any call on my cell phone before the accident," and you know that Way's testimony is false. You could build up Way's lie by asking him additional questions about not receiving a phone call, such as the following: "You specifically remember that you didn't get a call on your cell phone just prior to the accident, correct?" and "You're sure that you were not distracted by a call on your cell phone prior to the accident?"

These build-up questions make it very hard for Way to later get out of the lie by saying that he misunderstood your question at the deposition, or that he had a momentary lapse of memory. Of course, at trial you'd have to prove that Way was lying, perhaps by subpoenaing Way's cell phone bills or eliciting the information from the bystander or Way's secretary, who made the call.

4. Evaluating the Deponent's Credibility

Any information that casts doubt on the deponent's credibility can improve your settlement position and undermine the weight of the deponent's testimony before a judge or jury. Both forms of questions can help you evaluate a hostile deponent's credibility.

a. Demeanor and Manner of Answering

As you know, one aspect of credibility concerns a deponent's nonverbal demeanor and style of answering questions. Most judges and jurors regard a witness who is poised and confident when answering questions as credible, while a witness who seems nervous or who gives inappropriate answers lacks credibility. Thus, you can "test" a deponent's demeanor by observing any problems in how the deponent responds to questioner-centered as opposed to deponent-centered questions. For example, the deponent may seem hesitant and nervous, especially when called upon by deponent-centered questions to describe events in the deponent's own words. If so, you may decide that the witness's testimony will have diminished impact at trial.

In response to open-ended, deponent-centered questions, a deponent may give what comes across as lengthy "canned" (memorized) responses. A judge or jury is not likely to find that kind of testimony convincing—something you can point out as part of settlement negotiations before trial.

Example

You: What happened after you arrived at the scene of Humpty Dumpty's fall?

A: It was a mess. I'd say definitely it was a great fall, maybe the biggest fall since the Roman Empire. There were king's horses and king's men everywhere. I couldn't count them, but I'd say there were at least 20. When I first got there …

An answer such as this often comes across as a script that a witness has memorized, enabling you to argue that it lacks credibility.

Or, a deponent may also give only very short, conclusory answers in response to open, deponent-centered questions. This might suggest that the deponent lacks actual independent recall and that the deponent can only repeat specific bits of information fed to the deponent by your adversary.

Example

> You: *What happened after you arrived at the scene of Humpty Dumpty's fall?*
>
> A: *There was chaos.*
>
> You: *Can you describe the scene in more detail?*
>
> A: *Well, it was just a mess of men and horses.*
>
> You: *Anything else you can recall?*
>
> A: *What I've told you.*

Answers such as these in response to open-ended questions are so brief and conclusory that a judge or jury may doubt that the witness really recalls what happened.

On the other hand, in response to narrow, questioner-centered inquiries, a deponent may evince little knowledge of concrete details.

Example

> You: *What time did you arrive at the scene of Humpty Dumpty's fall?*
>
> A: *Sometime in the afternoon, around 2:00 or 3:00, I'm not really sure.*

> You: *How many king's horses did you see?*
>
> A: *I don't remember. Quite a few.*
>
> You: *How about king's men—how many of them did you see?*
>
> A: *It's hard to say. There was a lot going on.*

This witness's ability to recall concrete details is so poor that a judge or jury may give little weight to whatever information the deponent does remember.

Of course, a deponent's demeanor may improve dramatically from the deposition to the courtroom. This may be due to your opponent's "woodshedding" (meeting with and thoroughly rehearsing) a deponent before trial. But even so, you might be able to undermine a deponent's credibility at trial by reading into the record the not-so-credible deposition testimony.

Example

At trial, the deponent in the last example, above, testifies that "I saw 20 of the king's horses at the scene of Humpty Dumpty's fall." When cross-examining this witness, you could read into the trial record the following portion of the same witness's deposition:

> Q: *How many king's horses did you see?*
>
> A: *I don't remember. Quite a few.*

b. Motive of Ability to Perceive

A witness's credibility is often also affected by evidence bearing on a witness's motive or ability to testify. As you would expect, both basic forms of questions can be useful when you try to uncover evidence that will negatively affect a hostile deponent's credibility negatively.

Among the factors that commonly bear on a witness's credibility are the following:

- **Ability to perceive or observe.** For example, you may try to elicit evidence showing that it was too dark or a deponent was too far away to have seen or heard what the deponent claims to have seen or heard.

- **Motive to lie.** For example, evidence showing that a used car salesperson was under pressure to increase sales would support your claim that the salesperson lied about a car's condition in order to induce you to buy it.

- **Bias.** For example, evidence showing that the deponent stands to gain financially if your adversary wins the case would support your argument that the deponent is lying or misremembering what happened.

- **Contradiction.** For example, evidence that the deponent's testimony conflicts with what the deponent wrote in an earlier report would undermine the witness's credibility.

Example

You're involved in a personal injury case and are deposing a nonparty witness, a motorist who claims that you were weaving in and out of lanes of a busy highway just prior to the accident. One credibility issue you want to explore is the deponent's ability to have observed your driving. You may do so through:

- *A deponent-centered question: "Please describe how you were able to observe my car over a distance of a mile."*

- *A questioner-centered inquiry: "Did you observe any other late-model black Lexus sedans on the one-mile portion of highway preceding the accident?"*

Similarly, you may want to find out whether the motorist has become friendly with your adversary to such an extent that a judge or jury might believe that the motorist is biased. Again, you might ask:

- *A deponent-centered question: "Please describe your current relationship to the plaintiff."*

- *A questioner-centered inquiry: "How many times have you talked to the plaintiff during the last six months?"*

Common Helpful Questions

Most of your deposition questions will depend on the facts of your specific case. Here are some questions you can ask a deponent that are likely to be effective in every case:

"Why did you do (or say) that?" When the deponent testifies to doing or saying something, ask "why."

Example

Q: What happened next?

A: I went to the doctor.

Q: **Why did you go to the doctor?**

The answers to "why" questions can help you evaluate whether a deponent's story makes sense. You can also ask "why" questions about what other people did or said.

Example

Q: What did Joe do next?

A: Joe went to the doctor.

Q: **Why did Joe go to the doctor?**

At trial, evidence rules usually forbid questions about why other people behaved as they did, because they ask witnesses to speculate. You can ask such questions at a deposition, however.

"Have you told me everything you know?" or **"Is there anything else you can recall?"** As indicated earlier, an important deposition goal is to find out as much as you can about what an adverse witness will say if a case goes to trial. A good way to prevent witnesses from adding new information at trial is to use a "wrap-up" question that gives them every chance to mention the information at deposition.

Example

Q: Which employees did you talk about promoting in the meeting on the 23rd?

A: We discussed Ipsy Dixit and Sue Society.

Q: **Can you remember discussing any other employee at the meeting on the 23rd?**

A: No, just those two.

The purpose of the wrap-up question is to prevent the witness from testifying at trial to other employees whose promotion was discussed at the meeting on the 23rd. In the absence of the wrap-up question, you can't do much if the witness mentions additional employees in response to this question at trial. When you ask the witness, "Why didn't you mention that person's name at the deposition?" the witness might respond, "Because you didn't ask me."

"Can you give me any examples?"
Deponents often testify to generalities. To really find out what they might say if a case goes to trial, you need to probe those generalities.

Example

Q: Had you seen Johnson driving on other occasions?

A: Yes, Johnson always drove like a maniac?

Q: **Can you describe specific instances in which Johnson drove like a maniac?**

Asking for examples can be especially useful when deponents refer to conditions that extended over a lengthy period of time.

Common Helpful Questions (continued)

Example

Q: How did the accident affect you?

A: For one thing, I could hardly do anything because I had terrible back pain for months.

Q: **Can you give me any examples of when your back pain prevented you from doing something?**

"What do you mean by that?" Especially when they testify to opinions, people are prone to talk in terms of broad characterizations instead of describing specific behavior. Again, to really find out what a deponent is likely to say if a case goes to trial you should puncture those broad characterizations and ask for details.

Example

Q: How was Johnson driving just before the accident?

A: Johnson was driving like a maniac.

Q: **When you say that Johnson was driving like a maniac, what do you mean?**

"What have you heard about that?" At trial, the hearsay rule often prevents witnesses from testifying about what other people have told them. At deposition, however, you can ask deponents to testify to statements that other people have made to them. The answers can help you anticipate the testimony that your opponent will offer at trial. Moreover, you may develop leads to other people who can provide helpful information.

Example

Q: What took place during the meeting on the 23rd?

A: Sorry, I can't tell you. I wasn't present at that meeting.

Q: Were you ever told what happened during that meeting?

A: I did hear some things, yes.

Q: **What have you heard about what took place at the meeting?**

G. Using Documents

The path to litigation is typically strewn with documents such as contracts, reports, receipts, estimates, proposals, memoranda, and the like. As a result, during a deposition you'll undoubtedly question the deponent about one or more documents. This section offers suggestions on effective document-related questioning.

1. The Purposes of Document-Related Questioning

There are a variety of reasons to question a deponent about documents. One is simply that documents are part and parcel of the chronology of events. For example, perhaps the deponent attended a meeting that's important to your lawsuit, then wrote a memorandum summarizing the meeting. If so, you'll probably want to question the deponent about the document.

A second reason to question deponents about documents is that documents often carry great weight with judges and jurors. Unlike memories, the contents of documents remain constant over time. If you can show that some portion of a document supports your claim, you've probably boosted the strength of your case.

A third reason for document-related inquiries is to prove that the document is authentic. If you want to offer a document into evidence at trial, you need to show that it's genuine, or as attorneys say, to "authenticate" the document. (For a common type of "authentication" rule, see Federal Rule of Evidence 901.) Often, you can elicit the evidence you need to prove the document is genuine by showing it to the deponent and asking the deponent what it is, how and why it was prepared, and who prepared it.

Finally, showing documents to a deponent can help you elicit more case-related information. Many deponents can recall past events in greater detail when they can refresh their memories with documents pertaining to those events. For instance, a deponent may be better able to recall what was discussed at a particular meeting after reading an agenda that was prepared for the meeting.

2. Documents Brought to the Deposition by the Deponent

Following your preliminary questioning (see Section D, above), you might next ask the deponent to give you any documents the deponent brought to the deposition in response to your request in the Notice of Deposition, Request for Production of Documents, or Subpoena Duces Tecum. Keep these documents separate from any documents that you brought with you. You might want to tell the court reporter that you want to "go off the record" while you look through the documents. That allows the court reporter to relax and gives you time to review the documents and get a sense of their contents.

After you've had a chance to look over the documents the deponent has produced, you may want to question the deponent about:

- how the deponent went about collecting the documents produced at the deposition, and

- whether any documents you requested have been withheld, perhaps based on a claim of privilege.

For example, assume that you have filed a wrongful termination complaint against your former employer, Ad Agency, Inc. You are deposing your former supervisor, Sue Pervisor, who was directly involved in the decision to terminate your employment. Your Notice of Deposition asked Pervisor to bring the following documents to the deposition:

- your personnel file
- all documents related to your work on the Campbell account, and
- all documents that support or tend to support the company's claim that you did not perform satisfactorily on your job.

After reviewing the documents produced by Pervisor, your questioning might proceed as follows:

You: *I am showing you what's been marked for identification as Exhibit #1, a Notice of Deposition dated February 2. Do you see on Exhibit #1 where it asks you to produce my personnel file at this deposition?*

A: *Yes.*

You: *Did you obtain my personnel file in response to this request?*

A: *Yes.*

You: *Did you remove anything from my personnel file before bringing it to this deposition?*

A: *No.*

You: *When you looked at the file, did you do anything to make sure it was complete?*

A: *No, I just picked it up from personnel and I assumed it was complete and up to date.*

You: *Were any documents removed from the file before it was brought to this deposition today?*

A: *Not as far as I know.*

You: *Exhibit #1 also asks you to produce all the documents related to my work on the Campbell account. Did you do anything to collect documents that related to my work on the Campbell account?*

A: *Yes. I went through all of my files on the account and pulled out the documents that related to the work you performed on the account.*

You: *Did you also pull out any letters that the client sent to you about whether he was satisfied with Ad Agency's work on the account?*

A: *No, I didn't. I didn't think those letters related to your work on the account.*

You: *How did you go about determining which documents in your file responded to the request for all documents related to my work on the Campbell account?*

A: *Well, I just thought you wanted ...*

These questions will help you determine if the deponent has produced all the documents you requested. If the deponent has withheld documents or just neglected to include some documents that you think should have been turned over, you may be able to work out an arrangement with the defending counsel to have the missing documents produced at a second day of the deponent's deposition. If the deponent refuses to produce documents that you requested and to which you think you're entitled, you may have to file a written motion in court to obtain the withheld documents.

Putting a Refusal to Produce Documents on the Record

If the deponent fails to produce a requested document, put the deponent's refusal on the record in case you want to challenge the refusal in court later.

Example:

You're suing a car dealership whose salesperson allegedly misrepresented the condition of the car that you purchased. When arranging for the salesperson's deposition, you asked the salesperson to bring to the deposition any document the salesperson had been given within the three months preceding your purchase of the car indicating how many cars the dealership expected the salesperson to sell. At the deposition, the following dialogue takes place:

You: In the three months prior to my buying the car, did the dealership give you any document indicating how many cars the dealership expected you to sell?

A: It did.

You: Have you brought any such documents with you, as requested in the Notice of Deposition, Exhibit #1?

A: I have not.

You: How many such documents did you receive?

A: Two that I can remember.

You: And you haven't produced either of them?

A: That's right.

You: For the record, why have you failed to produce them?

A: I just feel they are private. They relate to my employment and have nothing to do with this case.

You: I am not trying to invade your privacy. But I think I am entitled to those documents. I'm not required to explain why I think I'm entitled to the documents, but in an effort to resolve the problem quickly, let me just say that I think they may show whether you were under pressure to sell cars at the time I bought a car. Will you produce those documents voluntarily?

A: No, I won't.

You: Very well. I'll continue with the deposition, but just so you know, I reserve the right to seek a court order requiring you to produce those documents, and if I get such an order, I'll ask the judge to order you to pay my court costs and my attorney's fees. Is that understood?

A: Yes.

You: And you still stick by your refusal?

A: Yes.

This testimony sufficiently documents the deponent's refusal to provide the records you seek. For further discussion of what to do when a deponent refuses to provide information, see Chapter 12.

3. Procedures for "Marking" Exhibits

To keep the record straight, comply with the following procedures whenever you question the deponent about any document. To illustrate these procedures, assume that you want to ask a deponent about the contents of a document entitled, "Minutes of June 6 meeting."

- First, identify the document on the record and ask the court reporter to "mark" it as an "exhibit for identification." Here, for example, you might say something like, "I have here a document entitled 'Minutes of June 6 meeting.' [To court reporter:] Could you please mark this document as Exhibit #3 for identification?"

- Then, referring to the document by its exhibit number, show the document to the deponent and ask the deponent to identify it if possible: "[Say the deponent's name], I'm handing you what has been marked Plaintiff's Exhibit #3 for identification. Can you tell me what Exhibit #3 is?" In this situation, the deponent might respond: "Yes, these are the minutes I prepared after the June 6 meeting."

- After the deponent identifies the document, refer to it during questioning by its exhibit number. For example, here you might ask the deponent to "Please look over Plaintiff's Exhibit #3 and then tell me as much as you can remember about what was discussed

during the June 6 meeting." (To avoid wasting time by going off the record while the deponent and then the defending lawyer take turns reading a document, bring along multiple copies so they can read through a document simultaneously.)

The deponent may be unable to identify an exhibit. In this example, perhaps the Minutes of June 6 Meeting were prepared by someone not known to the deponent. If so, the deponent will probably respond by saying something like, "No, I've never seen this document before." The document can still be marked as an exhibit and used later to refresh the deponent's memory during questioning. For example, assume that the deponent testifies that "I can't remember anything else that was discussed at the June 6 meeting." Whether or not the deponent wrote the minutes or knows who did, you can still ask the deponent to "Please take a look at Plaintiff's Exhibit #3 for identification and see if it refreshes your recollection as to what was discussed at the June 6 meeting."

4. Copying Original Documents

At the end of the deposition, the court reporter will collect the documents that have been marked as exhibits and attach those documents to the deposition transcript. To avoid turning over original documents to the court reporter, make copies of all the documents you will use before the deposition and have the reporter use the copies as attachments.

5. Documents and the Two Basic Forms of Questions

As with any other topic, you may use both deponent-centered and questioner-centered inquiries when asking about documents.

Examples

- *"I notice that Exhibit #3 refers to a report on employee disciplinary procedures prepared last year. Can you tell me what occurred during the discussion of this report?"* [deponent-centered question]

- *"I notice that Exhibit #3 refers to a report on employee disciplinary procedures prepared last year. Do you recall the approximate date of that report?"* [Questioner-centered inquiry]

H. Responding to an Evasive Witness

Hostile deponents often give evasive answers to try to minimize or withhold information that helps your case. This section discusses how to respond to the most common forms of evasive answers.

1. The "I Don't Remember" Answer

The most common refuge of the evasive witness is an "I don't remember" type of response. Evasive deponents will sometimes respond to your questions with answers such as:

- "I don't really recall much else."

- "I have no clear recollection of anything else."

- "I can't remember everything we talked about."

Of course, sometimes a deponent gives this sort of answer due to a legitimate inability to remember. Other times, however, the deponent uses such an answer to avoid disclosing damaging information while convincing him- or herself that it's not really lying because his or her memory is less than crystal clear. When you think that a deponent is using some version of an "I don't remember" response to be evasive you might ask for:

- **Documents.** Ask the deponent whether he or she is aware of any document that might help to refresh his or her memory. If so and if you have the document available, you can show the document to the deponent and perhaps obtain more information. If the document is not available and the testimony is critical, you can temporarily suspend the deposition until you obtain the document. (If the deponent won't produce it voluntarily, you may have to compel its production with a Request to Produce Documents or a Subpoena Duces Tecum.) Make sure that you complete all your other questioning before suspending a deposition for this purpose.

- **Everything the deponent can remember.** When a deponent says something like "I can't remember everything that happened" or "I don't remember exactly what he said at the meeting," ask the deponent to testify to everything that he or she can remember. For example, you might ask questions such as: "Even if you can't remember everything that happened, please tell me everything that you can remember" or " Please tell me everything that you do recall he said at the meeting."

- **Estimates.** When a deponent cannot remember a specific date or number, ask for a best estimate. For example, if a deponent cannot remember how often he or she went to the doctor for treatment of an injury, ask for his or her best estimate of the number of times he or she went for treatment.

You can also ask the deponent questions designed to narrow things down. Using the example above, you might ask the deponent if he or she went for treatment more than once, more than ten times, or more than 20 times. Or, if a deponent doesn't remember the date a particular event took place, you might ask if he or she remembers the week, month, or season when the meeting occurred.

2. The Nonresponsive Answer

Some deponents withhold information by appearing to answer a question without really doing so. When you're mid-deposition, such nonresponsive answers may seem to provide most of what you want. But when you want to use the information later, you will realize that the answer did not really respond to your question directly. Consider these examples:

You   *Did you see the light turn red?*

A: *I may have.*

You: *Did the bear go over the mountain?*

A: *Where else could it have gone?*

In the heat of the deposition, both responses may appear to provide your desired answer. Neither, however, constitutes a directly responsive answer. As a result, the impact of the information may be diminished if you seek to rely on it during a settlement discussion or at trial.

When a deponent gives a nonresponsive answer, politely point out the answer's inadequacy and ask your question again. With a particularly recalcitrant deponent, you may have to pursue the question more than once.

Example 1

You: *Did you see the light turn red?*

A: *I may have.*

You: *Excuse me, I'd like this clear for the record. Did you see the light turn red?*

A: *I suppose I did.*

You: *So your answer is yes, you did see the light turn red?*

A: *Yes.*

Example 2

You: *Did you see the bear go over the mountain?*

A: *Where else could it have gone?*

You: *Please, I need you to answer the question. Did you see the bear go over the mountain?*

A: *Yes, I did.*

I. Depositions Arranged by Your Opponent

This chapter has described the most common situation in which you're likely to depose a hostile witness: when you arrange for the deposition and question the deponent. Following your questioning, your adversary also has a right to question the deponent.

Sometimes, however, your adversary will set up the deposition of a witness who is hostile to you. Generally, this situation arises when your adversary is taking a deposition to "perpetuate" (preserve) testimony to the time of trial in case the witness should die, become seriously ill, or move a long distance away. (Perpetuation of testimony is covered in Chapter 2.) In such a situation, your opponent will examine the deponent first, then you'll have a chance to ask questions of your own.

Be sure to take advantage of the opportunity to ask questions—you probably won't get another chance to depose the hostile witness. If your opponent uses deposition testimony later in a pretrial motion or offers the deposition transcript into evidence at trial, you'll want to make sure that it includes any information the deponent knows that's helpful to your case. For example, you might want to:

- Ask about case-related topics that you think the deponent knows about but which the adversary avoided. Perhaps the adversary was trying to hide damaging evidence!

- Ask about any information you wrote down on your list of helpful evidence. (See Section C, above.) Whether your opponent or you arrange for a deposition, you'll want to make a list of helpful evidence that the deponent could speak to and then try to elicit that evidence through your questions.

- Using the common credibility factors mentioned above (see Section F). Try to undercut the impact of adverse evidence by asking questions to elicit evidence that undermines the deponent's credibility. ■

Chapter 12

Taking a Deposition: Responding to a Defending Attorney's Roadblocks

When you take a deposition, the opposing attorney will probably show up and defend it—and might use some lawyerly tricks to try to derail you. This chapter examines common roadblocks that the attorney might throw up to interfere with your ability to elicit testimony and explains how you might respond. Such roadblocks include:

- objections to your questions
- instructions to the deponent not to answer your questions, and
- attempts to coach the deponent.

A. Responding to Objections

Chapter 10 explains how the objection process works when you're defending a deposition. This section looks at the objection process from the other side. It explains how you might respond when the defending attorney objects to your questions.

1. What Should I Do When the Defending Attorney Objects to a Question?

The most important thing you can do when the defending attorney objects to a question is to ask the deponent to answer it. Unless the defending attorney instructs the deponent not to answer (a situation discussed in Section B, below), you are entitled to an answer to an objected-to question, whether or not the objection is valid. (See FRCP 30(c), which sets forth the general rule that testimony at deposition is taken subject to objections.)

The easiest way to obtain an answer is simply to repeat an objected-to question.

Example

You: Why did the chicken cross the road?

Defending attorney: Objection, calls for speculation.

You (to the deponent): Please answer the question. Why did the chicken cross the road?

Defending attorney: I've objected to that question as calling for speculation.

You: Please answer the question. Why did the chicken cross the road?

Deponent: Well, it seemed to me that the chicken wanted to get to the other side.

You: And what happened when the chicken got to the other side?

Deponent: Well …

In this example, the defending attorney makes what is almost certainly a proper objection (unless the deponent speaks chicken, the question does ask the deponent to speculate). Just as properly, you ignore the objection and politely but firmly insist on an answer. When the attorney repeats the objection (perhaps in an effort to intimidate you into withdrawing or changing your question), you continue to insist on an answer. Such persistence may be necessary if you are to probe for information thoroughly.

An alternative method of obtaining an answer following an objection is to ask the court reporter to read back the objected-to question. After the court reporter reads back the question, ask the deponent to answer it. That process goes something like this:

> You: *Why did the chicken cross the road?*
>
> Defending lawyer: *Objection, calls for speculation.*
>
> You: *Ms. Reporter, would you please read back my last question?*
>
> Reporter: *Question. Why did the chicken cross the road?*
>
> You (to the deponent): *Please answer the question.*
>
> Deponent: *Well, it seemed to me that the chicken wanted to get to the other side.*

Especially when the deposing party is self-represented, a defending attorney may raise more objections than normal to try to intimidate, distract, or fluster you. Your best response to this ploy is to simply insist on answers to your questions and refuse to argue with opposing counsel about whether an objection is valid.

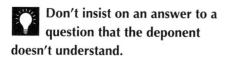 **Don't insist on an answer to a question that the deponent doesn't understand.**

The advice that you should insist on answers to objected-to questions is subject to one practical exception: Don't try to insist that a deponent answer a question that he or she does not understand. For example, assume that you ask a deponent, "Before that meeting, what was going on between you and Mr. Pell?" The defending lawyer may well object that this question is vague, and the deponent may understandably say something like, "I don't understand your question." In this instance, you should ask a more focused question. For example, you might rephrase the question above as follows: "Before that meeting, had you and Mr. Pell had any disagreements about whether to purchase the computers?"

2. Should I Respond to an Objection Once I Get an Answer?

If the objection is proper and you hope to use the deponent's answer later in the case (to support your position in a pretrial motion or at trial), you must "cure" (overcome) the objection by rephrasing your question. Under FRCP 32(a), you won't be able to use deposition testimony later in the case if your adversary properly objected at deposition to the question that produced the answer. (See Chapter 10 for more on deposition objections.)

Despite this barrier to the future use of objectionable testimony, your best bet is usually to ignore an objection altogether, insist on an answer to your question, and move on to your next question for all of the following reasons:

• If deposition testimony doesn't support your legal claims, you probably won't want to use it later in the case anyway. When you're deposing a hostile witness, most of the evidence you elicit will probably support your adversary's claims rather than yours.

- Overcoming evidentiary problems raised by objections often requires thorough knowledge of evidence rules, which you as a self-represented party are unlikely to possess. Indeed, experienced practicing lawyers often don't know how to overcome many deposition objections.

- Many evidentiary problems raised at deposition simply cannot be overcome, no matter how well you understand the rules of evidence.

- Overcoming evidentiary problems is important primarily when you want to use deposition testimony at trial. Since most cases settle prior to trial, your ability or inability to overcome objections at depositions is unlikely to affect the amount you receive or pay in settlement significantly.

- If the deponent testifies in person at trial (should the case get that far), you probably won't refer to the deposition testimony anyway. Consequently, the fact that there are uncured objections in the deposition transcript won't matter.

- It's usually to your advantage to concentrate on the deponent's testimony and what to ask next in light of what the deponent has already said. If you concentrate on trying to overcome objections, your attention will be diverted from the deponent's testimony. In fact, the defending lawyer may object at a deposition largely in the hope that objec-

tions will divert your attention away from the testimony. The lawyer may try to confuse or distract you by making you try to solve complex or frivolous evidence problems. By trying to cure objections, you encourage a lawyer following this strategy to make even more objections.

For all of these reasons, your best response is usually to ignore the defending lawyer's objections, insist on answers to objected-to questions, and continue your questioning.

3. If I Want to Overcome an Objection, How Can I Do So?

Despite the many reasons to ignore objections outlined in Section A2, above, you may decide that it makes sense to try to overcome an objection if:

- the answer you get to an objected-to question strongly supports your legal claims

- you believe that the defending attorney's objection is proper, and

- you believe that you know how to overcome the objection.

The subsections below identify common objections that the defending attorney may make and illustrate methods of curing them.

a. Objection: Compound Question

Compound questions are essentially two questions phrased as one.

Example

"Who was at the party and which of them had you met previously?"

If the defending attorney properly objects that a question is compound, you should find it easy to cure the problem by breaking the compound question into its constituent parts. The process may look like this:

You: Who was at the party and which of them had you met previously?

Defending attorney: Objection: Compound question.

You: Please answer the question.

A: I remember that Kevin, Debbie, and Hilary were at the party. I'd never met any of them before.

Assuming that this testimony supports your legal claims, you may cure the problem by breaking the compound question into two parts.

You: Please tell me again, who was at the party?

A: Kevin, Debbie, and Hilary.

You: And had you met any of them previously?

A: No.

b. Objection: Assumes Facts Not in Evidence

A question assumes facts not in evidence when it refers to facts to which a deponent has not previously testified (even if you "know" that the fact is accurate).

Example

You ask, "When you and Mr. Pell met before the termination meeting, what did you talk about?" But the deponent has not testified to meeting with Pell before the termination meeting.

Following an answer that you may want to use later, you might cure this objection by asking a separate question that results in the witness testifying to the fact you had assumed. The dialogue might go as follows:

You: When you and Mr. Pell met before the termination meeting, what did you talk about?

Defending attorney: Objection: Assumes facts not in evidence.

You: Please answer the question.

A: Pell just talked about a couple of times that you had been late to work.

If this answer helps your case, you might cure the problem by asking whether the assumed fact is true.

You: Did you and Mr. Pell meet before the termination meeting?

A: Yes.

You: And when you and Mr. Pell met before the termination meeting, what did you talk about?

A: Pell just talked about a couple of times that you had been late to work.

c. Objection: Vague

A question is vague when it does not make clear what information you are seeking.

Example

You ask, "Before that meeting, what was going on between you and Mr. Pell?"

The defending lawyer may well object that this question is vague, as it doesn't give the lawyer or the deponent an adequate indication as to the topic or time period you want the deponent to address. The deponent then may respond by saying something like, "I don't understand the question." If so, don't try to force the deponent to answer the question; rephrase your question to make it clearer.

However, if the deponent does answer the question and the answer is helpful, you can cure the problem with additional narrower questions specifically seeking the helpful evidence. The process might go like this:

You: Before that meeting, what was going on between you and Mr. Pell?

Defending attorney: Objection: Vague.

You: Can you answer the question?

A: Well, I'm not sure if this is what you you're asking about, but a couple of days before the meeting, Pell had gotten angry with me when we talked about purchasing new computers.

If this information is helpful, you might cure the vagueness problem with additional questions focused on the helpful information.

You: Did you and Mr. Pell talk about purchasing new computers before the meeting took place?

A: Yes, we did.

Q: And what was Mr. Pell's reaction to purchasing computers?

A: He got angry with me.

d. Objection: Calls for a Narrative Answer

A question "calls for a narrative" when it asks a deponent to describe a lengthy series of events, or when it is too broad in scope for the defending lawyer to anticipate what the deponent will say. The risk for the defending lawyer is that the deponent will refer to improper evidence before the lawyer can object to it.

Example

You ask, "Please tell me what happened at the meetings that were held to discuss the purchase of the new computer system."

The defending lawyer may object that the question calls for a narrative answer, because it asks the deponent to describe an entire series of events. If the answer reveals helpful information for your case, you could cure the problem by breaking up the single broad question into smaller chunks. The process may go as follows:

You: Please tell me what happened at the meetings that were held to discuss the purchase of the new computer system.

Defending attorney: Objection: Calls for a narrative answer.

You: Please answer the question.

A: Well, almost all the discussions concerned whether to go with a whole new system immediately, or stay with the current system for another 12 to 18 months, at which time new technology was supposed to be available.

If this information is helpful, you might cure the problem by exploring the topic with narrower questions.

You: Please tell me what happened at the first meeting at which the timing of the purchase of a new computer system was discussed.

e. Objection: Argumentative

A question is argumentative when you ask a deponent to respond to an argument you make—rather than just a question—that supports your legal claims.

Examples

• *"Doesn't the fact that you can't remember who was present at the meeting of July 24 show that you never were at that meeting?"*

• *"Ms. Green's report, which does not list you as attending the meeting, was written right after the meeting. Why shouldn't a judge believe Ms. Green's report rather than your testimony?"*

If the defending attorney makes an "argumentative" objection, and the deponent doesn't explain the inconsistency that underlies your argument, you can cure the problem by asking for an explanation in a nonargumentative way. The process may look like this:

You: Doesn't the fact that you can't remember who was present at the meeting of July 24 show that you never were at that meeting?

Defending attorney: Objection: Argumentative.

You: Please answer the question.

A: All I can do is repeat what I've already said—that I was at that meeting.

If it's helpful to your case to show that the deponent can't explain the inability to recall who was at the meeting, elicit the inability to explain with a nonargumentative question.

You: Can you explain to me why you are unable to recall who else was at the meeting?

A: No, I just can't remember who was present.

f. Objection: Leading

A "leading" question is one that suggests the answer you want the deponent to give. You can properly ask leading questions of deponents whom the law regards as hostile, such as your adversary or an employee or colleague of your adversary. (See Federal Rule of Evidence 611(c).) If the defending attorney objects to your question as leading when evidence rules clearly permit you to ask this type of question, you can ignore it; an improper objection to leading will not prevent you from using the answer later in the case. However, you cannot ordinarily ask leading questions of friendly witnesses or neutral nonparty deponents.

Example

You ask a neutral nonparty deponent who was at the scene of an auto accident in which you were involved, "You saw the green car run the stop sign, didn't you?"

If the defending lawyer objects that a question is leading, you can cure the problem by asking another question designed to produce the same answer that is not leading. The process would go like this:

You: You saw the green car run the stop sign, didn't you?

Defending attorney: Objection: Leading.

You: Please answer the question.

A: Yes, I did.

If this answer is helpful, you can cure the problem by eliciting the same information with a different question that does not lead the deponent.

You: What did you see the green car do?

A: I saw the green car run the stop sign.

The Federal Rules of Evidence (FRE)

The Federal Rules of Evidence (commonly referred to as the "FRE") are the rules that determine whether evidence will be admitted in federal court trials. But just as is true for the FRCP, most states pattern their evidence rules on the FRE. Thus, even if your case is in state court, the court will probably follow evidentiary rules that are very similar to the FRE. An in-depth analysis of evidence rules is beyond the scope of this book. (For more information, refer to the references listed on pages 10/9 and 10/10.)

---

g. Objection: Misquotes or Mischaracterizes the Testimony

The opposing attorney might object if he or she believes that your question misstates earlier testimony by the deponent.

Example

Earlier in the deposition, the deponent testified that you shouted at him during a performance review. You ask the deponent, "Do you recall what I said when I raised my voice during the performance review?" Your question mischaracterizes the deponent's testimony by substituting the phrase "raised my voice" for the testimony "shouted."

If the defending attorney objects and you want to cure the problem because the answer is helpful, you can ask the question again and either (1) use the exact language of the prior testimony or (2) delete all reference to the prior testimony. The process may go as follows:

You: *Do you recall what I said when I raised my voice during the performance review?*

Defending attorney: *Objection: The question misstates the testimony.*

You: *You may answer the question.*

A: *You said that you thought the process was unfair because you'd never been told about any of the problems.*

Assuming that this answer is helpful, you can cure the problem by asking the same question without mischaracterizing the earlier testimony. In the question below, you do so by removing any reference to the earlier testimony.

You: *What did I say during the performance review?*

A: *You said that you thought the process was unfair because you'd never been told about any of the problems.*

h. Objection: Lack of Personal Knowledge (or Lack of Foundation)

The opposing attorney is likely to make this objection when your prior questioning has not established that a deponent has firsthand information about the events to which you've asked the deponent to testify. (See Federal Rule of Evidence 602, which requires that for testimony to be admissible at trial, ordinary [nonexpert] witnesses must testify based on personal knowledge—meaning what they have personally seen, heard, smelled, or touched.)

Example

You ask, "What did Ms. Julian do after she left the meeting?" However, previous questioning has not established that the deponent was in a position to know what Ms. Julian did after the meeting.

If the defending attorney objects and you want to cure the problem because the answer is helpful, you will have to use additional questions to demonstrate that the deponent does have firsthand knowledge of the event to which the testimony relates. Your questioning may proceed as follows:

You: *What did Ms. Julian do after she left the meeting?*

Defending attorney: *Objection: Lack of personal knowledge.*

You: *You may answer the question.*

A: *She went right in to talk to Mr. Wilson.*

If you want to use this answer, you can cure the problem with additional questions demonstrating that the deponent has personal knowledge of where Ms. Julian went after the meeting.

Q: How do you know that Ms. Julian went right in to talk to Mr. Wilson?

A: Because I stayed behind for a moment, but then I caught up and went into his office with her.

i.   Objection: Calls for Speculation

A "speculation" objection raises a similar issue as an objection based on lack of personal knowledge: Both claim that a deponent lacks firsthand information. The defending attorney may object that a question "calls for speculation" when your question asks a deponent to testify about what someone else was thinking or why another person acted in a certain way.

Examples

- "Why did the chicken cross the road?"
- "Why did Mr. Pell decide to fire me?"
- "Why was Mona Lisa smiling?"

If the defending attorney objects and you want to cure the problem because the answer is helpful, you can ask the deponent to repeat the testimony in response to a question that does not ask the deponent to speculate. This exchange might go as follows:

You: Why did Mr. Pell decide to fire me?

Defending attorney: Objection: The question calls for speculation.

You: You may answer the question.

A: I remember that he said something about you being too old for the job.

If this is helpful testimony, you may cure the problem by rephrasing the question as follows:.

You: What did Mr. Pell say was the reason that I was being fired?

A: I remember that he said something about you being too old for the job.

j.   Objection: Improper Opinion

An "improper opinion" objection may occur when you haven't shown that a deponent has sufficient personal knowledge or expertise to support an opinion you've asked the deponent to give.

Example

You ask, "In your opinion, was the driver of the car that hit me under the influence of alcohol?" However, it's not clear from the record that the deponent observed the driver before, during, or after the accident.

If the defending attorney objects that you're asking for an improper opinion and you want to cure the problem because the answer is helpful, you'll need to ask additional questions to bring out the factors upon which the deponent's opinion is based, showing the deponent's personal knowledge of those factors. Your questioning might go as follows:

> You: *In your opinion, was the driver of the car that hit me under the influence of alcohol?*
>
> Defending attorney: *Objection: Improper opinion.*
>
> You: *You may answer the question.*
>
> A: *Yes, I thought that the driver was under the influence of alcohol.*

If this is helpful testimony, you can cure the problem by bringing out the deponent's firsthand knowledge of evidence that supports the opinion, and then eliciting the opinion again.

> You: *When did you actually have a chance to observe the driver of the car that hit me?*
>
> A: *It was right after you were hit—I came running over to offer help.*
>
> Q: *And how close were you to the driver?*
>
> A: *Just a few inches away, really.*
>
> Q: *And what did you notice about the driver?*
>
> A: *For one thing, he smelled strongly of alcohol. His eyes were red and watery, and when he spoke his speech was slurred.*
>
> You: *Based on these observations, do you have an opinion as to whether the driver was under the influence of alcohol?*
>
> A: *Yes, in my opinion he was.*

The defending lawyer may also properly make an "improper opinion" objection if you ask a lay (nonexpert) witness to give an opinion that only an expert witness is legally entitled to give. For example, only a medical expert could testify to an opinion that "the doctor's failure to diagnose the kidney stone constitutes medical malpractice." To cure this problem, you'd have to elicit evidence showing that the witness is qualified as an expert in the relevant field. (See Chapter 8 for a discussion of the qualifications necessary to be an expert witness.)

k. Objection: The Document Has Not Been Authenticated (or Lack of Foundation for the Document)

This objection asserts that you haven't previously shown (through the deponent's testimony) that a document you're asking the deponent about is "genuine"—that is, that it was authored or produced by the person you claim to be the author or producer. (For the text of a typical authentication rule, see Federal Rule of Evidence 901.)

Example

You ask, "Please look at this letter written by your Aunt Agnes and tell me if you've ever seen it before." Previous questioning has not established that Aunt Agnes wrote the letter.

If the defending attorney objects and you want to cure the problem because the answer is helpful, you'll need to elicit evidence demonstrating that the letter really was written by whom you said write it—Aunt Agnes, in this example.

Evidence rules allow numerous ways of authenticating documents. (Federal Rule of Evidence 901 has a big list, and even that list is not exclusive.) One way to do this is to show that the deponent recognizes handwriting. In the Aunt Agnes situation, then, your questioning may proceed as follows:

> You: *Please look at this letter written by your Aunt Agnes and tell me if you've ever seen it before.*
>
> Defending attorney: *Objection: Lack of authentication.*
>
> You: *You may answer the question.*
>
> A: *I have. That's a letter Agnes wrote to me last August.*

If this is helpful testimony, you can cure the problem by bringing out how the deponent recognizes the letter as one written by Aunt Agnes.

> You: *And how do you know that Agnes wrote the letter?*
>
> A: *Because I know her handwriting. I've gotten lots of letters from her over the years. That's her handwriting, and that's her signature.*

Of course, you may not be able to cure this defect in this way if the deponent really doesn't know whether a document is genuine. If this occurs and the authenticity of the document is not really in doubt, you can ask the defending lawyer to "stipulate to the document's authenticity" (voluntarily agree on the record that the docu-

ment is genuine). If the defending lawyer refuses either to withdraw the objection or to stipulate to authenticity, you'll have to authenticate the document through some other means if you hope to use the helpful testimony in a pretrial motion or at trial. (One method that attorneys often use is to mail a "Request for Admission," asking an adversary to admit that a document is genuine. For discussion of this method, see Chapter 9.)

I.   Objection: Hearsay

A hearsay problem may arise whenever you ask a deponent to testify about a statement that the deponent or any other person made previously, outside of the deposition in order to prove that the statement is true. (See Federal Rule of Evidence 801.)

Examples

- *You ask, "What did the person standing next to you say following the accident?" If the deponent testifies that the bystander said, "The green car ran the stop sign," the bystander's statement is probably inadmissible hearsay if you want to use it to prove that the green car ran the stop sign.*

- *You ask, "What did your boss tell you after the meeting?" If the deponent testifies that the boss said, "Jones Co. agreed to sell us the widgets for $2 each," and you want to use this statement to prove that this was the the agreement, the boss's statement is probably hearsay.*

As discussed in Chapter 10, Subsection E5c, the hearsay rule is complicated and riddled with exceptions. One significant and long-established exception to the hearsay rule (called the "admissions exemption" in the FRE) makes one party's statements admissible when they are offered into evidence by the other party. The exception extends to statements made by a party's employees or agents. (See Federal Rule of Evidence 801.) Therefore, if you ask the deponent about a statement made by your adversary or an employee or agent of your adversary, the hearsay rule will probably not be a problem: A hearsay objection would probably be invalid in this situation, and you could safely ignore it.

When a deponent testifies to a statement made by someone other than your adversary, however, a hearsay objection may prevent your use of the statement later. To attempt to cure the hearsay problem, you could try to bring out additional evidence establishing one of the other numerous exceptions to the hearsay rule. If an exception applies, you can use the deposition testimony later notwithstanding the hearsay objection. (For a list of the most common exceptions to the hearsay rule, see Federal Rules of Evidence 803 and 804.)

However, the hearsay rule is extremely complex. Especially when an objection is based on hearsay, your best response may be to get your answer and move on.

Should you wish to overcome a hearsay objection, the following example illustrates how you might elicit additional testimony to establish the basis for a hearsay exception. The hearsay exception for "present sense impressions" makes statements describing events that are made during or immediately after the events themselves admissible as evidence. (See Federal Rule of Evidence 803(1).) You might then cure a hearsay problem by offering testimony that shows that a statement was made during or immediately after the event to which it relates.

For example, assume that in an auto accident case, you want to ask the deponent about a statement made by a bystander who saw the accident. (The bystander is unavailable, so you can get the bystander's statement into evidence only by having this deponent testify about it.) A portion of your questioning may go as follows:

You: Do you recall any statement being made to you after the collision?

Defending attorney: Objection: Hearsay.

You: You can go ahead and answer the question.

A: *Yes. There was a tall blond fellow next to me. Right after I heard the crash, he turned to me and said that the Buick ran the red light.*

If this is helpful testimony, you can cure the problem by asking additional questions to show that the statement qualifies as a "present sense impression."

> You: *How much time elapsed between the time of the collision and the time this fellow said that the Buick ran the red light?*
>
> A: *Gee, I'd say it couldn't have been more than a few seconds.*

The deponent's testimony that the bystander's statement followed the collision by "a few seconds" probably qualifies the bystander's statement as a "present sense impression." You could therefore use the deponent's testimony about the bystander's statement in a pretrial motion or offer it into evidence at trial.

 Many references discuss hearsay exceptions.

For a further discussion of common hearsay exceptions, see *Represent Yourself in Court*, by Paul Bergman & Sara Berman-Barrett (Nolo). A multitude of books and outlines for lawyers and law students explaining the hearsay rule and its exceptions exists; one book that you may find helpful is *Federal Rules of Evidence in a Nutshell*, by Michael Graham (West Group). Recall, however, that you're normally better off getting all the information you can rather than worrying about how to cure an objection. This advice is especially true for hearsay problems.

4. Are There Any Objections That I Probably Can't Cure, So I Should Ignore?

Yes. The few common objections described in the subsections below are likely to be "uncurable." In other words, you probably won't be able to ask additional questions at a deposition to overcome them. Thus, your best response is to ignore these objections. Simply obtain answers and move on.

a. Objection: Asked and Answered

This objection asserts that you have already asked the objected-to question earlier in the deposition, and that the deponent has answered it. Nevertheless, following an "asked and answered" objection you'll normally ask the deponent to simply answer the question. Even if the objection is valid, you can probably use the deponent's earlier deposition answer later. And if the objection is improper—that is, if the deponent's current answer is different—the "asked and answered" objection obviously won't prevent use of this different answer later in the case.

b. Objection: Irrelevant

This objection asserts that the information you seek has no bearing on the issues in your case. (See Federal Rule of Evidence 401.) A related objection is that "the relevance of information is slight and is outweighed by the danger of unfair prejudice." (See Federal Rule of Evidence 403.) Usually, the danger of unfair prejudice amounts to a claim that evidence will appeal primarily to a juror's biases and emotions.

The defending attorney is unlikely to make either of these objections, because they are typically "preserved" (able to be raised later) regardless of whether they are made at the time of a deposition. If one of these objections is made, however, it is almost always incurable. If the information you seek is irrelevant, or if its relevance is outweighed by the risk of undue prejudice, further deposition questioning won't fix the problem. You may ask for an answer, but you will be able to use the answer later only if the judge overrules these objections.

5. How Do I Cure an Objection to an Answer?

The defending attorney may also object to a deponent's answer—rather than to your question—for many of the same reasons set forth in Sections A3 and A4, above (for example, that an answer is speculative or irrelevant). In such a situation, you can cure the problem in exactly the same way as if the attorney had objected to your question rather than to the deponent's answer.

One objection that can be made only to an answer and not to a question is that the answer is "nonresponsive." Evidence rules require that a deponent's answers respond directly to the questions asked. So, if a deponent gives an answer that does not respond to your question, the defending attorney may object to the answer and move to strike (remove) it from the record, on the ground that the answer is nonresponsive.

Example

You: Why did the chicken cross the road?

A: Many chickens were crossing the road that day.

Defending attorney: Objection: That answer is nonresponsive. I move to strike it.

If you want to be able to use a deponent's answer later, you can usually cure a "nonresponsive" objection by asking a new question to which the answer will be responsive.

Example

You are a defendant representing yourself in a lawsuit filed against you by Blue Prince, a building contractor who did remodeling work on your house. Your defense is that you should not have to pay the balance of the contract price because some of Prince's work did not meet contract standards. You are deposing an employee of the lumber company where Prince purchased the wood used in your remodeling job.

You: When Prince first contacted you about buying lumber for this job, what type of wood did Prince ask to purchase?

A: Prince said that he had promised you that he would use cedar siding for the outside wall.

Defending attorney: Objection: Move to strike. The answer is nonresponsive.

This objection appears to be proper. Your question asked about what type of wood the contractor asked to purchase; the deponent's answer refers to a promise the contractor made to you. Since the nonresponsive answer is helpful, however, you may decide to cure the objection. If so, you might proceed as follows:

> You: *In this initial conversation you had with Prince, did Prince mention what type of wood Prince had promised to use on the job?*
>
> A: *Yes. Prince said that he had promised you that he would use cedar siding for the outside wall.*

Having overcome the nonresponsive problem, you should then return to your initial inquiry:

> Q: *And what type of wood did Prince actually ask to purchase?*
>
> A: *Prince asked to purchase pine siding.*
>
> Q: *What is the difference in the cost of pine siding as opposed to cedar siding?*
>
> A: *Cedar siding costs much more …*

B. Responding to Instructions Not to Answer

In some circumstances, the defending attorney may both object and instruct the deponent not to answer a question. The defending attorney can properly instruct a deponent not to answer only if:

- the defending attorney represents the deponent, and

- your question either

  - asks the deponent to divulge privileged information, or

  - asks the deponent to disclose private information and, under the circumstances, constitutes harassment.

If you think that the defending attorney has properly instructed the deponent not to answer, you should simply move on to another question. If, however, you believe that the defending attorney has improperly instructed the deponent not to answer a question, the subsections below explain how you might respond. An instruction not to answer would be improper if:

- The defending attorney does not represent the deponent. The defending attorney cannot instruct a witness or other non-party deponent whom that attorney does not represent to refuse to answer a question. (Of course, a nonparty deponent may take a hint from the defending attorney's objection and refuse to answer anyway; see Chapter 7.)

- Your question is improper for reasons that don't involve privilege or privacy. For example, the defending attorney can object but cannot instruct a deponent to refuse to answer on the ground that a question calls for "speculation" or "hearsay" or is in some other way improper.

When the defending attorney improperly instructs a deponent not to answer a question, there are several steps you can take to try to force a deponent to answer, up to and including suspending the deposition and filing a written "Motion to Compel Answers" in court. This motion asks a judge to order the deponent to answer your question. Filing a Motion to Compel Answers is time consuming and possibly expensive if you have to hire a lawyer to do it. (But see "Immediate Hearings by Phone" in Section B3, below, for an inexpensive alternative to going to court that might be available in your locality.) To try to resolve the dispute, and to strengthen your position if you do have to go to court, you should take the following steps before suspending the deposition.

1. Ask the Defending Attorney to Withdraw the Instruction

When faced with what you believe to be an improper instruction not to answer, your first step is to plainly state on the record that the instruction not to answer is improper, and give a reason for your contention. It's possible that your failure to roll over will lead the defending attorney to withdraw the instruction not to answer, saving you the trouble, expense, and uncertainty of seeking a court order. (In addition, FRCP 37(a)(2)(B) requires that you attempt to resolve discovery disputes in good faith before going to court.) Also, a judge will be more likely to sanction (fine or in some other way penalize) the defending attorney for an improper instruction

not to answer if you have attempted to resolve the matter amicably during the deposition. (See FRCP 37(a)(4).)

Example 1

Instruction not to answer based on improper claim of work product privilege: *Assume that you are a homeowner and are suing a car rental company for renting a car to an underage driver who crashed into your yard and caused property damage. You are deposing Lynn Herman, an employee of the rental car agency who investigated the accident. The following testimony unfolds:*

> You: *Ms. Herman, in the course of your investigation, did you talk to any witness about the accident?*

> Defending attorney (representing the car rental company): *Objection: Work product privilege. Ms. Herman talked to witnesses at my suggestion and what she learned is therefore attorney work product. I instruct Ms. Herman not to answer the question.*

> You: *I don't think the question violates the work product privilege. I'm not asking the deponent to testify to the content of any written statement she prepared for you. Therefore what I'm asking about is not within the work product rule.*

> Defending lawyer: *I'm still instructing the witness not to answer, because she was assigned by me to investigate on behalf of the car rental company.*

In this example, you correctly point out that the work product privilege does not apply. (See Chapter 7 for more on this privilege.) You've stated on the record that you disagree with the instruction not to answer, and you have given a reason for your position. However, if the defending attorney persists in instructing the deponent not to answer, you'll have to go to court and ask a judge to order the deponent to answer your question (unless phone-in dispute resolution procedures are available in your locality; see "Immediate Hearings by Phone" in Section B3, below).

Example 2

Improper instruction not to answer following an objection not based on privilege: *In the same case and deponent, the defending attorney instructs the deponent not to answer a question that calls for hearsay:*

> You: *Ms. Herman, in the course of your investigation, did you interview any witnesses to the accident?*
>
> A: *I did. I talked to a Ms. Pine and a Mr. Wilson.*
>
> Q: *And what did Ms. Pine tell you?*
>
> Defending attorney: *Objection: Hearsay. I instruct Ms. Herman not to answer the question.*
>
> You: *Counsel, I've done my homework and as I'm sure you know, it's improper for you*

> *to instruct the witness not to answer in this situation. Under FRCP 30(c) and 30(d)(1), which is the law in this court, the deponent has to answer subject to your objection since the question doesn't ask the witness to disclose privileged information. I even have a copy of the rule right here. A judge can rule on your objection later if I ever want to use the answer, but I'm entitled to an answer to my question now.*
>
> Defending attorney: *My hearsay objection stands, but I'll allow the witness to answer.*

In this example your response is accurate, and your argument succeeds. You'll get an answer without having to involve the court system.

2. Put the Deponent's Refusal to Answer on the Record

If the defending lawyer continues to improperly instruct a witness not to answer, the written record kept by the court reporter must indicate that the deponent has actually refused to answer your question before you can go to court to successfully move to compel answers. In addition, if you can clearly link the deponent's refusal to answer to the lawyer's instruction, chances go way up that a judge will sanction the defending lawyer for the improper behavior.

Example

You are again deposing Ms. Herman in the car accident case, and the defending lawyer has persisted in improperly instructing Ms. Herman not to answer based on work product privilege. To make the record clear that the court's intervention is the only way that you'll get an answer to your question, you should continue as follows:

> You: *Ms. Herman, do you refuse to answer my question about whether after the accident you obtained witness statements from anyone?*
>
> A: *Yes I do.*
>
> You: *And are you basing that refusal to answer on your attorney's instruction not to answer?*
>
> A: *Yes I am.*

You now have an adequate record for filing a motion to compel answers or using a phone-in dispute resolution procedure, should you choose to do so.

3. Decide Whether to Suspend the Deposition and Go to Court

Following the two steps above puts you in a position to suspend the deposition and file a Motion to Compel Answers in court if you choose to do so. However, do not automatically suspend a deposition and file a motion when you believe that the defending lawyer has improperly instructed the deponent not to answer. You should be reluctant to go to court because:

• It's expensive and time consuming. As a result, even many lawyers forgo making Motions to Compel Answers in the face of improper instructions not to answer. (Of course, this isn't a problem if you can use a phone-in procedure.)

• Courts tend to be very picky about how and when you can file motions, even down to the type of paper you can use. If you make a mistake, the court may not consider your motion; at the very least, the hearing may be delayed.

• Unless the answer you expect the deponent to give is absolutely vital to the outcome of the case, the expense and trouble of going to court is likely to far outweigh the benefit of the answer.

Consequently, instead of immediately suspending a deposition when the defending attorney gives the deponent what you believe to be an improper instruction not to answer, you should continue with the deposition until you've completed your questioning. Once you've gotten all the information you can, decide whether you need answers to any questions that you believe the deponent has been improperly instructed not to answer. (Also see "Immediate Hearings by Phone," below.)

To preserve your right to make a Motion to Compel Answers in court, at the conclusion of your questioning and while you're still "on the record," say something like the following:

I reserve the right to resume the deposition after moving to compel answers to questions that the deponent refused to answer earlier in the deposition.

Preserving your right to go to court does not commit you to doing so. After you've had a chance to think about the situation and perhaps consult with a lawyer, you can decide whether to make a Motion to Compel Answers.

On the next page is a sample Motion to Compel Answers that you can adapt to the circumstances of your case. Consult your local court rules for proper format and other filing requirements.

Immediate Hearings by Phone

Judges and magistrates who rule on Motions to Compel Answers are increasingly willing to resolve disputes about instructions not to answer deposition questions over the telephone, during a recess in the deposition. The court reporter reads to the judge or magistrate the questions that the deponent refuses to answer, and then both you and the defending lawyer can argue about whether an instruction not to answer is proper. This sensible procedure allows the judge or magistrate to rule immediately, so the deposition can then resume promptly. Where available, this phone-in procedure can save the considerable time, money, and inconvenience of formal written motions. Your court clerk should be able to tell you whether and under what circumstances telephone conferencing is available to sort out deposition arguments.

SAMPLE

MOTION TO COMPEL ANSWERS

(Case Caption)

Plaintiff Marilyn Onassis moves this court for an Order compelling defendant Aristotle Monroe to answer deposition questions. In support of this Motion, Plaintiff states as follows:

1. On February 2, 20xx, Plaintiff took the deposition of defendant Monroe.

2. The defendant failed to answer the following *[insert the number of questions]* questions:

[Here, insert the text of the questions that the deponent refused to answer. You'll get this information from the reporter's transcript, which you'll need to have in hand before making a Motion to Compel.]

3. The questions that the deponent refused to answer did not ask for privileged information. Under FRCP 30(c) and 30(d)(1), therefore, defendant Monroe was obligated to answer the questions subject to objection, if appropriate.

4. Plaintiff Onassis tried to resolve the dispute in good faith. In each instance, Plaintiff advised defendant's counsel that counsel's instruction not to answer was improper under FRCP 30(c) and 30(d)(1), and asked counsel to withdraw the instruction. Counsel refused to do so and defendant refused to answer based on counsel's instructions.

Wherefore, Plaintiff Onassis requests that this Court order the defendant to appear for another session of the deposition, to answer the questions that the defendant previously refused to answer as well as any additional and related questions that do not call for privileged information and to award Plaintiff reasonable expenses, including attorney's fees, under FRCP 37(a)(4).

Dated: _____   Respectfully Submitted,

Marilyn Onassis

Marilyn Onassis
Plaintiff in Pro Se

C. Responding to Coaching of the Deponent

FRCP 30(c) requires attorneys to behave as professionally and courteously during a deposition as in open court. By and large, attorneys fulfill these obligations. But especially when facing a self-represented party, a defending lawyer might be tempted to engage in improper coaching of the deponent.

Coaching occurs when the defending attorney by word or actions suggests answers to a deponent. The attorney can legitimately discuss a deponent's expected testimony before a deposition. But once a deposition is underway, it is improper for the attorney to attempt to guide a deponent's responses. The subsections below examine some common coaching methods and how you might respond.

 Videotaped depositions make most lawyers behave.

Though videotaping adds to a deposition's expense, it is an effective way to reduce the likelihood that a defending attorney will engage in improper behavior, such as coaching. If an argument develops over whether an attorney acted improperly, you can show the tape to the judge. For further discussion of videotaping depositions, see Chapter 14.

1. Speaking Objections

FRCP 30(d)(1) requires that objections be stated in a concise and nonargumentative fash-ion. "Speaking objections" (lectures or harangues) are improper.

Example

- *Properly phrased objection: "Objection: Vague."*

- *Improper speaking objection: "Objection: Vague and ambiguous. How can you expect this witness to know what you're driving at when you ask questions like that? If you will ask a specific question that the witness can answer, instead of wasting everybody's time, we can get this deposition over in a reasonable amount of time."*

One big reason why speaking objections are improper is that a defending attorney might use them to coach the deponent to give a particular response. In the example above, the lawyer's speaking objection may be an attempt to signal the deponent to respond to your question by saying, "I don't understand the question."

Unless the defending attorney continuously makes speaking objections, you should probably respond to them no differently than you would to proper objections. (See Section A, above.) That is, first insist on an answer. Then, if the underlying objection is proper (your question really was vague), you can consider curing the problem if the answer is helpful.

In an extreme situation, where speaking objections are so prevalent that they greatly prolong the deposition and seriously disrupt your questioning, consider asking a magistrate or referee to resolve the problem over the phone, if your local court has such a procedure.

If phone-in dispute resolution is unavailable, or if it doesn't succeed in stopping the improper behavior, you might terminate the deposition and seek a protective order and sanctions. FRCP 26(c), 30(d)(4), 30(d)(3), and 37(a)(4) provide that a judge may make a protective order if "justice requires" to protect you or a deponent from annoyance, embarrassment, oppression, undue burden, or expense in connection with the conduct of depositions. However, most judges strongly dislike becoming embroiled in discovery battles. If you seek a protective order for isolated or trivial disruptions, you'll probably end up paying sanctions to the defending lawyer. And before seeking a protective order, remember that FRCP 26(c) requires you to make a good faith effort to work out the matter. For example, before seeking a protective order based on excessive speaking objections, you might say something like this to the defending lawyer:

> *Counsel, I've been ignoring your improper objections for some time now. But as you should know better than me, FRCP 30(d)(1) requires you to object in a concise and nonargumentative manner. I have a copy of the rule right here if you want to see it. I think you're just trying to harass me because I'm not a lawyer. But if you continue to make long arguments every time you object, I'll have to stop the*

> *deposition and go to court and seek a protective order and sanctions. Will you agree to object according to the rules?*

2. Mid-Questioning Conferences

The defending attorney is generally prohibited from conferring with the deponent while you are in the process of asking questions and obtaining answers. (The one exception to this rule allows deponents to talk to their attorneys to seek advice about whether information is privileged. See Chapter 7 for a discussion of the attorney-client and other privileges.)

The following examples illustrate three kinds of improper conferences mid-question.

Examples

- Deponent seeks help from lawyer.

  You: Why did the chicken cross the road?

  A: I'd like to talk to my attorney before I answer that question.

- Lawyer seeks conference with deponent.

  You: Why did the chicken cross the road?

  Defending lawyer: Just a moment, don't answer that yet. I'd like a quick word with my client before she answers that question.

- Lawyer gives mid-deposition advice to deponent.

  You: Why did the chicken cross the road?

  A: It looked like the chicken wanted to get to the other side. Actually, the chicken started across the road twice before going all the way across.

Defending attorney: It's best to just answer the question, don't volunteer information that hasn't been asked for.

Despite the fact that rules forbid lawyer/deponent conferences mid-questioning, such as those illustrated above, such conferences frequently occur, and experienced lawyers do not try to prevent every one. Mid-questioning conferences often serve the interests of both parties by clearing up misunderstandings and thereby expediting questioning. Thus, as a self-represented party, you'll want to exercise judgment when deciding how to react to mid-questioning conferences. Such a conference might be appropriate to:

- resolve concerns about when the deposition will end, or

- clarify minor uncertainties.

Example 1

You: What, if anything, did Sara say after the chicken crossed the road?

A: She said that it looked like the chicken was just trying to get to the other side.

[Deponent then whispers to his counsel in a voice that the reporter cannot hear.]

Defending attorney: My client has just advised me that he has an appointment at 5:00 p.m. He wants to know if the deposition will be concluded in time for him to make that appointment. If not, he'd like to take a break soon so he can call and cancel (or we can

suspend the deposition at 4:00 so he can make the appointment).

Example 2

You: How could it have been the chicken who crossed the road when it was really the bear that wanted to see what was on the other side?

[Deponent looks totally confused and briefly whispers to the deponent's attorney.]

Defending attorney: I'm sorry, my client is having difficulty understanding your question. Are you trying to find out whether my client saw the chicken cross the road?

In each of these examples, it probably makes sense to ignore what may technically be an improper conference because the defending lawyer does not appear to be trying to feed information to the deponent. At most, you may want to say something like, "I appreciate that you're both trying to help the deposition go smoothly. But in the future, I would appreciate it if the deponent will follow the rules and speak directly with me if she needs a break or is confused about one of my questions."

The subsections below explain alternatives commonly available to you when you believe that the defending lawyer is trying to use mid-questioning conferences to improperly coach a deponent.

a. Deny Permission for a Conference

Either the deponent or the lawyer may ask for permission to hold a mid-questioning conference before the deponent answers a question. If you believe that coaching is likely to take place during the conference, politely decline to give permission. This scenario may unfold as follows:

> *You: Why did the chicken cross the road?*
>
> *A: May I talk to my attorney before I answer that question?*
>
> *You: I prefer that you just answer my question, thank you. If you're not clear what I'm asking, let me know and I'll try to make the question clearer.*

Of course, you cannot physically stop the deponent and defending attorney from conferring before answering your question. If your attempt to deny permission for a mid-questioning conference is unsuccessful, in the event that conferences occur repeatedly, your only alternative is to move for a protective order.

b. Lay the Groundwork for a Protective Order (Put Mid-Questioning Conferences on the Record)

When the opposing lawyer engages in a whispered conference with the deponent, the court reporter may be unable to hear or transcribe what is said. Thus, the written transcript record probably will not reflect that a conference has taken place unless you indicate for the record what happened. This scenario might go as follows:

> *You: Mr. Bean, what happened after the chicken crossed the road?*
>
> *Defending attorney: Excuse me just a moment. (Assume that at this point the adversary's lawyer has a whispered conference with the deponent.)*
>
> *You: Let the record reflect that counsel is now conferring with the deponent. Counsel, you are not entitled to confer with your client during my examination unless your conference is necessary to determine whether or not to assert a privilege. This question clearly does not call for privileged information. If your client feels my question is unclear, please tell Mr. Bean to tell me that the question is unclear and we can try to solve that problem. But you are not entitled to confer with your client before the client answers this question.*

Again, some attorneys may try to take advantage of your self-represented status by insisting that they have a right to confer with the deponent. If the opposing attorney's behavior persists, you can threaten to seek a protective order. This type of scenario might proceed as follows:

Defending attorney (after you've asked the attorney not to confer with the deponent, as above): I am conferring with my client to make sure the client understands the question. I think I'm entitled to do that.

You: You should know better than me that FRCP 30(c) prohibits you from conferring with the deponent. Depositions are supposed to proceed like trial, and of course you are not entitled to confer with your client during my examination at trial. I have a copy of the rule right here. Please do not try to confer with your client during my questioning.

Defending attorney: You're being hyper-technical because you don't really understand the rules. My job is to make sure that the record is clear and that my client understands your poorly phrased question before she answers it. That makes for a clear record. That's all I'm doing.

You: I'm sorry, I disagree. If you improperly confer with your client again during my examination, I'll note it for the record, and I reserve the right to decide whether I will suspend the deposition and go to court to seek a protective order and sanctions.

If improper conferences continue, you will ultimately have to decide if the problem is serious enough to warrant the time and expense of going to seek a protective order prohibiting such conferences.

c. Conferences During a Recess

Recesses are certain to occur during any deposition lasting more than an hour or two. The court reporter will need a break from transcribing testimony, and the defending attorney is likely to call for a break to keep the deponent fresh and attentive. And, of course, any participant may request a bathroom break or a short recess to make a phone call.

Neither the deponent nor the defending attorney is supposed to call for a break for the purpose of discussing how to answer a question. Consequently, you may try to delay taking a recess if you believe that the purpose of an attorney's request is to interrupt an important topic in order to coach a deponent. For example, you may respond to a request for a break as follows:

You: And where did the chicken go after crossing the road?

Defending attorney: We'd like to take a break. My client has been testifying for nearly an hour now and I need to use the restroom. So let's take a ten-minute break, Okay?

You: I'm happy to take a break, but I'd like an answer to my question first.

Defending attorney: Sorry, but my client and I are taking a break. (They get up and leave the room.)

As in this example, you cannot physically stop the deponent and defending attorney from taking a break and leaving the room. Consequently, if your attempt to delay the recess fails, you may have to ignore this behavior.

A somewhat more aggressive option you could take—especially if this behavior occurs repeatedly—that lays the groundwork for seeking a protective order is to note for the record that you objected to the recess and indicate any reasons that lead you to think that the lawyer is using the recess request as an excuse to coach the deponent. For example, you might say something along these lines:

> *"I'd like the record to reflect that the attorney and the deponent have left the room despite my request that the deponent answer the question that was pending at the time they left. Moreover, this is the third time that a recess, supposedly to use the restroom, has been taken over my objection in the past hour, and in each instance I was asking about the relationship between the deponent and the Farnley Company."*

Again, however, you should think about seeking a protective order only if the deponent's attorney uses the recess ploy constantly and your questioning is seriously disrupted.

D. The Bottom Line

This chapter has identified deposition obstacles that a defending attorney may throw in your path. However, when deciding how you might respond to any of these forms of improper behavior, the "bottom line" is that judges generally do not want to supervise depositions closely. Like attorneys, you'll probably have to endure technical violations and efforts to make you uncomfortable in the course of taking a deposition. Keep in mind that motions to compel answers and protective orders are time consuming and difficult to obtain, and that judges have wide discretion when deciding whether to issue them. Usually, your best alternative is to keep your cool, try to ask proper questions, ignore objections, and persist until you've gotten the information to which you think you're entitled. ■

Chapter 13

Taking a Deposition: Deposing a "Friendly" Witness

This chapter briefly looks at when and how you might depose a "friendly" witness (one whose evidence supports your legal claims and who is willing to talk to you informally). Ordinarily, you should not depose friendly witnesses. You'd simply be eliciting information you could get much more cheaply and quickly in an informal interview. And, you'd be sharing the information that helps your case with your opponent's lawyer, who would almost certainly defend the deposition.

Deposing a friendly witness can make sense, however, when you want to use a deposition to "perpetuate" (preserve) the witness's testimony for you to use at trial.

A. When to Depose a Friendly Witness

Consider deposing a friendly witness when both of the following circumstances are present:

- the witness has information that is essential to the success of your legal claims or defenses, and

- the witness will probably be unavailable to testify in person if the case goes to trial.

Deposing a friendly witness under these circumstances provides you with a transcript of testimony that you can refer to during settlement negotiations and read into evidence at trial in lieu of the witness's live testimony. While deposition testimony is not normally admissible

as evidence at trial, such testimony is admissible if the deponent is "legally unavailable" to testify in person at the time of trial. For example, a deponent who is deceased or too ill to come to court at the time of trial is legally unavailable. So, too, is a deponent who moves to another state and refuses to come back to testify at trial, because civil courts in one state have no power to compel a person who lives in a different state to attend a trial. (See Chapter 2 for further discussion of using deposition testimony at trial.)

Example

You've been sued by Hy Kerr, who was allegedly attacked by your dog when walking by your property. Ida Stade, who lives nearby, has told you that she saw what happened and that your dog bit Hy only after Hy had taunted and thrown rocks at the dog for several minutes. Since you didn't personally see the incident, Ida's testimony is critical to your defense.

However, Ida plans to move across country and won't be available to testify in person should the case come to trial. Moreover, Hy's claims are grossly inflated and he has resisted all settlement efforts.

You might depose Ida in order to perpetuate her testimony. Doing so would allow you to offer Ida's deposition testimony into evidence at trial if in fact she is unavailable to testify in person at that time.

You Can Take a Deposition Before You File a Lawsuit

FRCP 27 provides that you can take a deposition to perpetuate testimony even before a lawsuit is filed as long as you have the permission of a judge. To seek a judge's permission, you must file a written request in court called a "Petition to Perpetuate Testimony of (name of deponent) Prior to Filing Suit" that explains the circumstances that warrant a prelawsuit deposition. For example, a judge might grant permission to depose an important witness who is terminally ill and likely to die even before you can file a lawsuit. Or a judge might let you depose a witness who is about to move a long distance. If a judge grants permission for a prelawsuit deposition, you have to give written notice of the deposition to your likely adversaries, so that they can attend the deposition if they want to do so.

B. Offering Deposition Testimony Into Evidence

You can normally offer deposition testimony into evidence at trial in one of three ways:

- you can read the questions and answers to the judge or jury

- you can have an assistant (or even the court clerk) read the deponent's answers while you read the questions, or

- if the deposition has been videotaped, you can play the videotape for the judge or jury. (See Chapter 14 for a discussion of videotaping depositions.)

To save time in a case tried before a judge without a jury, the judge may require you to simply submit the deposition booklet into evidence for the judge to read privately before deciding the case.

C. Eliciting All Favorable Evidence

When deposing a hostile witness, one of your goals should be to find out all case-related information known to the deponent. (See Chapter 11.) By contrast, when deposing a friendly witness, your goal is more limited. You want the friendly deponent to testify only to the evidence that supports your legal claims or defenses. Since you're using the deposition as a substitute for live testimony, it makes sense to try to have only favorable information in the transcript. (Of course, if your adversary defends the deposition, your adversary will have an opportunity to bring out unfavorable information, which may also be read into evidence at trial.)

Example

You take Ida's deposition in the dog-biting example above. Ida testifies that she lives two blocks away from you. You neglect to have her testify that she had not met you prior to the dog bite incident. If you offer Ida's deposition testimony into evidence, a judge or jury may think that Ida was biased in your favor: Because she lives so close to you, they might assume that she knew you previously. True, you could testify that you'd never met Ida prior to the incident, but to corroborate (back up) your testimony on this point, you'd want to question Ida about this during her deposition.

D. Complying With Evidence Rules

When you depose a friendly witness, it's important that the form of the testimony complies with trial evidence rules. Otherwise, the trial judge may exclude deposition testimony that was helpful to you. Following the two rules of thumb below will help you avoid the most common errors that might lead a judge to exclude the deposition testimony of a friendly witness:

1. Don't Ask Leading Questions

A leading question is a question that suggests the answer you want the deponent to give. At trial, you cannot ask leading questions of a friendly witness. (See Federal Rule of Evidence 611(c).) Therefore, if the opposing lawyer objects that a question is leading, you'll have to rephrase it so that it doesn't lead the deponent.

Example

You ask the deponent—a friend who was a passenger in your car at the time of an auto accident in which you were involved, "You saw the green car run the stop sign, didn't you?" If the defending lawyer objects that the question is leading, cure the problem by asking another question that is not leading. The process would go like this:

You: You saw the green car run the stop sign, right?

Defending attorney: Objection: Leading.

You: What did you see the green car do?

A: The green car ran the stop sign.

2. Demonstrate the Deponent's Personal Knowledge

Evidence rules require that witnesses have personal knowledge of the evidence to which they testify. (See Federal Rule of Evidence 602.) Therefore, if your adversary's lawyer objects that the deponent "lacks personal knowledge," you'll have to ask questions that demonstrate how the deponent knows what he or she is testifying about.

Example

You ask, "What did Ms. Julian do after she left the meeting?" However, previous questioning has not established that the deponent was in a position to know what Ms. Julian did after the meeting.

If the defending attorney objects, to cure the problem you'll need to ask additional questions to demonstrate how the deponent knows what Ms. Julian did after she left the meeting. Your questioning may proceed as follows:

You: What did Ms. Julian do after she left the meeting?

Defending attorney: Objection: Lack of personal knowledge.

A: She went right in to talk to Mr. Wilson.

Q: How do you know that Ms. Julian went right in to talk to Mr. Wilson?

A: Because I stayed behind for a moment, but then I caught up and went into his office with her.

These two rules of thumb will help you avoid the most common problems that may prevent you from using a friendly witness's deposition testimony at trial. For a discussion of other objections that your adversary may make and suggestions for methods of overcoming them, see Chapter 12. ■

Chapter 14

Videotaped Depositions

This chapter explains procedures and tactics for videotaped depositions. If you're representing yourself, the suggestions below will help you take or defend a videotaped deposition effectively. And if you're a deponent, this chapter will help you understand what to expect if your deposition will be videotaped.

Traditionally, deposition testimony has been taken down manually by court reporters, who later transcribe it into booklets. Most depositions are still recorded this way. However, discovery rules in most localities now also authorize the videotaping of depositions. (See, for example, FRCP 30(b)(2).) As a result, deposition testimony may be recorded manually, videotaped, or both.

As a self-representing party, the principal reasons for requesting that a deposition be videotaped are:

- **To have greater impact at trial.** Evidence rules sometimes permit you to introduce all or part of a deposition into evidence at trial. (See Chapter 2.) If so, showing the deponent's actual deposition testimony is likely to have a greater impact on a judge or juror than reading the same testimony into the record from a written transcript.

Example

You're the defendant in a personal injury case growing out of a collision between your truck and the plaintiff's car. You depose Bo Loney; the deposition is both videotaped and transcribed manually. During the deposition,

Loney testifies that "I couldn't really tell how fast the truck was going." When called by the plaintiff at trial, however, Loney testifies that your truck was traveling "at least 50 m.p.h." moments before the collision.

On cross-examination of Loney, you would undoubtedly try to attack his credibility by having the judge or jury hear Loney's conflicting deposition testimony. While you could read the conflicting deposition testimony into evidence, you'd probably prefer to show a clip of Loney testifying, "I couldn't really tell how fast the truck was going." Because a videotape allows a judge or jury to see Loney contradict himself out of his own mouth, the videotape is likely to have more impact than you reading from a transcript.

- **To control an obstreperous lawyer.** Videotaping tends to discourage improper behavior by the lawyer for your adversary. For example, a lawyer is far less likely to try to bully a deponent who supports your legal claims or coach a deponent who supports your opponent when a camera is waiting to capture the lawyer's tone of voice and nonverbal behavior. And if a lawyer engages in improper behavior nevertheless, the visual record may be more convincing than a written transcript if you later ask a judge to sanction (penalize) the lawyer or prohibit the lawyer from using the deposition at trial. (See Chapter 12 for further discussion of how to respond to an attorney's improper behavior at a deposition.)

Example

In the same personal injury case, you are again deposing Bo Loney. The plaintiff's attorney, Jess Chure, sometimes improperly coaches Loney by pointing to portions of a document when Loney seems uncertain about how to answer a question. If the deposition is transcribed manually, you could make a record of Chure's improper behavior by saying something like, "I'd like the record to reflect that attorney Chure pointed out information on a document to Mr. Loney just before Mr. Loney answered that last question." However, a judge might react more sternly if a videotape captures Chure in the act of coaching the deponent.

Of course, the presence of a video camera doesn't change the basic deposition ground rules. For example, regardless of whether a deposition is to be videotaped or transcribed (or both), the deponent will be under oath. However, videotaping presents a few unique concerns, which we cover in this chapter. If you're representing yourself and considering videotaping a deposition, the information in this chapter can help you decide when it makes sense to do so, how to arrange for videotaping, and how to take a videotaped deposition effectively. If you're a witness whose deposition will be videotaped, this chapter provides tips for testifying effectively "on camera."

A. The Rules of Videotaped Depositions

The sections below summarize the basic ground rules that govern videotaped depositions.

1. Authorizing Rule

FRCP 30(b)(2) and similar rules in practically every state authorize parties to videotape depositions.

2. Either Party Can Request Videotaping

FRCP 30(b)(3) allows either party to request that a deposition be videotaped. If you want a deposition you're taking to be videotaped, FRCP 30(b)(2) requires that your notice setting up the deposition indicate this. You would also have to pay the costs of videotaping. In many localities, you can have a deposition recorded both by transcribing and by videotaping it. The drawback is that you'll have to pay for both recording methods. Nevertheless, if testimony is crucial and a lot of money is at stake, you may want both a videotape and a transcript at hand. (For example, you'll find a written transcript more convenient to use if you want to incorporate deposition testimony into a pretrial motion.)

If you're defending a deposition arranged by your adversary, Rule 30(b)(3) also gives you the right to insist that the deposition be videotaped. If your adversary has arranged for a deposition that will be recorded stenographically by a court reporter, you can mail out a notice stating that the deposition will also be videotaped. Of course, since you asked for it, you would pay the cost of videotaping, while your adversary would pay for the stenographic court reporter.

Videotaped Deposition Costs

Most court reporting services that videotape depositions charge by the hour. If you request videotaping, expect to pay approximately $80 to $100 per hour. (You may have to pay for a minimum number of hours regardless of the actual length of the deposition.) In addition, you'll pay an extra $15 or so for the videotape itself. By contrast, the fee for manually transcribing a deposition is usually based on the deposition's page length. Expect to pay about $5 to $6 per page of deposition testimony; a day of deposition testimony may well consume over 100 pages.

---

3. Only Parties Can Request Videotaping

You can request that a deposition be videotaped only if you're a party taking or defending a deposition. If you're a nonparty deponent, you have no right to request that your deposition be videotaped. (Sorry—if you're a nonparty deponent who's a would-be actor, you'll just have to arrange for a screen test on your own time!)

4. A Court Officer Must Be Present

A court officer—either a court reporter or some other person licensed to administer oaths—must be present throughout every deposition, whether it's being recorded stenographically, by videotape, or both. (FRCP 30(b)(4).) If a deposition is both videotaped and transcribed, one court reporter often both supervises the videotaping and transcribes the deposition.

5. Videotape Deposition Sites

Licensed court reporting services schedule videotaped depositions in specially-equipped conference rooms. Some attorneys who take a high volume of depositions also have videotape-equipped conference rooms in their offices. But no matter where a videotaped deposition takes place, it still must be presided over by an officer licensed to administer the oath.

6. Guidance for Videotaping

Many factors can potentially affect the impression that a videotaped deposition might give a judge or juror of a deponent's credibility. For example, credibility may differ depending on whether a deponent is shown in tight close-ups or from farther away. And a videotape's potential to prevent an attorney from using gestures to coach a deponent may depend on whether the attorney is included when the camera frames the picture.

Nevertheless, rules authorizing videotaped depositions typically provide little guidance as to how to actually conduct the taping. For example, FRCP 30(b)(4) simply provides that the appearance or demeanor of a deponent or an attorney shall not be distorted through camera or sound recording techniques. Because the rules relating to the conduct of videotaped depositions are so vague, if you have special concerns about a videotaped deposition that you're going to take, defend, or participate in, you can probably ask the officer to set up the camera in a way that meets your needs.

Example

You're a self-represented party whose deposition is about to be videotaped. The lighting is such that you have alternating streaks of dark shadows running across your face. You might ask the officer to adjust the seating arrangements or the camera angle, to prevent the shadows from distorting your appearance and conveying a menacing demeanor.

Other types of adjustments you might want to make include:

- If you're concerned that an adversary's lawyer will engage in improper behavior during the deposition, ask the videotape operator to include the attorney in the picture.

- If you have a physical problem (for example, a facial scar) that you would prefer to minimize, ask the officer to set up the camera in a way that will not draw attention to the problem.

⚠ State laws and regulations on videotaping may vary.

If you have concerns about videotaping a particular deposition, check the local rules in your state to make sure that they allow whatever special requests you want to make.

When the camera and all participants are in place, the officer will start the tape rolling, administer the oath, and then make other statements for the record. For example, the officer may recite (a) the officer's name and business address, (b) the date, time, and place of the deposition, (c) the deponent's name, and (d) the names of all persons present. If the length of the deposition requires more than one videotape, the officer will recess the deposition briefly to change tapes. After inserting and starting a new tape, the officer will repeat some of these same recitals.

When questioning concludes, the officer will state for the record that the deposition is complete. The deponent can ask to review the videotape and make any necessary corrections. (For a discussion of how to make post-deposition corrections, see Chapter 4.) Any party can secure a copy of the videotape by paying a "reasonable" copying fee to the court officer who presided over the videotaping. (FRCP 30(f).)

B. When Should You Videotape a Deposition?

This section highlights two key questions you should ask yourself when considering whether to videotape a deposition. Ordinarily, it will make sense for you to bear the added expense of videotaping only if you can answer "yes" to one of these questions.

1. Are You Taking the Deposition in Order to Perpetuate a Helpful Witness's Testimony?

As explained in Chapter 13, generally you depose a "friendly" witness (one whose testimony helps your case and who is willing to talk to you informally) only when the witness's testimony is crucial to your case and you have good reason to believe that the witness may be unavailable to testify in person at trial. In that event, you may be able to present the helpful deposition testimony to the judge or jury at trial in lieu of the deponent's live testimony.

If you are about to depose a friendly witness, therefore, opting for videotape may make sense. As a general rule, showing testimony on a courtroom screen is likely to have greater impact on a judge or jury than reading that same testimony from a transcript.

Nevertheless, don't automatically choose to videotape a friendly witness's deposition. First, consider each of the following issues carefully:

- Is the case really likely to go to trial? Only if the case goes to trial can you benefit from the ability to show the deponent's testimony to a judge or jury. If a case settles before trial (as the overwhelming percentage of cases do), the fact that a deposition was videotaped rather than transcribed is of little importance. In short, if you expect the case to settle, videotaping is usually unnecessary.

- Is the deponent really unlikely to be available to testify in person at the trial? If the deponent testifies at the trial, you'll probably have no opportunity to show the deposition videotape to the judge or jury. If you expect the witness to show up for trial, videotaping "just in case" may be a needless expense.

- Does the value of the case merit the extra expense of videotaping? The smaller the amount you can reasonably expect to gain or lose, the less the reason to videotape.

If you can answer "yes" to each of these questions, it's probably a good idea to videotape a deposition that you take to perpetuate a friendly witness's testimony.

Should You Videotape an Adverse Witness's Deposition Testimony?

Unless you are concerned about controlling an obstreperous lawyer, the general answer is "no." If you depose a hostile witness, it's likely that much of what the witness has to say will hurt your legal claims. If so, you'll probably add to the impact of your adversary's case if the witness is unavailable to testify in person at trial and the adversary shows the videotape that you paid for!

The one situation in which it may be to your advantage to have a videotape rather than a written transcript of an adverse witness's deposition is when your case goes to trial, the adverse witness testifies at the trial, and the adverse witness's trial testimony contradicts his or her deposition testimony. Evidence rules would then allow you to attack the adverse witness's credibility by proving to the judge or jury that the witness's story has changed. If so, your attack may have more impact if you show a video clip of the witness testifying differently than if you read the contradictory testimony from the deposition transcript.

However, there is a huge practical problem with this strategy. You probably won't know before trial whether the witness will contradict the deposition testimony and if so, in what way. Thus, if the witness does change his or her testimony, you'd have the almost impossible job of quickly locating the contradictory portion of a videotaped deposition in the middle of trial. Certainly a judge is not going to take kindly to your fumbling through a lengthy videotape in an attempt to find the contradictory testimony.

Realistically, to be useful, you'd have to go to the additional trouble and expense of converting the videotape to a CD-ROM in advance of the trial. You could then generate a bar code and index for each line of deposition testimony, and bring the CD-ROM to the trial. To locate the deposition testimony that conflicts with the adverse witness's trial testimony, you would sweep a wand across the appropriate bar code. The corresponding portion of the deposition would then immediately show on a screen for the judge or jury to see.

While some attorneys with big-bucks litigation practices routinely videotape depositions and convert the videos to CD-ROMs, this is too much trouble and expense for most self-represented parties to go through on the chance of impeaching an adverse witness with deposition testimony.

2. Is Videotaping Necessary to Control an Obstreperous Lawyer?

Another reason for you to videotape a deposition is to discourage the adversary's lawyer from coaching a deponent or using other improper behavior to try to disrupt a deposition or intimidate you or a deponent. Fortunately, you can expect most lawyers to behave as professionally at private depositions as in public courtrooms. However, your adversary's lawyer may be an exception. You may have advance warning that your adversary's lawyer is likely to behave improperly to try to take advantage of the fact that you are representing yourself. For example:

- perhaps a friend or lawyer you know has told you to expect the worst

- perhaps you've observed the lawyer behave improperly during earlier depositions or other proceedings, or

- perhaps the lawyer has told you that he is going to "make your life a living hell" if you don't accept a modest settlement.

If you have good reason to expect improper behavior by the opposing lawyer, the witness is an important one, and the amount in dispute justifies the added expense, then consider videotaping a deposition.

C. Disadvantages of Videotaping

Even if you're perpetuating an important friendly witness's testimony, or you think improper behavior by your adversary's lawyer is likely, consider the following common disadvantages of videotaping before deciding to videotape.

The first obvious disadvantage is the expense. Videotaping is likely to add hundreds of dollars to a deposition's cost, especially if you're also paying a court stenographer to transcribe the testimony.

You could, of course, request that the deposition be videotaped but not transcribed. (While videotaping will probably cost more than transcribing, at least you don't have to pay for both.) The downside of this, however, is that you won't have a printed version of the deponent's testimony. And if you want to cite deposition testimony in a pretrial motion, or use a deposition to help prepare a witness for trial, a videotape is not as convenient as a printed transcript. You might prepare an "unofficial" transcript from the videotape yourself so that you have a ready source of testimony for a witness to read. However, transcribing what might be hours of questions and answers would be extremely burdensome.

Another disadvantage of videotaping results if a friendly deponent whom you expect to provide strong testimony on your behalf doesn't testify as well as you'd hoped. For example, if your key witness looks nervous on camera or hesitates frequently before answering, you might be better off reading the testimony to a judge or jury at trial than showing the videotape of the witness testifying. (Hesitations and nervous mannerisms don't show up on a written transcript!) Conducting a predeposition video practice session (see Section D, below) can help you spot these problems ahead of time.

D. Taking an Effective Videotaped Deposition

The sections below assume that you're representing yourself and plan to videotape the deposition of a friendly witness. Following the suggestions may make your taping more effective.

1. Videotape the Practice Session

As explained in Chapter 10, you may be able to meet with a friendly witness in advance to prepare the witness for deposition questioning. At that time, you can conduct a "mock deposition" by asking the types of questions you intend to ask at the deposition. If the deposition will be videotaped, it's a good idea to videotape the mock deposition as well. Looking at the practice videotape will give you and the deponent a chance to correct visual "flaws" that are often unconscious but might damage the deponent's credibility. (And if, despite practice, the witness comes across as nervous or uncertain on camera, you might opt for traditional transcribing in lieu of videotaping.)

Example

Viewing the videotape of a practice deposition, you and the deponent notice that the deponent has a tendency to look up at the ceiling rather than directly into the camera, and to swivel back and forth in the chair. If repeated during the actual deposition, these mannerisms might hurt the deponent's credibility were the videotape to be shown at trial. Seeing these nervous mannerisms might help the deponent eliminate them.

2. Discuss What to Wear

How the deponent dresses matters more in a videotaped than in a transcribed deposition. Dressing "to the nines" isn't necessary. However, a deponent's manner of dress should at least reflect the fact that the witness takes the deposition seriously and respects the legal system. If the importance of the deposition merits it, you may follow the lead of some lawyers and consult a professional videographer about what type or color of clothing creates the most favorable impression on tape before advising a deponent on what to wear to the deposition.

3. Decide Upon "Production Values"

As any experienced viewer of amateur video-tapes knows, not all tapes are of equal quality. If you've requested that a deposition be video-taped and want the videotape to have maximum impact on a judge or jury, you want the picture and sound to be of good quality. Consistent with rules like FRCP 30(b)(4) (which forbids distortion of a deponent's or an attorney's appearance or demeanor through camera or sound recording techniques), you can ask the camera operator to arrange the scene to your liking. For example, you might want only the deponent shown in the picture. If two cameras are available, you may want a "split screen" showing you, the adversary's lawyer, and the deponent in the picture at the same time. Either setup would be proper (neither would create a rule-breaking "distortion").

Also, remember that in the typical deposition, at least three people need to be heard clearly—you, the deponent, and the opposing lawyer (or party). Check on the sound quality and make sure that at least these three people can be heard clearly on the tape. If multiple microphones will be used, ask the videographer to use a "sound mixer," which can individually control the volume of each speaker's microphone. Try to have the microphones positioned so as to avoid picking up background noise from incidental activity in or outside of the deposition room.

Proper lighting is also essential to a high-quality videotape. If the lighting is too dark, your friendly deponent may come across on camera as a bit sinister! Look at the picture before the deposition starts, and ask for better lighting if necessary.

The deponent may have a natural tendency to look at you when testifying. To help a friendly deponent establish "eye contact" with judges or jurors who might view the videotape, remind the deponent to look directly into the camera when answering your questions. The request will be easier for the deponent to carry out if the camera is set up in such a way that the deponent can easily move his or her head between you and the camera. (In "big" cases, some attorneys even pay for multiple cameras that allow for a variety of different camera angles. Changing from one angle to another from time to time makes a tape look more professional and may help maintain a judge's or jury's interest.) You might also ask the videographer to zoom in on critical documents or exhibits.

If your adversary raises any objections to your desired taping procedure, try to work out an agreed-upon procedure ahead of time and recite the agreement on the record at the start of the deposition. If you cannot work out an agreement, the deposition should continue subject to the adversary's objections. However, you may be prohibited from showing the videotape in court if a judge ultimately rules that your procedures distorted the deponent or your adversary. This is another reason to have a court reporter transcribe the deposition as a backup. (Note: Some of the options described above may not be available from the court reporting service you retain to videotape your deposition, or may be available only for higher fees.)

E. Defending a Videotaped Deposition

If you're a self-represented party defending a videotaped deposition of a friendly witness to be taken by your adversary, you'll want to make sure that the videotape in no way distorts the deponent's testimony. The following suggestions can help you achieve that goal.

1. Ask for a "Dry Run"

Before the deposition begins, ask your adversary to conduct a short off-the-record "dry run." To encourage your adversary to agree to a dry run, suggest that it can be very brief (a minute or two), and that it can be based upon questions totally unrelated to the dispute. By seeing and listening to the deponent as the deponent will appear on the videotape, you can make sure that the videotape presents the deponent fairly. If your adversary refuses your request for a dry run, note the refusal for the record once the videotape is rolling. However, the reality is that a judge is unlikely to forbid your adversary from

using a videotape simply because the adversary refused your request for a dry run.

If you have any objections to the lighting, sound, camera angles, zoom shots, use of multiple cameras, or any other taping procedures, try to resolve them before the deposition begins. If you cannot reach a satisfactory arrangement on these issues, state your objections at the start of the deposition, after the videotape has begun rolling. You can raise these same objections later if your adversary tries to use the videotape in connection with a motion or at trial. If you do not put these objections on the record at the start of the deposition, or as soon thereafter as you become aware of any objectionable procedures, a judge will probably rule that you have waived your right to object.

2. Display the Time and Date

Most recording equipment comes equipped with a switch that allows the videographer to display the date and the elapsed time of the deposition continuously in a corner of the picture. Ask the videographer to switch this on, so that you can easily identify any portions of the deposition that your adversary edits out of the finished tape.

Editing Videotaped Depositions for Use at Trial

Parties typically have to edit videotaped depositions before they are shown to judges or juries at trial. Editing is often necessary because some portions are redundant or inadmissible under trial evidence rules. For example, if a judge agrees with your objection that a portion of videotaped testimony is inadmissible hearsay, that portion of the tape would have to be deleted before the tape could be shown to the jury. Before the judge finally decides what portion of a videotape may be shown at trial, the party seeking to show the videotape has to provide the judge and the adversary with a transcript of the portion that the party seeks to show. (See FRCP 32(c). Either an "official" transcript or an unofficial copy made from the videotape suffices for this purpose.) If you think that your adversary's editing unfairly distorts the testimony (for example, leaves out explanations that qualify the portion that the adversary wants to show), you can ask that additional portions be shown. You would have to provide the judge and your adversary with a written transcript of these additional portions.

3. Avoid Mid-Questioning Conferences

It's generally improper for you to confer with a friendly deponent during deposition questioning. It is particularly important to avoid improper conferences in a videotaped deposition. A judge or juror who sees you conferring with a deponent may lose trust in the deponent's credibility. Also realize that with a videotape running, if you or the deponent whisper something embarrassing or damaging that would not be heard by a court reporter at a stenographically recorded deposition (and therefore would not become part of the transcript), it might be picked up by the microphone and become part of the videotape record. In short, if you need to confer with the deponent, be sure you take a formal break and that the tape is not rolling.

4. Take Regular Breaks

Request regular breaks (say, about five minutes per hour) to help a friendly deponent stay fresh and give complete and accurate testimony. The need for regular breaks is even more important in a videotaped deposition. If the judge and jury see the deponent visibly wilting as the deposition wears on, it could damage the deponent's credibility.

5. Prevent Improper Use of the Videotape

You or the deponent may be fearful that your adversary will attempt to use the videotape to embarrass or financially harm you or the deponent. For example, if a deponent's testimony concerns your business's trade secrets, you would not want any of your competitors gaining access to the videotape. In such a situation, ask your adversary to stipulate (agree) in writing not to make the videotape available to unauthorized parties. (Your adversary might be liable to you for any damages you suffer as a result of a breach of the agreement.)

If your adversary refuses to stipulate, you might have to seek a protective order from a judge that the tape not be shared with unauthorized persons. (For further discussion of protective orders, see Chapter 10.)

It may be a good idea to get a similar stipulation for the written deposition transcripts, however the risk of misuse may be higher with videotaped depositions. Videotapes are just as easily copied as transcripts, numerous people can view a single showing of a videotape, and disclosure of private information can be more damaging or embarrassing when it happens in a visual medium. ■

Glossary

Admonition. Preliminary matter that attorney usually reviews with deponent at the outset of a deposition. Typically, an admonition explains deposition procedures and demonstrates that a deponent understands "the rules of the game" and is in good physical and mental condition to testify.

Adverse witness. See "hostile witness."

Authentication. Evidence demonstrating that a document is genuine.

Coaching. Improper efforts to influence a deponent's answers.

Contempt of court. Violation of a judge's order, punishable by a fine or, in rare cases, imprisonment.

Court reporter. The person who officially presides over a deposition by swearing in the witness and recording and transcribing the testimony.

Credibility. Believability, either of a witness or of a witness's testimony.

Curing an objection. Eliciting additional evidence or rephrasing a question to overcome an adversary's objection to deposition testimony.

Defendant. The litigant from whom a plaintiff seeks money damages and/or other remedies.

Defending a deposition. A party's presence at a deposition taken by the adversary. A party defending a deposition can take notes on testimony, object to questions, and ask follow-up questions.

Deponent. A witness whose deposition is taken.

Deponent-centered question. Open-style question encouraging a deponent to describe events in the deponent's own words.

Deposition. Oral questioning under oath prior to trial, usually in an office setting.

Designated deponent procedure. Furnishing an organization with a list of topics and asking the organization to designate and make available for depositions the one or more representatives who are knowledgeable about those topics.

Discovery. The process by which parties to lawsuits can gather information from their adversaries and others by compelling them to answer questions and turn over documents before trial.

Expert. Witness with "specialized knowledge" who is retained to provide opinions about case-related issues that would be helpful to people who lack that specialized knowledge.

Federal Rules of Civil Procedure (FRCP). The rules that govern discovery and many other aspects of civil procedure in all federal court cases. Almost all states have identical or very similar discovery rules.

Forensic expert. Another name for an expert witness, signifying his or her task of translating specialized knowledge into testimony.

Friendly witness. A witness whose information supports a party's legal claims or defenses and who voluntarily discusses a case with that party.

Hearsay evidence. Oral or written assertion made by someone other than the deponent, when offered to prove the accuracy of the assertions. Though hearsay evidence is often inadmissible at trial, it is normally proper to ask deponents to testify to hearsay at depositions.

Hostile witness. A witness whose testimony is adverse to a party and who usually will not agree to discuss a case voluntarily with the party.

Impeachment. Evidence offered to attack a witness's credibility.

Incurable objection. Objection that is preserved for trial even if it is not made at deposition.

Informal discovery. Seeking information from a witness who voluntarily agrees to provide it.

Interested nonparty witness. A person who is neither a plaintiff nor a defendant but who has an emotional or financial stake in a case's outcome.

Interrogatories. Written questions sent by one party to the opposing party, who must provide written answers under oath, generally within 30 days. Parties may not serve interrogatories on nonparty witnesses.

Lay witness. Ordinary, "percipient," nonexpert witness; a person who saw, heard, or otherwise has firsthand knowledge about the dispute.

Leading question. A question that either by its wording or through the questioner's tone of voice suggests the answer the deponent should give.

Leapfrog questioning. Questions that rapidly shift from one topic to another, without regard to chronology.

Litigant. A party to a legal case, usually called a "plaintiff" or a "defendant."

Litigation. The process for resolving legal disputes, from initial complaint through final appeal.

Meet and confer. A discussion between parties seeking to resolve a dispute about discovery procedures. Laws in most jurisdictions require parties to meet and confer before seeking relief in court.

Motion. A formal request for a legal ruling.

Nonparty witness. Individual who has information relevant to a lawsuit and whom parties can compel to attend and testify at depositions and to turn over documents for inspection and copying, but who has no formal involvement in a lawsuit.

Objection. A claim that a rule of evidence such as the hearsay rule would make testimony or a document inadmissible at trial.

Offer into evidence. Ask a judge to rule that testimony or a tangible exhibit is an official part of the trial record and can be considered when arriving at a verdict.

Party. An individual or entity (corporation, partnership, and the like) named as the plaintiff or defendant in a lawsuit.

Perjury. A lie under oath concerning a material (important) matter.

Perpetuating testimony. Deposing a friendly witness who is likely to be unavailable to testify if a case goes to trial.

Plaintiff. The litigant who initiates a legal dispute.

Preserved objection. Objection that may be made at trial even if it is not made at deposition.

Primary material. The text of actual law.

Privilege against self-incrimination. The constitutional right of a person to refuse to answer questions when those answers might be used against the person in a criminal prosecution.

Privileged information. Information that parties and persons do not have to reveal in a lawsuit; includes certain private and confidential information, such as attorney-client communications.

Pro se party (or litigant). A party who is self-represented. In civil cases, all parties (both plaintiffs and defendants) have the right to represent themselves.

Protective order. Order that a judge may make to protect any party or person from "annoyance, embarrassment, oppression, or undue burden or expense."

Quash a subpoena. A judge's order that a subpoena is invalid.

Questioner-centered question. Narrow-style question seeking specific pieces of information by including most of the factual information in the question.

The record. The transcript or videotape of everything that occurred "on the record" during a deposition. "The record" does not include conversations or events that take place during the time that the deposing party has asked the court stenographer or videotape operator to go "off the record."

Request for Admissions. Written request that one party sends to the opposing party, asking the recipient to admit the accuracy of certain documents or the truth of certain stated facts.

Request for Production of Documents. Written demand sent by one party to the opposing party to compel the inspection, copying, and/or testing of records, documents, and tangible objects in the opposing party's possession. Like Interrogatories, a Request for Production of Documents can be sent only to opposing parties, not to nonparty witnesses.

Sanction. Penalty a judge can impose on a party (or a party's attorney) for violation of discovery rules, ranging from a monetary fine to dismissal of the lawsuit.

Secondary material. Court opinions and books that interpret or explain legal rules (the "primary materials").

Speaking objection. Improper form of objection that, instead of simply identifying an evidence rule violation, includes a more extensive legal argument.

Stipulation. Agreement between parties that may be placed on the record of a deposition.

Subpoena. Court order served by a party on a nonparty witness compelling the production, inspection, and copying of documents and records in the witness's possession. A "Subpoena re Deposition" orders a witness to attend a deposition. A "Subpoena Duces Tecum re Depo-

sition" orders a witness to attend a deposition with the documents, records, or tangible items described in the subpoena.

Summary judgment motion. A written motion in court asking a judge to terminate a lawsuit short of trial.

Voluntary disclosure. Information that a party must disclose to an adversary without waiting for the adversary to ask for it.

Work product. A lawyer's or self-represented party's trial preparation materials; usually these do not have to be disclosed to an adversary. ■

Appendix 1

Excerpts From the Federal Rules of Civil Procedure (FRCP)

Section V: Depositions and Discovery

Rule 26. General Provisions Governing Discovery; Duty of Disclosure

(a) Required Disclosures; Methods to Discover Additional Matter.

(1) Initial Disclosures.

Except in categories of proceedings specified in Rule 26(a)(1)(E), or to the extent otherwise stipulated or directed by order, a party must, without awaiting a discovery request, provide to other parties:

(A) the name and, if known, the address and telephone number of each individual likely to have discoverable information that the disclosing party may use to support its claims or defenses, unless solely for impeachment, identifying the subjects of the information;

(B) a copy of, or a description by category and location of, all documents, data compilations, and tangible things that are in the posses-

sion, custody, or control of the party and that the disclosing party may use to support its claims or defenses, unless solely for impeachment;

(C) a computation of any category of damages claimed by the disclosing party, making available for inspection and copying as under Rule 34 the documents or other evidentiary material, not privileged or protected from disclosure, on which such computation is based, including materials bearing on the nature and extent of injuries suffered; and

(D) for inspection and copying as under Rule 34 any insurance agreement under which any person carrying on an insurance business may be liable to satisfy part or all of a judgment which may be entered in the action or to indemnify or reimburse for payments made to satisfy the judgment.

(E) The following categories of proceedings are exempt from initial disclosure under Rule 26(a)(1):

(i) an action for review on an administrative record;

(ii) a petition for habeas corpus or other proceeding to challenge a criminal conviction or sentence;

(iii) an action brought without counsel by a person in custody of the United States, a state, or a state subdivision;

(iv) an action to enforce or quash an administrative summons or subpoena;

(v) an action by the United States to recover benefit payments;

(vi) an action by the United States to collect on a student loan guaranteed by the United States;

(vii) a proceeding ancillary to proceedings in other courts; and

(viii) an action to enforce an arbitration award.

These disclosures must be made at or within 14 days after the Rule 26(f) conference unless a different time is set by stipulation or court order, or unless a party objects during the conference that initial disclosures are not appropriate in the circumstances of the action and states the objection in the Rule 26(f) discovery plan. In ruling on the objection, the court must determine what disclosures—if any—are to be made, and set the time for disclosure. Any party first served or otherwise joined after the Rule 26(f) conference must make these disclosures within 30 days after being served or joined unless a different time is set by stipulation or court

order. A party must make its initial disclosures based on the information then reasonably available to it and is not excused from making its disclosures because it has not fully completed its investigation of the case or because it challenges the sufficiency of another party's disclosures or because another party has not made its disclosures.

(2) Disclosure of Expert Testimony.

(A) In addition to the disclosures required by paragraph (1), a party shall disclose to other parties the identity of any person who may be used at trial to present evidence under Rules 702, 703, or 705 of the Federal Rules of Evidence.

(B) Except as otherwise stipulated or directed by the court, this disclosure shall, with respect to a witness who is retained or specially employed to provide expert testimony in the case or whose duties as an employee of the party regularly involve giving expert testimony, be accompanied by a written report prepared and signed by the witness. The report shall contain a complete statement of all opinions to be expressed and the basis and reasons therefor; the data or other information considered by the witness in forming the opinions; any exhibits to be used as a summary of or support for the opinions; the qualifications of the witness, including a list of all publications authored by the witness within the preceding ten years; the compensation to be paid for the study and testimony; and a listing of any other cases in which the witness has testified as an expert at trial or by deposition within the preceding four years.

(C) These disclosures shall be made at the times and in the sequence directed by the court. In the absence of other directions from the court or stipulation by the parties, the disclosures shall be made at least 90 days before the trial date or the date the case is to be ready for trial or, if the evidence is intended solely to contradict or rebut evidence on the same subject matter identified by another party under paragraph (2)(B), within 30 days after the disclosure made by the other party. The parties shall supplement these disclosures when required under subdivision (e)(1).

(3) Pretrial Disclosures.

In addition to the disclosures required by Rule 26(a)(1) and (2), a party must provide to other parties and promptly file with the court the following information regarding the evidence that it may present at trial other than solely for impeachment:

(A) the name and, if not previously provided, the address and telephone number of each witness, separately identifying those whom the party expects to present and those whom the party may call if the need arises;

(B) the designation of those witnesses whose testimony is expected to be presented by means of a deposition and, if not taken stenographically, a transcript of the pertinent portions of the deposition testimony; and

(C) an appropriate identification of each document or other exhibit, including summaries of other evidence, separately identifying those which the party expects to offer and those which the party may offer if the need arises.

Unless otherwise directed by the court, these disclosures shall be made at least 30 days before trial. Within 14 days thereafter, unless a different time is specified by the court, a party may serve and file a list disclosing (i) any objections to the use under Rule 32(a) of a deposition designated by another party under Rule 26(a)(3)(B), and (ii) any objection, together with the grounds therefor, that may be made to the admissibility of materials identified under Rule 26(a)(3)(C). Objections not so disclosed, other than objections under Rules 402 and 403 of the Federal Rules of Evidence, are waived unless excused by the court for good cause.

(4) Form of Disclosures.

Unless the court orders otherwise, all disclosures under Rules 26(a)(1) through (3) must be made in writing, signed and served.

(5) Methods to Discover Additional Matter.

Parties may obtain discovery by one or more of the following methods: depositions upon oral examination or written questions; written interrogatories; production of documents or things or permission to enter upon land or other property under Rule 34 or 45(a)(1)(C), for inspection and other purposes; physical and mental examinations; and requests for admission.

(b) Discovery Scope and Limits.

Unless otherwise limited by order of the court in accordance with these rules, the scope of discovery is as follows:

(1) In General.

Parties may obtain discovery regarding any matter, not privileged, that is relevant to the claim or defense of the any party, including the existence, description, nature, custody, condition, and location of any books, documents, or other tangible things and the identity and location of persons having knowledge of any discoverable matter. For good cause, the court may order discovery of any matter relevant to the subject matter involved in the action. Relevant information need not be admissible at trial if the discovery appears reasonably calculated to lead to the discovery of admissible evidence. All discovery is subject to the limitations imposed by Rule 26(b)(2)(i), (ii), and (iii).

(2) Limitations.

By order, the court may alter the limits in these rules on the number of depositions and interrogatories or the length of depositions under Rule 30. By order or local rule, the court may also limit the number of requests under Rule 36. The frequency or extent of use of the discovery methods otherwise permitted under these rules and by any local rule shall be limited by the court if it determines that: (i) the discovery sought is unreasonably cumulative or duplicative, or is obtainable from some other source that is more convenient, less burdensome, or less expensive; (ii) the party seeking discovery has had ample opportunity by discovery in the action to obtain the information sought; or (iii) the burden or expense of the proposed discovery outweighs its likely benefit, taking into account the needs of the case, the amount in controversy, the parties' resources, the importance of the issues at stake in the litigation, and the importance of the proposed discovery in resolving the issues. The court may act upon its own initiative after reasonable notice or pursuant to a motion under subdivision (c).

(3) Trial Preparation: Materials.

Subject to the provisions of subdivision (b)(4) of this rule, a party may obtain discovery of documents and tangible things otherwise discoverable under subdivision (b)(1) of this rule and prepared in anticipation of litigation or for trial by or for another party or by or for that other party's representative (including the other party's attorney, consultant, surety, indemnitor, insurer, or agent) only upon a showing that the party seeking discovery has substantial need of the materials in the preparation of the party's case and that the party is unable without undue hardship to obtain the substantial equivalent of the materials by other means. In ordering discovery of such materials when the required showing has been made, the court shall protect against disclosure of the mental impressions, conclusions, opinions, or legal theories of an attorney or other representative of a party concerning the litigation.

A party may obtain without the required showing a statement concerning the action or its subject matter previously made by that party. Upon request, a person not a party may obtain without the required showing a statement concerning the action or its subject matter previously made by that person. If the request is refused, the person may move for a court order. The provisions of Rule 37(a)(4) apply to the award of expenses incurred in relation to the motion. For purposes of this paragraph, a statement previously made is (A) a written statement signed or otherwise adopted or approved by the person making it, or (B) a stenographic, mechanical, electrical, or other recording, or a transcription thereof, which is a substantially verbatim recital of an oral statement by the person making it and contemporaneously recorded.

(4) Trial Preparation: Experts.

(A) A party may depose any person who has been identified as an expert whose opinions may be presented at trial. If a report from the expert is required under subdivision (a)(2)(B), the deposition shall not be conducted until after the report is provided.

(B) A party may, through interrogatories or by deposition, discover facts known or opinions held by an expert who has been retained or specially employed by another party in anticipation of litigation or preparation for trial and who is not expected to be called as a witness at trial, only as provided in Rule 35(b) or upon a showing of exceptional circumstances under which it is impracticable for the party seeking discovery

to obtain facts or opinions on the same subject by other means.

(C) Unless manifest injustice would result, (i) the court shall require that the party seeking discovery pay the expert a reasonable fee for time spent in responding to discovery under this subdivision; and (ii) with respect to discovery obtained under subdivision (b)(4)(B) of this rule the court shall require the party seeking discovery to pay the other party a fair portion of the fees and expenses reasonably incurred by the latter party in obtaining facts and opinions from the expert.

(5) Claims of Privilege or Protection of Trial Preparation Materials.

When a party withholds information otherwise discoverable under these rules by claiming that it is privileged or subject to protection as trial preparation material, the party shall make the claim expressly and shall describe the nature of the documents, communications, or things not produced or disclosed in a manner that, without revealing information itself privileged or protected, will enable other parties to assess the applicability of the privilege or protection.

(c) Protective Orders.

Upon motion by a party or by the person from whom discovery is sought, accompanied by a certification that the movant has in good faith conferred or attempted to confer with other affected parties in an effort to resolve the dispute without court action, and for good cause shown, the court in which the action is pending or alternatively, on matters relating to a deposition, the court in the district where the deposition is to be taken may make any order which justice requires to protect a party or person from annoyance, embarrassment, oppression, or undue burden or expense, including one or more of the following:

(1) that the disclosure or discovery not be had;

(2) that the disclosure or discovery may be had only on specified terms and conditions, including a designation of the time or place;

(3) that the discovery may be had only by a method of discovery other than that selected by the party seeking discovery;

(4) that certain matters not be inquired into, or that the scope of the disclosure or discovery be limited to certain matters;

(5) that discovery be conducted with no one present except persons designated by the court;

(6) that a deposition, after being sealed, be opened only by order of the court;

(7) that a trade secret or other confidential research, development, or commercial information not be revealed or be revealed only in a designated way; and

(8) that the parties simultaneously file specified documents or information enclosed in sealed envelopes to be opened as directed by the court.

If the motion for a protective order is denied in whole or in part, the court may, on such terms and conditions as are just, order that any party or other person provide or permit discovery. The provisions of Rule 37(a)(4) apply to the award of expenses incurred in relation to the motion.

(d) Timing and Sequence of Discovery.

Except in categories of proceeding exempted from initial disclosure under Rule 26(a)(1)(E), or when authorized under these rules or by order or agreement of the parties, a party may not seek discovery from any source before the parties have met and conferred as required by Rule 26(f). Unless the court upon motion, for the convenience of parties and witnesses and in the interests of justice, orders otherwise, methods of discovery may be used in any sequence, and the fact that a party is conducting discovery, whether by deposition or otherwise, shall not operate to delay any other party's discovery.

(e) Supplementation of Disclosures and Responses.

A party who has made a disclosure under subdivision (a) or responded to a request for discovery with a disclosure or response is under a duty to supplement or correct the disclosure or response to include information thereafter acquired if ordered by the court or in the following circumstances:

(1) A party is under a duty to supplement at appropriate intervals its disclosures under

subdivision (a) if the party learns that in some material respect the information disclosed is incomplete or incorrect and if the additional or corrective information has not otherwise been made known to the other parties during the discovery process or in writing. With respect to testimony of an expert from whom a report is required under subdivision (a)(2)(B) the duty extends both to information contained in the report and to information provided through a deposition of the expert, and any additions or other changes to this information shall be disclosed by the time the party's disclosures under Rule 26(a)(3) are due.

(2) A party is under a duty seasonably to amend a prior response to an interrogatory, request for production, or request for admission if the party learns that the response is in some material respect incomplete or incorrect and if the additional or corrective information has not otherwise been made known to the other parties during the discovery process or in writing.

(f) Conference of Parties; Planning for Discovery.

Except in categories of proceedings exempted from initial disclosure under Rule 26(a)(1)(E) or when otherwise ordered, the parties must, as soon as practicable and in any event at least 21 days before a scheduling conference is held or a scheduling order is due under Rule 16(b), confer to consider the nature and basis of their claims and defenses and the possibilities for a prompt settlement or resolution of the case, to make or arrange for the disclosures required by Rule 26(a)(1), and to develop a proposed discovery plan that indicates the parties' views and proposals concerning:

(1) what changes should be made in the timing, form, or requirement for disclosures under Rule 26(a), including a statement as to when disclosures under Rule 26(a)(1) were made or will be made;

(2) the subjects on which discovery may be needed, when discovery should be completed, and whether discovery should be conducted in phases or be limited to or focused upon particular issues;

(3) what changes should be made in the limitations on discovery imposed under these rules or by local rule, and what other limitations should be imposed; and

(4) any other orders that should be entered by the court under Rule 26(c) or under Rule 16(b) and (c).

The attorneys of record and all unrepresented parties that have appeared in the case are jointly responsible for arranging the conference, for attempting in good faith to agree on the proposed discovery plan, and for submitting to the court within 14 days after the conference a written report outlining the plan.

A court may order that the parties or attorneys attend the conference in person. If necessary to comply with its expedited schedule for Rule 16(b) conferences, a court may by local rule (i) require that the conference between the parties occur fewer than 21 days before the scheduling conference is held or a scheduling order is due under Rule 16(b), and (ii) require that the written report outlining the discovery plan be filed fewer than 14 days after the conference between the parties, or excuse the parties from submitting a written report and permit them to report orally on their discovery plan at the Rule 16(b) conference.

(g) Signing of Disclosures, Discovery Requests, Responses, and Objections.

(1) Every disclosure made pursuant to subdivision (a)(1) or subdivision (a)(3) shall be signed by at least one attorney of record in the attorney's individual name, whose address shall be stated. An unrepresented party shall sign the disclosure and state the party's address. The signature of the attorney or party constitutes a certification that to the best of the signer's knowledge, information, and belief, formed after a reasonable inquiry, the disclosure is complete and correct as of the time it is made.

(2) Every discovery request, response, or objection made by a party represented by an attorney shall be signed by at least one attorney of record in the attorney's individual name, whose address shall be stated. An unrepresented party shall sign the request, response, or objection and state the party's address. The signature of the attorney or party constitutes a certification that to the best of the signer's knowledge, information, and belief, formed after a reasonable inquiry, the request, response, or objection is:

(A) consistent with these rules and warranted by existing law or a good faith argument for the extension, modification, or reversal of existing law;

(B) not interposed for any improper purpose, such as to harass or to cause unnecessary delay or needless increase in the cost of litigation; and

(C) not unreasonable or unduly burdensome or expensive, given the needs of the case, the discovery already had in the case, the amount in controversy, and the importance of the issues at stake in the litigation.

If a request, response, or objection is not signed, it shall be stricken unless it is signed promptly after the omission is called to the attention of the party making the request, response, or objection, and a party shall not be obligated to take any action with respect to it until it is signed.

(3) If without substantial justification a certification is made in violation of the rule, the court, upon motion or upon its own initiative, shall impose upon the person who made the certification, the party on whose behalf the disclosure, request, response, or objection is made, or both, an appropriate sanction, which may include an order to pay the amount of the reasonable expenses incurred because of the violation, including a reasonable attorney's fee.

Rule 27. Depositions Before Action or Pending Appeal

(a) Before Action.

(1) Petition.

A person who desires to perpetuate testimony regarding any matter that may be cognizable in any court of the United States may file a verified petition in the United States district court in the district of the residence of any expected adverse party. The petition shall be entitled in the name of the petitioner and shall show: 1, that the petitioner expects to be a party to an action cognizable in a court of the United States but is presently unable to bring it or cause it to be brought; 2, the subject matter of the expected action and the petitioner's interest therein; 3, the facts which the petitioner desires to establish by the proposed testimony and the reasons for desiring to perpetuate it; 4, the names or a description of the persons the petitioner expects will be adverse parties and their addresses so far as known; and 5, the names and addresses of the persons to be examined and the substance of the testimony which the petitioner expects to elicit from each, and shall ask for an order authorizing the petitioner to take the depositions of the persons to be examined named in the petition, for the purpose of perpetuating their testimony.

(2) Notice and Service.

The petitioner shall thereafter serve a notice upon each person named in the petition as an expected adverse party, together with a copy of the petition, stating that the petitioner will apply to the court, at a time and place named therein, for the order described in the petition. At least 20 days before the date of hearing the notice shall be served either within or without the district or state in the manner provided in Rule 4(d) for service of summons; but if such service cannot with due diligence be made upon any expected adverse party named in the petition, the court may make such order as is just for service by publication or otherwise, and shall appoint, for persons not served in the manner provided in Rule 4(d), an attorney who shall represent them, and, in case they are not otherwise represented, shall cross-examine the deponent. If any expected adverse party is a minor or incompetent the provisions of Rule 17(c) apply.

(3) Order and Examination.

If the court is satisfied that the perpetuation of the testimony may prevent a failure or delay of justice, it shall make an order designating or describing the persons whose depositions may be taken and specifying the subject matter of the examination and whether the depositions shall be taken upon oral examination or written interrogatories.

The depositions may then be taken in accordance with these rules; and the court may make orders of the character provided for by Rules 34 and 35. For the purpose of applying these rules to depositions for perpetuating testimony, each reference therein to the court in which the action is pending shall be deemed to refer to the court in which the petition for such deposition was filed.

(4) Use of Deposition.

If a deposition to perpetuate testimony is taken under these rules or if, although not so taken, it would be admissible in evidence in the courts of the state in which it is taken, it may be used in any action involving the same subject matter subsequently brought in a United States district court, in accordance with the provisions of Rule 32(a).

(b) Pending Appeal.

If an appeal has been taken from a judgment of a district court or before the taking of an appeal if the time therefor has not expired, the district court in which the judgment was rendered may allow the taking of the depositions of witnesses to perpetuate their testimony for use in the event of further proceedings in the district court. In such case the party who desires to perpetuate the testimony may make a motion in the district court for leave to take the depositions, upon the same notice and service thereof as if the action was pending in the district court. The motion shall show (1) the names and addresses of persons to be examined and the substance of the testimony which the party expects to elicit from each; (2) the reasons for perpetuating their testimony. If the court finds that the perpetuation of the testimony is proper to avoid a failure or delay of justice, it may make an order allowing the depositions to be taken and may make orders of the character provided for by Rules 34 and 35, and thereupon the depositions may be taken and used in the same manner and under the same conditions as are prescribed in these rules for depositions taken in actions pending in the district court.

(c) Perpetuation by Action.

This rule does not limit the power of a court to entertain an action to perpetuate testimony.

Rule 28. Persons Before Whom Depositions May Be Taken

(a) Within the United States.

Within the United States or within a territory or insular possession subject to the jurisdiction of the United States, depositions shall be taken before an officer authorized to administer oaths by the laws of the United States or of the place where the examination is held, or before a person appointed by the court in which the action is pending.

A person so appointed has power to administer oaths and take testimony. The term officer as used in Rules 30, 31, and 32 includes a person appointed by the court or designated by the parties under Rule 29.

(b) In Foreign Countries.

Depositions may be taken in a foreign country (1) pursuant to any applicable treaty or convention, or (2) pursuant to a letter of request (whether or not captioned a letter rogatory), or (3) on notice before a person authorized to administer oaths in the place where the examination is held, either by the law thereof or by the law of the United States, or (4) before a person commissioned by the court, and a person so commissioned shall have the power by virtue of the commission to administer any necessary oath and take testimony. A commission or a letter of request shall be issued on application and notice and on terms that are just and appropriate. It is not requisite to the issuance of a commission or a letter of request that the taking of the deposition in any other manner is impracticable or inconvenient; and both a commission and a letter of request may be issued in proper cases. A notice or commission may designate the person before whom the deposition is to be taken either by name or descriptive title. A letter of request may be addressed "To the Appropriate Authority in [here name the country]." When a letter of request or any other device is used pursuant to any applicable treaty or convention, it shall be captioned in the form prescribed by that treaty or convention. Evidence obtained in response to a letter of request need not be excluded merely because it is not a verbatim transcript, because the testimony was not taken under oath, or because of any similar departure from the requirements for depositions taken within the United States under these rules.

(c) Disqualification for Interest.

No deposition shall be taken before a person who is a relative or employee or attorney or counsel of any of the parties, or is a relative or employee of such attorney or counsel, or is financially interested in the action.

Rule 29. Stipulations Regarding Discovery Procedure

Unless otherwise directed by the court, the parties may by written stipulation (1) provide that depositions may be taken before any person, at any time or place, upon any notice, and in any manner and when so taken may be used like other depositions, and (2) modify other procedures governing or limitations placed upon discovery, except that stipulations extending the time provided in Rules 33, 34, and 36 for responses to discovery may, if they would interfere with any time set for completion of discovery, for hearing of a motion, or for trial, be made only with the approval of the court.

Rule 30. Depositions Upon Oral Examination

(a) When Depositions May Be Taken; When Leave Required.

(1) A party may take the testimony of any person, including a party, by deposition upon oral examination without leave of court except as provided in paragraph (2). The attendance of witnesses may be compelled by subpoena as provided in Rule 45.

(2) A party must obtain leave of court, which shall be granted to the extent consistent with the principles stated in Rule 26(b)(2), if the person to be examined is confined in prison or if, without the written stipulation of the parties:

(A) a proposed deposition would result in more than ten depositions being taken under this rule or Rule 31 by the plaintiffs, or by the defendants, or by third-party defendants;

(B) the person to be examined already has been deposed in the case; or

(C) a party seeks to take a deposition before the time specified in Rule 26(d) unless the notice contains a certification, with supporting facts, that the person to be examined is expected to leave the United States and be unavailable for examination in this country unless deposed before that time.

(b) Notice of Examination: General Requirements; Method of Recording; Production of Documents and Things; Deposition of Organization; Deposition by Telephone.

(1) A party desiring to take the deposition of any person upon oral examination shall give reasonable notice in writing to every other party to the action. The notice shall state the time and place for taking the deposition and the name and address of each person to be examined, if known, and, if the name is not known, a general description sufficient to identify the person or the particular class or group to which the person belongs. If a subpoena duces tecum is to be served on the person to be examined, the designation of the materials to be produced as set forth in the subpoena shall be attached to, or included in, the notice.

(2) The party taking the deposition shall state in the notice the method by which the testimony shall be recorded. Unless the court orders otherwise, it may be recorded by sound, sound-and-visual, or stenographic means, and the party taking the deposition shall bear the cost of the recording. Any party may arrange for a transcription to be made from the recording of a deposition taken by nonstenographic means.

(3) With prior notice to the deponent and other parties, any party may designate another method to record the deponent's testimony in addition to the method specified by the person taking the deposition. The additional record or transcript shall be made at that party's expense unless the court otherwise orders.

(4) Unless otherwise agreed by the parties, a deposition shall be conducted before an officer appointed or designated under Rule 28 and shall begin with a statement on the record by the officer that includes (A) the officer's name and business address; (B) the date, time, and place of the deposition; (C) the name of the deponent; (D) the administration of the oath or affirmation to the deponent; and (E) an identification of all persons present. If the deposition is recorded other than stenographically, the officer shall repeat items (A) through (C) at the beginning of each unit of recorded tape or other recording medium. The appearance or demeanor of deponents or attorneys shall not be distorted through camera or sound-recording techniques. At the end of the deposition, the officer shall state on the record that the deposition is complete and shall set forth any stipulations made by counsel concerning the custody of the tran-

script or recording and the exhibits, or concerning other pertinent matters.

(5) The notice to a party deponent may be accompanied by a request made in compliance with Rule 34 for the production of documents and tangible things at the taking of the deposition. The procedure of Rule 34 shall apply to the request.

(6) A party may in the party's notice and in a subpoena name as the deponent a public or private corporation or a partnership or association or governmental agency and describe with reasonable particularity the matters on which examination is requested. In that event, the organization so named shall designate one or more officers, directors, or managing agents, or other persons who consent to testify on its behalf, and may set forth, for each person designated, the matters on which the person will testify. A subpoena shall advise a non-party organization of its duty to make such a designation. The persons so designated shall testify as to matters known or reasonably available to the organization. This subdivision (b)(6) does not preclude taking a deposition by any other procedure authorized in these rules.

(7) The parties may stipulate in writing or the court may upon motion order that a deposition be taken by telephone or other remote electronic means. For the purposes of this rule and Rules 28(a), 37(a)(1), and 37(b)(1), a deposition taken by such means is taken in the district and at the place where the deponent is to answer questions.

(c) Examination and Cross-Examination; Record of Examination; Oath; Objections.

Examination and cross-examination of witnesses may proceed as permitted at the trial under the provisions of the Federal Rules of Evidence except Rules 103 and 615. The officer before whom the deposition is to be taken shall put the witness on oath or affirmation and shall personally, or by someone acting under the officer's direction and in the officer's presence, record the testimony of the witness. The testimony shall be taken stenographically or recorded by any other method authorized by subdivision (b)(2) of this rule. All objections made at the time of the examination to the qualifications of the officer taking the deposition, to the manner of taking it, to the evidence presented, to the conduct of any party, or to any other aspect of the proceedings shall be noted by the officer upon the record of the deposition; but the examination shall proceed, with the testimony being taken subject to the objections. In lieu of participating in the oral examination, parties may serve written questions in a sealed envelope on the party taking the deposition and the party taking the deposition shall transmit them to the officer, who shall propound them to the witness and record the answers verbatim.

(d) Schedule and Duration; Motion to Terminate or Limit Examination.

(1) Any objection during a deposition shall be stated concisely and in a non-argumentative and non-suggestive manner. A party may instruct a deponent not to answer only when

necessary to preserve a privilege, to enforce a limitation directed by the court, or to present a motion under Rule 30(d)(4).

(2) Unless otherwise authorized by the court or stipulated by the parties, a deposition is limited to one day of seven hours. The court must allow additional time consistent with Rule 26(b)(2) if needed for a fair examination of the deponent or if the deponent or another person, or other circumstance, impedes or delays the examination.

(3) If the court finds that any impediment, delay, or other conduct has frustrated the fair examination of the deponent, it may impose upon the persons responsible an appropriate sanction, including the reasonable costs and attorney's fees incurred by any parties as a result thereof.

(4) At any time during a deposition, on motion of a party or of the deponent and upon a showing that the examination is being conducted in bad faith or in such manner as unreasonably to annoy, embarrass, or oppress the deponent or party, the court in which the action is pending or the court in the district where the deposition is being taken may order the officer conducting the examination to cease forthwith from taking the deposition, or may limit the scope and manner of the taking of the deposition as provided in Rule 26(c). If the order made terminates the examination, it may be resumed thereafter only upon the order of the court in which the action is pending. Upon demand of the objecting party or deponent, the taking of the deposition shall be suspended for the time necessary to make a motion for an order. The provisions of Rule 37(a)(4) apply to the award of expenses incurred in relation to the motion.

(e) Review by Witness; Changes; Signing.

If requested by the deponent or a party before completion of the deposition, the deponent shall have 30 days after being notified by the officer that the transcript or recording is available in which to review the transcript or recording and, if there are changes in form or substance, to sign a statement reciting such changes and the reasons given by the deponent for making them. The officer shall indicate in the certificate prescribed by subdivision (f)(1) whether any review was requested and, if so, shall append any changes made by the deponent during the period allowed.

(f) Certification and Delivery by Officer; Exhibits; Copies.

(1) The officer must certify that the witness was duly sworn by the officer and that the deposition is a true record of the testimony given by the witness. This certificate must be in writing and accompany the record of the deposition. Unless otherwise ordered by the court, the officer must securely seal the deposition in an envelope or package indorsed with the title of the action and marked 'Deposition of [here insert name of witness]' and must promptly send it to the attorney who arranged for the transcript or proceeding, who must store it under conditions that will protect it against loss, destruction, tampering, or deterioration. Documents and

things produced for inspection during the examination of the witness, must upon the request of a party, be marked for identification and annexed to the deposition and may be inspected and copied by any party, except that if the person producing the materials desires to retain them the person may (A) offer copies to be marked for identification and annexed to the deposition and to serve thereafter as originals if the person affords to all parties fair opportunity to verify the copies by comparison with the originals, or (B) offer the originals to be marked for identification, after giving to each party an opportunity to inspect and copy them, in which event the materials may then be used in the same manner as if annexed to the deposition. Any party may move for an order that the original be annexed to and returned with the deposition to the court, pending final disposition of the case.

(2) Unless otherwise ordered by the court or agreed by the parties, the officer shall retain stenographic notes of any deposition taken stenographically or a copy of the recording of any deposition taken by another method. Upon payment of reasonable charges therefor, the officer shall furnish a copy of the transcript or other recording of the deposition to any party or to the deponent.

(3) The party taking the deposition shall give prompt notice of its filing to all other parties.

(g) Failure to Attend or to Serve Subpoena; Expenses.

(1) If the party giving the notice of the taking of a deposition fails to attend and proceed therewith and another party attends in person or by attorney pursuant to the notice, the court may order the party giving the notice to pay to such other party the reasonable expenses incurred by that party and that party's attorney in attending, including reasonable attorney's fees.

(2) If the party giving the notice of the taking of a deposition of a witness fails to serve a subpoena upon the witness and the witness because of such failure does not attend, and if another party attends in person or by attorney because that party expects the deposition of that witness to be taken, the court may order the party giving the notice to pay to such other party the reasonable expenses incurred by that party and that party's attorney in attending, including reasonable attorney's fees.

Rule 32. Use of Depositions in Court Proceedings

(a) Use of Depositions.

At the trial or upon the hearing of a motion or an interlocutory proceeding, any part or all of a deposition, so far as admissible under the rules of evidence applied as though the witness were then present and testifying, may be used against any party who was present or represented at the taking of the deposition or who had reasonable notice thereof, in accordance with any of the following provisions:

(1) Any deposition may be used by any party for the purpose of contradicting or im-

peaching the testimony of deponent as a witness, or for any other purpose permitted by the Federal Rules of Evidence.

(2) The deposition of a party or of anyone who at the time of taking the deposition was an officer, director, or managing agent, or a person designated under Rule 30(b)(6) or 31(a) to testify on behalf of a public or private corporation, partnership or association or governmental agency which is a party may be used by an adverse party for any purpose.

(3) The deposition of a witness, whether or not a party, may be used by any party for any purpose if the court finds:

(A) that the witness is dead; or

(B) that the witness is at a greater distance than 100 miles from the place of trial or hearing, or is out of the United States, unless it appears that the absence of the witness was procured by the party offering the deposition; or

(C) that the witness is unable to attend or testify because of age, illness, infirmity, or imprisonment; or

(D) that the party offering the deposition has been unable to procure the attendance of the witness by subpoena; or

(E) upon application and notice, that such exceptional circumstances exist as to make it desirable, in the interest of justice and with due regard to the importance of presenting the testimony of witnesses orally in open court, to allow the deposition to be used.

A deposition taken without leave of court pursuant to a notice under Rule 30(a)(2)(C)

shall not be used against a party who demonstrates that, when served with the notice, it was unable through the exercise of diligence to obtain counsel to represent it at the taking of the deposition; nor shall a deposition be used against a party who, having received less than 11 days notice of a deposition, has promptly upon receiving such notice filed a motion for a protective order under Rule 26(c)(2) requesting that the deposition not be held or be held at a different time or place and such motion is pending at the time the deposition is held.

(4) If only part of a deposition is offered in evidence by a party, an adverse party may require the offeror to introduce any other part which ought in fairness to be considered with the part introduced, and any party may introduce any other parts.

Substitution of parties pursuant to Rule 25 does not affect the right to use depositions previously taken; and, when an action has been brought in any court of the United States or of any State and another action involving the same subject matter is afterward brought between the same parties or their representatives or successors in interest, all depositions lawfully taken and duly filed in the former action may be used in the latter as if originally taken therefor. A deposition previously taken may also be used as permitted by the Federal Rules of Evidence.

(b) Objections to Admissibility.

Subject to the provisions of Rule 28(b) and subdivision (d)(3) of this rule, objection may be made at the trial or hearing to receiving in evidence any deposition or part thereof for any reason which would require the exclusion of the evidence if the witness were then present and testifying.

(c) Form of Presentation.

Except as otherwise directed by the court, a party offering deposition testimony pursuant to this rule may offer it in stenographic or non-stenographic form, but, if in nonstenographic form, the party shall also provide the court with a transcript of the portions so offered. On request of any party in a case tried before a jury, deposition testimony offered other than for impeachment purposes shall be presented in nonstenographic form, if available, unless the court for good cause orders otherwise.

(d) Effect of Errors and Irregularities in Depositions.

(1) As to Notice.

All errors and irregularities in the notice for taking a deposition are waived unless written objection is promptly served upon the party giving the notice.

(2) As to Disqualification of Officer.

Objection to taking a deposition because of disqualification of the officer before whom it is to be taken is waived unless made before the taking of the deposition begins or as soon thereafter as the disqualification becomes known or could be discovered with reasonable diligence.

(3) As to Taking of Deposition.

(A) Objections to the competency of a witness or to the competency, relevancy, or materiality of testimony are not waived by failure to make them before or during the taking of the deposition, unless the ground of the objection is one which might have been obviated or removed if presented at that time.

(B) Errors and irregularities occurring at the oral examination in the manner of taking the deposition, in the form of the questions or answers, in the oath or affirmation, or in the conduct of parties, and errors of any kind which might be obviated, removed, or cured if promptly presented, are waived unless seasonable objection thereto is made at the taking of the deposition.

(C) Objections to the form of written questions submitted under Rule 31 are waived unless served in writing upon the party propounding them within the time allowed for serving the succeeding cross or other questions and within 5 days after service of the last questions authorized.

(4) As to Completion and Return of Deposition.

Errors and irregularities in the manner in which the testimony is transcribed or the deposition is prepared, signed, certified, sealed, indorsed, transmitted, filed, or otherwise dealt with by the officer under Rules 30 and 31 are waived unless a motion to suppress the deposition or some part thereof is made with reasonable promptness after such defect is, or with due diligence might have been, ascertained.

Rule 33. Interrogatories to Parties

(a) Availability.

Without leave of court or written stipulation, any party may serve upon any other party written interrogatories, not exceeding 25 in number including all discrete subparts, to be answered by the party served or, if the party served is a public or private corporation or a partnership or association or governmental agency, by any officer or agent, who shall furnish such information as is available to the party. Leave to serve additional interrogatories shall be granted to the extent consistent with the principles of Rule 26(b)(2). Without leave of court or written stipulation, interrogatories may not be served before the time specified in Rule 26(d).

(b) Answers and Objections.

(1) Each interrogatory shall be answered separately and fully in writing under oath, unless it is objected to, in which event the objecting party shall state the reasons for objection and shall answer to the extent the interrogatory is not objectionable.

(2) The answers are to be signed by the person making them, and the objections signed by the attorney making them.

(3) The party upon whom the interrogatories have been served shall serve a copy of the answers, and objections if any, within 30 days after the service of the interrogatories. A shorter or longer time may be directed by the court or, in the absence of such an order, agreed to in writing by the parties subject to Rule 29.

(4) All grounds for an objection to an interrogatory shall be stated with specificity. Any ground not stated in a timely objection is waived unless the party's failure to object is excused by the court for good cause shown.

(5) The party submitting the interrogatories may move for an order under Rule 37(a) with respect to any objection to or other failure to answer an interrogatory.

(c) Scope; Use at Trial.

Interrogatories may relate to any matter which can be inquired into under Rule 26(b)(1), and the answers may be used to the extent permitted by the rules of evidence.

An interrogatory otherwise proper is not necessarily objectionable merely because an answer to the interrogatory involves an opinion or contention that relates to fact or the application of law to fact, but the court may order that such an interrogatory need not be answered until after designated discovery has been completed or until a pre-trial conference or other later time.

(d) Option to Produce Business Records.

Where the answer to an interrogatory may be derived or ascertained from the business records of the party upon whom the interrogatory has been served or from an examination, audit or inspection of such business records, including a compilation, abstract or summary thereof, and the burden of deriving or ascertaining the answer is substantially the same for the party serving the interrogatory as for the party served, it is a sufficient answer to such interrogatory to specify the records from which the answer may be derived or ascertained and to afford to the party serving the interrogatory reasonable opportunity to examine, audit, or inspect such records and to make copies, compilations, abstracts, or summaries. A specification shall be in sufficient detail to permit the interrogating party to locate and to identify, as readily as can the party served, the records from which the answer may be ascertained.

Rule 34. Production of Documents and Things and Entry Upon Land for Inspection and Other Purposes

(a) Scope.

Any party may serve on any other party a request (1) to produce and permit the party making the request, or someone acting on the requestor's behalf, to inspect and copy, any designated documents (including writings, drawings, graphs, charts, photographs, phonorecords, and other data compilations from which information can be obtained, translated, if necessary, by the respondent through detection devices into reasonably usable form), or to inspect and copy, test, or sample any tangible things which constitute or contain matters within the scope of Rule 26(b) and which are in the possession, custody or control of the party upon whom the request is served; or (2) to permit entry upon designated land or other property in the possession or control of the party upon whom the request is served for the purpose of inspection and measuring, surveying, photographing, testing, or sampling the prop-

erty or any designated object or operation thereon, within the scope of Rule 26(b).

(b) Procedure.

The request shall set forth, either by individual item or by category, the items to be inspected, and describe each with reasonable particularity. The request shall specify a reasonable time, place, and manner of making the inspection and performing the related acts. Without leave of court or written stipulation, a request may not be served before the time specified in Rule 26(d).

The party upon whom the request is served shall serve a written response within 30 days after the service of the request. A shorter or longer time may be directed by the court or, in the absence of such an order, agreed to in writing by the parties, subject to Rule 29. The response shall state, with respect to each item or category, that inspection and related activities will be permitted as requested, unless the request is objected to, in which event the reasons for the objection shall be stated. If objection is made to part of an item or category, the part shall be specified and inspection permitted of the remaining parts. The party submitting the request may move for an order under Rule 37(a) with respect to any objection to or other failure to respond to the request or any part thereof, or any failure to permit inspection as requested.

A party who produces documents for inspection shall produce them as they are kept in the usual course of business or shall organize and label them to correspond with the categories in the request.

(c) Persons Not Parties.

A person not a party to the action may be compelled to produce documents and things or to submit to an inspection as provided in Rule 45.

Rule 36. Requests for Admission

(a) Request for Admission.

A party may serve upon any other party a written request for the admission, for purposes of the pending action only, of the truth of any matters within the scope of Rule 26(b)(1) set forth in the request that relate to statements or opinions of fact or of the application of law to fact, including the genuineness of any documents described in the request. Copies of documents shall be served with the request unless they have been or are otherwise furnished or made available for inspection and copying. Without leave of court or written stipulation, requests for admission may not be served before the time specified in Rule 26(d).

Each matter of which an admission is requested shall be separately set forth. The matter is admitted unless, within 30 days after service of the request, or within such shorter or longer time as the court may allow or as the parties may agree to in writing, subject to Rule 29, the party to whom the request is directed serves upon the party requesting the admission a written answer or objection addressed to the matter, signed by the party or by the party's attorney. If objection is made, the reasons therefor shall be stated. The answer shall specifically deny the matter or set forth in detail the reasons why the answering party cannot truthfully admit or deny the matter. A denial shall fairly meet the substance of the requested admission, and when good faith requires that a party qualify an answer or deny only a part of the matter of which an admission is requested, the party shall specify so much of it as is true and qualify or deny the remainder. An answering party may not give lack of information or knowledge as a reason for failure to admit or deny unless the party states that the party has made reasonable inquiry and that the information known or readily obtainable by the party is insufficient to enable the party to admit or deny. A party who considers that a matter of which an admission has been requested presents a genuine issue for trial may not, on that ground alone, object to the request; the party may, subject to the provisions of Rule 37(c), deny the matter or set forth reasons why the party cannot admit or deny it.

The party who has requested the admissions may move to determine the sufficiency of the answers or objections. Unless the court determines that an objection is justified, it shall order that an answer be served. If the court determines that an answer does not comply with the requirements of this rule, it may order either that the matter is admitted or that an amended answer be served. The court may, in lieu of these orders, determine that final disposition of the request be made at a pre-trial conference or at a designated time prior to trial. The provisions of Rule 37(a) (4) apply to the award of expenses incurred in relation to the motion.

(b) Effect of Admission.

Any matter admitted under this rule is conclusively established unless the court on motion permits withdrawal or amendment of the admission. Subject to the provision of Rule 16 governing amendment of a pretrial order, the court may permit withdrawal or amendment when the presentation of the merits of the action will be subserved thereby and the party who obtained the admission fails to satisfy the court that withdrawal or amendment will prejudice that party in maintaining the action or defense on the merits. Any admission made by a party under this rule is for the purpose of the pending action only and is not an admission for any other purpose nor may it be used against the party in any other proceeding.

Rule 37. Failure to Make or Cooperate in Discovery; Sanctions

(a) Motion for Order Compelling Disclosure or Discovery.

A party, upon reasonable notice to other parties and all persons affected thereby, may apply for an order compelling disclosure or discovery as follows:

(1) Appropriate Court.

An application for an order to a party shall be made to the court in which the action is pending. An application for an order to a person who is not a party shall be made to the court in the district where the discovery is being, or is to be, taken.

(2) Motion.

(A) If a party fails to make a disclosure required by Rule 26(a), any other party may move to compel disclosure and for appropriate sanctions. The motion must include a certification that the movant has in good faith conferred or attempted to confer with the party not making the disclosure in an effort to secure the disclosure without court action.

(B) If a deponent fails to answer a question propounded or submitted under Rules 30 or 31, or a corporation or other entity fails to make a designation under Rule 30(b)(6) or 31(a), or a party fails to answer an interrogatory submitted under Rule 33, or if a party, in response to a request for inspection submitted under Rule 34, fails to respond that inspection will be permitted as requested or fails to permit inspection as requested, the discovering party may move for an order compelling an answer, or a designation, or an order compelling inspection in accordance with the request. The motion must include a certification that the movant has in good faith conferred or attempted to confer with the person or party failing to make the discovery in an effort to secure the information or material without court action. When taking a deposition on oral examination, the proponent of the question may complete or adjourn the examination before applying for an order.

(3) Evasive or Incomplete Disclosure, Answer, or Response.

For purposes of this subdivision an evasive or incomplete disclosure, answer, or response is to be treated as a failure to disclose, answer, or respond.

(4) Expenses and Sanctions.

(A) If the motion is granted or if the disclosure or requested discovery is provided after the motion was filed, the court shall, after affording an opportunity to be heard, require the party or deponent whose conduct necessitated the motion or the party or attorney advising such conduct or both of them to pay to the moving party the reasonable expenses incurred in making the motion, including attorney's fees, unless the court finds that the motion was filed without the movant's first making a good faith effort to obtain the disclosure or discovery without court action, or that the opposing party's nondisclosure, response, or objection was substantially justified, or that other circumstances make an award of expenses unjust.

(B) If the motion is denied, the court may enter any protective order authorized under Rule 26(c) and shall, after affording an opportunity to be heard, require the moving party or the attorney filing the motion or both of them to pay to the party or deponent who opposed the motion the reasonable expenses incurred in opposing the motion, including attorney's fees, unless the court finds that the making of the motion was substantially justified or that other circumstances make an award of expenses unjust.

(C) If the motion is granted in part and denied in part, the court may enter any protective order authorized under Rule 26(c) and may, af-

ter affording an opportunity to be heard, apportion the reasonable expenses incurred in relation to the motion among the parties and persons in a just manner.

(b) Failure to Comply With Order.

(1) Sanctions by Court in District Where Deposition is Taken.

If a deponent fails to be sworn or to answer a question after being directed to do so by the court in the district in which the deposition is being taken, the failure may be considered a contempt of that court.

(2) Sanctions by Court in Which Action Is Pending.

If a party or an officer, director, or managing agent of a party or a person designated under Rule 30(b)(6) or 31(a) to testify on behalf of a party fails to obey an order to provide or permit discovery, including an order made under subdivision (a) of this rule or Rule 35, or if a party fails to obey an order entered under Rule 26(f), the court in which the action is pending may make such orders in regard to the failure as are just, and among others the following:

(A) An order that the matters regarding which the order was made or any other designated facts shall be taken to be established for the purposes of the action in accordance with the claim of the party obtaining the order;

(B) An order refusing to allow the disobedient party to support or oppose designated claims or defenses, or prohibiting that party from introducing designated matters in evidence;

(C) An order striking out pleadings or parts thereof, or staying further proceedings until the order is obeyed, or dismissing the action or proceeding or any part thereof, or rendering a judgment by default against the disobedient party;

(D) In lieu of any of the foregoing orders or in addition thereto, an order treating as a contempt of court the failure to obey any orders except an order to submit to a physical or mental examination;

(E) Where a party has failed to comply with an order under Rule 35(a) requiring that party to produce another for examination, such orders as are listed in paragraphs (A), (B), and (C) of this subdivision, unless the party failing to comply shows that that party is unable to produce such person for examination.

In lieu of any of the foregoing orders or in addition thereto, the court shall require the party failing to obey the order or the attorney advising that party or both to pay the reasonable expenses, including attorney's fees, caused by the failure, unless the court finds that the failure was substantially justified or that other circumstances make an award of expenses unjust.

(c) Failure to Disclose; False or Misleading Disclosure; Refusal to Admit.

(1) A party that without substantial justification fails to disclose information required by Rule 26(a) or 26(e)(1), or to amend a prior reponse to discovery as required by Rule 26(e)(2), is not, unless such failure is harmless, permitted to use as evidence at a trial, at a hearing, or on a motion any witness or information not so disclosed. In addition to or in lieu of this sanction, the court, on motion and after affording an opportunity to be heard, may impose other appropriate sanctions. In addition to requiring payment of reasonable expenses, including attorney's fees, caused by the failure, these sanctions may include any of the sanctions authorized under Rule 37(b)(2)(A), (B), and (C) and may include informing the jury of the failure to make the disclosure.

(2) If a party fails to admit the genuineness of any document or the truth of any matter as requested under Rule 36, and if the party requesting the admissions thereafter proves the genuineness of the document or the truth of the matter, the requesting party may apply to the court for an order requiring the other party to pay the reasonable expenses incurred in making that proof, including reasonable attorney's fees. The court shall make the order unless it finds that (A) the request was held objectionable pursuant to Rule 36(a), or (B) the admission sought was of no substantial importance, or (C) the party failing to admit had reasonable ground to believe that the party might prevail on the matter, or (D) there was other good reason for the failure to admit.

(d) Failure of Party to Attend at Own Deposition or Serve Answers to Interrogatories or Respond to Request for Inspection.

If a party or an officer, director, or managing agent of a party or a person designated under Rule 30(b)(6) or 31(a) to testify on behalf of a party fails (1) to appear before the officer who is to take the deposition, after being served with a proper notice, or (2) to serve answers or objections to interrogatories submitted under Rule 33, after proper service of the interrogatories, or (3) to serve a written response to a request for inspection submitted under Rule 34, after proper service of the request, the court in which the action is pending on motion may make such orders in regard to the failure as are just, and among others it may take any action authorized under subparagraphs (A), (B), and (C) of subdivision (b)(2) of this rule. Any motion specifying a failure under clause (2) or (3) of this subdivision shall include a certification that the movant has in good faith conferred or attempted to confer with the party failing to answer or respond in an effort to obtain such answer or response without court action. In lieu of any order or in addition thereto, the court shall require the party failing to act or the attorney advising that party or both to pay the reasonable expenses, including attorney's fees, caused by the failure unless the court finds that the failure was substantially justified or that other circumstances make an award of expenses unjust.

The failure to act described in this subdivision may not be excused on the ground that the discovery sought is objectionable unless the party failing to act has a pending motion for a protective order as provided by Rule 26(c).

(e) [Abrogated]

(f) [Repealed]

(g) Failure to Participate in the Framing of a Discovery Plan.

If a party or a party's attorney fails to participate in good faith in the development and submission of a proposed discovery plan as required by Rule 26(f), the court may, after opportunity for hearing, require such party or attorney to pay to any other party the reasonable expenses, including attorney's fees, caused by the failure.

Rule 45. Subpoena

(a) Form; Issuance.

(1) Every subpoena shall

(A) state the name of the court from which it is issued; and

(B) state the title of the action, the name of the court in which it is pending, and its civil action number; and

(C) command each person to whom it is directed to attend and give testimony or to produce and permit inspection and copying of designated books, documents or tangible things in the possession, custody or control of that person, or to permit inspection of premises, at a time and place therein specified; and

(D) set forth the text of subdivisions (c) and (d) of this rule. A command to produce evidence or to permit inspection may be joined with a command to appear at trial or hearing or at deposition, or may be issued separately.

(2) A subpoena commanding attendance at a trial or hearing shall issue from the court for the district in which the hearing or trial is to be held. A subpoena for attendance at a deposition

shall issue from the court for the district designated by the notice of deposition as the district in which the deposition is to be taken. If separate from a subpoena commanding the attendance of a person, a subpoena for production or inspection shall issue from the court for the district in which the production or inspection is to be made.

(3) The clerk shall issue a subpoena, signed but otherwise in blank, to a party requesting it, who shall complete it before service. An attorney as officer of the court may also issue and sign a subpoena on behalf of

(A) a court in which the attorney is authorized to practice; or

(B) a court for a district in which a deposition or production is compelled by the subpoena, if the deposition or production pertains to an action pending in a court in which the attorney is authorized to practice.

(b) Service.

(1) A subpoena may be served by any person who is not a party and is not less than 18 years of age. Service of a subpoena upon a person named therein shall be made by delivering a copy thereof to such person and, if the person's attendance is commanded, by tendering to that person the fees for one day's attendance and the mileage allowed by law. When the subpoena is issued on behalf of the United States or an officer or agency thereof, fees and mileage need not be tendered. Prior notice of any commanded production of documents and things or inspection of premises before trial shall be

served on each party in the manner prescribed by Rule 5(b).

(2) Subject to the provisions of clause (ii) of subparagraph (c)(3)(A) of this rule, a subpoena may be served at any place within the district of the court by which it is issued, or at any place without the district that is within 100 miles of the place of the deposition, hearing, trial, production, or inspection specified in the subpoena or at any place within the state where a state statute or rule of court permits service of a subpoena issued by a state court of general jurisdiction sitting in the place of the deposition, hearing, trial, production, or inspection specified in the subpoena. When a statute of the United States provides therefor, the court upon proper application and cause shown may authorize the service of a subpoena at any other place. A subpoena directed to a witness in a foreign country who is a national or resident of the United States shall issue under the circumstances and in the manner and be served as provided in Title 28, U.S.C. § 1783.

(3) Proof of service when necessary shall be made by filing with the clerk of the court by which the subpoena is issued a statement of the date and manner of service and of the names of the persons served, certified by the person who made the service.

(c) Protection of Persons Subject to Subpoenas.

(1) A party or an attorney responsible for the issuance and service of a subpoena shall take reasonable steps to avoid imposing undue

burden or expense on a person subject to that subpoena. The court on behalf of which the subpoena was issued shall enforce this duty and impose upon the party or attorney in breach of this duty an appropriate sanction, which may include, but is not limited to, lost earnings and a reasonable attorney's fee.

(2) (A) A person commanded to produce and permit inspection and copying of designated books, papers, documents or tangible things, or inspection of premises need not appear in person at the place of production or inspection unless commanded to appear for deposition, hearing or trial.

(B) Subject to paragraph (d)(2) of this rule, a person commanded to produce and permit inspection and copying may, within 14 days after service of the subpoena or before the time specified for compliance if such time is less than 14 days after service, serve upon the party or attorney designated in the subpoena written objection to inspection or copying of any or all of the designated materials or of the premises. If objection is made, the party serving the subpoena shall not be entitled to inspect and copy the materials or inspect the premises except pursuant to an order of the court by which the subpoena was issued. If objection has been made, the party serving the subpoena may, upon notice to the person commanded to produce, move at any time for an order to compel the production. Such an order to compel production shall protect any person who is not a party or an officer of a party from significant expense resulting from the inspection and copying commanded.

(3) (A) On timely motion, the court by which a subpoena was issued shall quash or modify the subpoena if it

(i) fails to allow reasonable time for compliance;

(ii) requires a person who is not a party or an officer of a party to travel to a place more than 100 miles from the place where that person resides, is employed or regularly transacts business in person, except that, subject to the provisions of clause (c)(3)(B)(iii) of this rule, such a person may in order to attend trial be commanded to travel from any such place within the state in which the trial is held, or

(iii) requires disclosure of privileged or other protected matter and no exception or waiver applies, or

(iv) subjects a person to undue burden.

(B) If a subpoena

(i) requires disclosure of a trade secret or other confidential research, development, or commercial information,

or

(ii) requires disclosure of an unretained expert's opinion or information not describing specific events or occurrences in dispute and resulting from the expert's study made not at the request of any party, or

(iii) requires a person who is not a party or an officer of a party to incur substantial expense to travel more than 100 miles to attend trial, the court may, to protect a person subject to or affected by the subpoena, quash or modify the subpoena or, if the party in whose behalf the subpoena is issued shows a substantial need for the testimony or material that cannot be otherwise met without undue hardship and assures that the person to whom the subpoena is addressed will be reasonably compensated, the court may order appearance or production only upon specified conditions.

(d) Duties in Responding to Subpoena.

(1) A person responding to a subpoena to produce documents shall produce them as they are kept in the usual course of business or shall organize and label them to correspond with the categories in the demand.

(2) When information subject to a subpoena is withheld on a claim that it is privileged or subject to protection as trial preparation materials, the claim shall be made expressly and shall be supported by a description of the nature of the documents, communications, or things not produced that is sufficient to enable the demanding party to contest the claim.

(e) Contempt.

Failure by any person without adequate excuse to obey a subpoena served upon that person may be deemed a contempt of the court from which the subpoena issued. An adequate cause for failure to obey exists when a subpoena purports to require a non-party to attend or produce at a place not within the limits provided by clause (ii) of subparagraph (c)(3)(A).

■

Appendix 2

State Discovery and Deposition Rules

This appendix tells you where to find your state's discovery and deposition rules. For reasons explained in the introduction, our discussion of discovery and deposition rules and procedures is based primarily on Rules 26 through 37 of the Federal Rules of Civil Procedure (FRCP). In fact, many states use the same numbering and organization as the FRCP.

Even though federal and state rules are similar, if you are a party to a state court case, you need to read your state rules. Follow the instructions below and refer to the table, "State Discovery and Deposition Rules," to locate your state's rules, either in the library ("Print Citation") or, when available, on the Web ("Online Location").

In the library. In some states, court rules are contained within the state's entire set of statutes, or laws, often called the state's "code." If

this is true for your state, you'll find the rules in one of the volumes of the multivolume state code. Often, the publishers helpfully print the words "Court Rules" on the spine of the particular volume that contains them. Even if you don't find that hint, it's still easy to locate the rules—just find the volume that contains the numbered cite of the rules. For example, if you're looking for California's rules, you'll find them within the Code of Civil Procedure, which itself is part of the entire state's code, in the volume that contains Sections 2016 to 2036.

In other states, the rules are published in separate books, often shelved at the end of the state code. Again, the title "Court Rules" or "Rules of Court" will tip you off. If you have difficulty locating the rules, be sure to ask the librarian. Requests to consult the rules are very common, and the librarian is sure to know exactly where they are.

On the Web. Many state courts have posted their rules online. By the time you use this book, more courts will have joined the trend. If your state rules are not online, be sure to check the National Center for State Courts (www.ncsc.dni.us), which has links to all the state courts. Once there, you'll be able to link to your state court and see whether rules have been added. Another helpful site is the Litigator's Internet Resource Guide: Rules of Court (www.llrx.com/columns/litigat.htm).

 Check for local rules, too.

Your local court may impose additional requirements not covered by your state's rules. Be sure to ask the clerk of the court for copies of any local discovery and deposition rules before proceeding.

STATE DISCOVERY AND DEPOSITION RULES

State	Relation to FRCP	Print Citation	Online Location
ALABAMA	Similar	ARCP R 26–37	The rules are not currently available online.
ALASKA	Similar	Alaska R. Civ. Proc. 26–37	www.state.ak.us/courts/home.htm. Click on Court Rules, then on Civil Procedure. Scroll down to Rules 26 through 37.
ARIZONA	Similar	Ariz St RCP R 26–37	www.supreme.state.az.us. Click on Opinions/Rules/Orders, then on Arizona Rules of Court. Select Current Rules, then Arizona Rules of Civil Procedure, and then Depositions and Discovery to view Rules 26 through 37.
ARKANSAS	Similar	ARCP Rule 26–37	http://courts.state.ar.us. Click on Court Rules & Administrative Orders. Choose Rules of Civil Procedure from the pull-down menu, Rules 26 through 37.
CALIFORNIA	Different	California Code of Civil Procedure §§ 2016 to 2036	www.leginfo.ca.gov. Click on California Law, then Code of Civil Procedure. Scroll down to Sections 2016 through 2036.
COLORADO	Similar	C.R.C.P. 26–37	www.courts.state.co.us/index.htm. Under the Self Help Center tab, click on Rules of the Court, then choose Search all Colorado Rules. Select Colorado Court Rules, then Colorado Rules of Civil Procedure, and go to Chapter 4 (Disclosure and Discovery) to browse Rules 26 through 37.
CONNECTICUT	Different	Conn. Super. Ct. Rules 13-1 to 13-32	www.jud.state.ct.us. Click on Law Libraries, then Connecticut Court Rules Practice Book. Select Connecticut Practice Book 2005—Part 1. Scroll down to Chapter 13 to view Rules 13-1 through 13-32.

State	Relation to FRCP	Print Citation	Online Location
DELAWARE	Similar	Del. Super. Ct. Civ. R. 26–37	*http://courts.state.de.us.* Click on Superior Court, then choose Rules of Procedure on the drop-down menu. Under Superior Court, click on Civil Procedures, then scroll down to browse Rules 26 through 37.
DISTRICT OF COLUMBIA	Identical	D.C. SCR-Civil Rule 26–37	
FLORIDA	Different	FRCP 1.280–1.380	*http://phonl.com/fl_law.* Click on Florida Rules of Civil Procedure to browse Rules 1.280 through 1.380.
GEORGIA	Similar	Ga. Code Ann. §§ 9-11-26 to 9-11-37	*www.ganet.state.ga.us.* Click on the Government tab, then Laws & Regulations, and then Laws of the State of Georgia. Select Georgia Code Title 9, Chapter 11 and browse through Sections 26 through 37.
HAWAII	Similar	HRCP, Rules 26–37	*www.state.hi.us.* Click on Government and then on the State Government drop-down menu and select Judiciary. Under Legal References, choose Rules, then scroll down to Rules 26 through 37.
IDAHO	Similar	I.R.C.P., Rules 26–37	*www2.state.id.us/judicial.* Under the Frequently Requested heading, click on Rules. Then click on Idaho Rules of Civil Procedure and scroll down to Rules 26 through 37.
ILLINOIS	Different	Supreme Ct., R. 201 to 224 (Supreme Court)	*www.state.il.us/court/supreme court.* Select the Government tab and then click on the link for Judiciary. Select Illinois Supreme Court, then Illinois Court Documents, and then Supreme Court Rules. Once in the Rules section, select Article II and scroll down to browse Rules 201 through 224.

State	Relation to FRCP	Print Citation	Online Location
INDIANA	Similar	Ind. TR 26–37 (Rules of Trial Procedure)	*www.in.gov.* On the right side of the page, under the State heading, click on State Courts. Click on Law Library and then on the link for Rules of Court on the left side of the page. Then select Trial Procedure to view Rules 26 through 37.
IOWA	Different	IRCP 121–166	*www.judicial.state.ia.us.* Next to the Court Rules tab, click on Iowa Court Rules. Click on the link to the Iowa Court Rules and scroll down to browse Iowa Rules of Civil Procedure 1.501 through 1.517.
KANSAS	Similar	Kan. Stat. Ann. §§ 60-226 to 60-237	*www.kslegislature.org/legsrv-statutes/index.do.* In the box provided, enter 60-226 and click on Get Statute to view Sections 60-226 through 60-237 of the Kansas Statutes Annotated.
KENTUCKY	Similar	KRCP 26–37	*www.louisvillelaw.com/courts/rules.htm.* Click on Civil Procedure (our site), then on Section V, Depositions and Discovery, to view Rules 26 through 37.
LOUISIANA	Different	La. CCP §§ 1421 to 1475	
MAINE	Similar	ME R RCP R 26–37	*www.courts.state.me.us/index.html.* Click on Rules, Forms, Fees & Publications, then on Court Rules. Select Maine Rules of Civil Procedure and scroll down to Section V to view Rules 26 through 37.

State	Relation to FRCP	Print Citation	Online Location
MARYLAND	Different	Md Rule 2-401 to 2-434	*www.courts.state.md.us.* Click on State Law Library, then at the top of the screen, click on Maryland Rules of Procedure compliments of Lexis-Nexis. On the left side of the screen, expand the Maryland Rules box, then click on the MARYLAND RULES tab that is in all capital letters. Select Civil Procedure–Circuit Court and scroll down to Chapter 400 to Rules 2-401 through 2-434. Note that the Maryland Law Library site is currently under construction.
MASSACHUSETTS	Similar	ALM R. Civ. P. Rules 26–37	*www.mass.gov/courts.* Click on Resources, then Law Libraries. Under the Laws, Regulations and Cases heading, click on Mass. Court Rules and Fees, and then select Massachusetts Rules of Civil Procedure. Scroll down to see Rules 26 through 37.
MICHIGAN	Different	MCR 2.301–2.316	*courtofappeals.mijud.net.* Under the About the Court drop-down menu, click on Court Rules, then elect Link to Rules. On the left side of the screen, expand the Chapter 2 Civil Procedures box and then the Subchapter 2.300 box. Click on Rule 2.301 and scroll down to see Rules 2.301 through 2.316.
MINNESOTA	Similar	Minn. Dist. Ct. Gen. Rule 26.01 to 37.04	*www.courts.state.mn.us.* Click on Court Rules, then Minnesota Rules of Civil Procedure. Scroll down to view Rules 26 through 37.
MISSISSIPPI	Similar	M.R.C.P. 26–37	*www.mssc.state.ms.us.* Click on Rules, then Mississippi Rules of Civil Procedure. On the left side of the page, scroll down to Rules 26 through 37.

State	Relation to FRCP	Print Citation	Online Location
MISSOURI	Different	S. Ct. Rule 56.01 to 61.01 (Supreme Court)	*www.courts.mo.gov.* Click on Supreme Court, then Orders/Rules, then Missouri Court Rules. Select Rules Online and then click on the arrow next to Rules of Civil Procedure – Rules Governing Civil Procedure in the Circuit Courts. Scroll down in the list that appears to browse Rules 56 through 61.
MONTANA	Similar	Mont. Code Ann. § 25 Ch. 20, Rules 26–37	*http://leg.state.mt.us.* Click on Montana Code and Constitution at the bottom of the page. Then click on the most recent version of the Montana Code Annotated. Select Title 25 (Civil Procedure), Chapter 20 (Rules of Civil Procedure). You will find Rules 26 through 37 in Part V of Chapter 20.
NEBRASKA	Different	Neb. Rev. Stat. §§ 25-1240 to 25-1245; *§§ 25-1268, 25-1273.01 (Many are repealed.)*	*http://unicam.state.ne.us.* Next to the Laws of Nebraska tab, select Statutes & Constitution. Along the left side of the screen, click on the Statutes folder. Click on the folder next to Chapter 25 Courts; Civil Procedure and then select View Chapter (just below the search box). Go to Sections 1240 through 1245, Section 1268, and Section 1273.
NEVADA	Similar	Nev. R.C.P 26–37	*www.leg.state.nv.us.* Click on the Law Library tab, then Court Rules. Select Nevada Rules of Civil Procedure and scroll down to view Rules 26 through 37.
NEW HAMPSHIRE	Different	N.H. Superior Ct. 35–44	*www.courts.state.nh.us/index.htm.* Click on Court Rules, then Rules of Practice and Procedure in the Probate Courts of the State of New Hampshire. Scroll down to Rules 35 through 44.

State	Relation to FRCP	Print Citation	Online Location
NEW JERSEY	Different	N.J. Court Rules R. 4:10-1 to 4:25-7 (Superior, Tax, & Surrogate Courts)	*www.njlawnet.com*. Under New Jersey Law on the left side, click on Court Rules. Click on Part IV, then scroll down to to Chapter III to get to Rules 4:10-1 through 4025-7.
NEW MEXICO	Similar	N.M. Dist. Ct. R.C.P. 1-026	*http://legis.state.nm.us*. Under Other Resources, click on Statutes, then on Start Here. On the left side, click on the folder next to New Mexico Statutes and Court Rules, and then on Contents of Judicial Volumes. Select Rules of Civil Procedure for the District Courts. Article 5 contains Rules 1-026 through 1-037.
NEW YORK	Different	N.Y. CPLR §§ 3101–3140	*www.law.cornell.edu*. Go to the tab Constitution & Codes, then click on State Constitution & Codes. Select New York from the list, then click on Statutes. Scroll down to Civil Practice Law & Rules. Select Article 31, then scroll down to Statutes 3101 through 3140.
NORTH CAROLINA	Similar	N.C. Gen. Stat § 1A-1 Rules 26–37	*www.ncga.state.nc.us*. On the right side of the screen, click on NC Statutes. Under Browse, select Table of Contents, then select Chapter 1A-Rules of Civil Procedure. Scroll down and click on Article 5–Depositions and Discovery to access Rules 26 through 37.
NORTH DAKOTA	Similar	N.D.R. Civ. P. Rules 26–37	*www.court.state.nd.us*. Select Rules from the menu on the left side of the screen, then click on Civil Procedure, North Dakota Rules of. Select Part V: Depositions and Discovery and scroll to Rules 26 through 37.

State	Relation to FRCP	Print Citation	Online Location
OHIO	Similar	OH Civ. R. 26–37	*www.sconet.state.oh.us.* Click on Ohio Rules of Court, then Rules of Civil Procedure. Scroll down to Rules 26 through 37.
OKLAHOMA	Similar	Okla. Stat. Ann. tit. 12, §§ 3226 to 3237	*www.lsb.state.ok.us.* Click on Oklahoma Statutes & Constitution, then on Oklahoma Statutes – Titles 1-85. Select Title 12 and scroll down to Sections 3226 through 3237.
OREGON	Different	ORCP 36–46	*www.leg.state.or.us.* Click on Bills/Laws, then scroll down under Laws to Oregon Revised Statutes. Click on Oregon Rules of Civil Procedure and scroll to Rules 36 through 46.
PENNSYLVANIA	Different	Pa. R.C.P. Rules 4001 to 4025	*www.pacode.com.* Click on Browse, then select Title 231. Select Part I (General), then Chapter 4000 to view Rules 4001 through 4025.
RHODE ISLAND	Similar	RI R.C.P. 26–37	*www.courts.state.ri.us.* Click on Site Map, then under the District Court heading, click on Rules of Procedure. Select Civil Rules of Procedure and scroll down to Rules 26 through 37.
SOUTH CAROLINA	Similar	S.C. Rules of Civ Proc. 26–37	*www.judicial.state.sc.us.* On the left side of the screen, click on Court Rules. Again on the left side of the screen, select Civil Procedure. Then scroll down to view Rules 26 through 37.
SOUTH DAKOTA	Similar	S.D. Codified Laws Ann. §§ 15-6-26 to 15-6-37	*http://legis.state.sd.us.* Click on Codified Laws, then select Title List from under the Statutes heading. Click on Title 15, then click on Chapter 6. Scroll down to Part 5 to get to Rules 26 through 37.

State	Relation to FRCP	Print Citation	Online Location
TENNESSEE	Similar	Tenn. Civ. Proc. Rules 26–37	*www.lrwlaw.com.* Select Online Library, then Tennessee Law. Under Court Rules, click on Tennessee Rules of Civil Procedure, and scroll down to Rules 26 through 37.
TEXAS	Different	TX. RCP Rules 176 to 215	
UTAH	Similar	URCP 26–37	*www.utcourts.gov.* Click on Court Resources, then Court Rules. Select Rules of Civil Procedure and scroll down to Rules 26 through 37.
VERMONT	Similar	V.R.C.P. 26–37	*www.leg.state.vt.us.* On the left side of the screen, click on Vermont Statutes, then Vermont Statutes and Court Rules at LexisNexis. On the left side of the screen, click on the Vermont Court Rules folder, then on Rules of Civil Procedure. Scroll down to Part V to get to Rules 26 through 37.
VIRGINIA	Different	Va. Sup. Ct. R 4:1 to 4:14 (Supreme Court)	*www.courts.state.va.us/main.htm.* Click on Supreme Court of Virginia, then Amendments to the Rules of Court. Select Rules of Court (searchable) and enter 4: in the search box to view Rules 4:1 through 4:14.
WASHINGTON	Similar	Rules 26–37 (Superior Court)	*www.courts.wa.gov.* Click on Court Rules, then on Rules for Superior Court. Select Superior Court Civil Rules, then scroll down to Rules 26 through 37.
WEST VIRGINIA	Similar	W. Va. R.C.P. Rules 26–37	*www.legis.state.wv.us.* On the drop-down menu under WV Code click on Magistrate Rules. Then on the left side of the screen select Section V under Rules of Civil Procedure to view Rules 26 through 37.

State	Relation to FRCP	Print Citation	Online Location
WISCONSIN	Different	Wis. Stat. Ann. §§ 804.01 to 804.12	*www.legis.state.wi.us.* Click on Wisconsin Law, then Statutes. In the Go to a Specific Statute box, type ch. 804. Scroll down to browse the rules at Sections 804.1 through 804.12.
WYOMING	Identical	W.R.C.P. Rules 26–37	*http://courts.state.wy.us.* On the left side of the screen, click on Court Rules, then Wyoming Rules of Civil Procedure. Scroll down to Rules 26 through 37. ∎

Appendix 3

Sample Forms

Sample Form #1: Deposition Subpoena
(Requiring attendance of nonparty witness at deposition.)

Sample Form #2: Deposition Subpoena Duces Tecum
(Requiring attendance of nonparty witness at deposition and production of documents.)

Sample Form #3: Notice of Deposition of a Nonparty Witness and Proof of Service by Mail
(This notice must be served on all parties by the party taking the deposition.)

Sample Form #4: Notice of Deposition of a Party and Proof of Service by Mail
(This notice must be served on all parties by the party taking the deposition.)

Sample Form #5: Notice of Deposition of a Party Requiring the Party to Produce Documents at the Deposition and Proof of Service by Mail
(This notice must be served on all parties at least 35 days prior to the deposition by the party taking the deposition.)

Sample Form #6: Request for Production of Documents and Proof of Service by Mail
(This request may be sent only to a party and the request must be served by the requesting party on all other parties at least 35 days prior to the date indicated for the production of the documents.)

DEPOSITION SUBPOENA

(Requiring attendance of nonparty witness at deposition)

DEPOSITION SUBPOENA

Issued by the

UNITED STATES DISTRICT COURT

Central District of California

SUBPOENA IN A CIVIL CASE

David A. Binder, Plaintiff

CASE NO. 1234567

V.

Susan Prager, Defendant

TO: Casey Shearer

YOU ARE COMMANDED to appear at the place, date, and time specified below to testify at the taking of a deposition in the above case.

PLACE OF DEPOSITION	DATE AND TIME
9512 Sawyer Street, Los Angeles, CA 90035	9:00 a.m. June 2, 20xx

YOU ARE COMMANDED to produce and permit inspection and copying of the following documents or objects at the place, date, and time specified below [list of documents or objects]:

PLACE	DATE AND TIME

YOU ARE COMMANDED to permit inspection and copying of the following premises at the place, date, and time specified below.

PREMISES	DATE AND TIME

Any organization not a party to this suit subpoenaed for the taking of a deposition shall designate one or more officers, directors, or managing agents, or other persons who consent on its behalf, and may set forth, for each person designated, the matters on which the person will testify. Federal Rules of Civil Procedure, 30(b)(6).

ISSUING OFFICER SIGNATURE AND TITLE	DATE
David A. Binder, Plaintiff in Pro Se	May 10, 20xx

ISSUING OFFICER'S NAME, ADDRESS, AND PHONE NUMBER

David A. Binder, 123 State Street, Los Angeles, CA 90037 Telephone (310) 204-5555

PROOF OF SERVICE

DATE SERVED	PLACE
May 11, 20xx	604 24th Street, Santa Monica, CA 90078
SERVED ON (PRINT NAME)	MANNER OF SERVICE
Casey Shearer	Personally delivered to Casey Shearer at his home.
SERVED BY (PRINT NAME)	TITLE
Orin Moore	

DECLARATION OF SERVER

I declare under penalty of perjury under the laws of the United States of America that the foregoing information contained in the Proof of Service is true and correct.

Executed on <u>May 11, 20xx</u>
         DATE

_____
    SIGNATURE OF SERVER

<u>301 Middlebury Street</u>
<u>Los Angeles, CA 90099</u>
ADDRESS OF SERVER

DEPOSITION SUBPOENA DUCES TECUM

(Requiring attendance of nonparty witness at deposition and production of documents)

DEPOSITION SUBPOENA

Issued by the

UNITED STATES DISTRICT COURT

Central District of California

SUBPOENA IN A CIVIL CASE

David A. Binder, Plaintiff

V.

CASE NO. 1234567

Susan Prager, Defendant

TO: Casey Shearer

YOU ARE COMMANDED to appear at the place, date, and time specified below to testify at the taking of a deposition in the above case.

PLACE OF DEPOSITION	DATE AND TIME
9512 Sawyer Street, Los Angeles, CA 90035	9:00 a.m. June 2, 20xx

YOU ARE COMMANDED to produce and permit inspection and copying of the following documents or objects at the place, date, and time specified below [list of documents or objects]:

All invoices relating to remodeling work done by Casey Shearer on the house located at 1717 Browning Street, Los Angeles , CA

PLACE	DATE AND TIME
9512 Sawyer Street, Los Angeles, CA 90035	9:00 a.m. June 2, 20xx

YOU ARE COMMANDED to permit inspection and copying of the following premises at the place, date, and time specified below.

PREMISES	DATE AND TIME

Any organization not a party to this suit subpoenaed for the taking of a deposition shall designate one or more officers, directors, or managing agents, or other persons who consent on its behalf, and may set forth, for each person designated, the matters on which the person will testify. Federal Rules of Civil Procedure, 30(b)(6).

ISSUING OFFICER SIGNATURE AND TITLE	DATE
David A. Binder, Plaintiff in Pro Se	May 10, 20XX

ISSUING OFFICER'S NAME, ADDRESS, AND PHONE NUMBER

David A. Binder, 123 State Street, Los Angeles, CA 90037 Telephone (310) 204-5555

PROOF OF SERVICE

DATE SERVED	PLACE
May 11, 20xx	604 24th Street, Santa Monica, CA 90078

SERVED ON (PRINT NAME)	MANNER OF SERVICE
Casey Shearer	Personally delivered to Casey Shearer at his home.

SERVED BY (PRINT NAME)	TITLE
Orin Moore	

DECLARATION OF SERVER

I declare under penalty of perjury under the laws of the United States of America that the foregoing information contained in the Proof of Service is true and correct.

Executed on <u>May 11, 20xx</u>
        DATE

_____
SIGNATURE OF SERVER

<u>301 Middlebury Street</u>
<u>Los Angeles, CA 90099</u>
ADDRESS OF SERVER

NOTICE OF DEPOSITION OF A NONPARTY WITNESS AND PROOF OF SERVICE BY MAIL

(This notice must be served on all parties by the party taking the deposition.)

David A. Binder
123 State Street
Los Angeles, CA
Plaintiff in Pro Se
Telephone (310) 204-5579

UNITED STATES DISTRICT COURT

FOR THE CENTRAL DISTRICT OF CALIFORNIA

David A. Binder		CASE NO.1234567
Plaintiff,	)	
	)	NOTICE OF DEPOSITION
	)	
V.	)	
	)	
Susan Prager	)	
	)	
Defendant	)	
	)	
_____	)	

TO EACH PARTY AND THEIR ATTORNEY OF RECORD IN THIS CASE:

YOU ARE NOTIFIED THAT: The deposition of Casey Shearer will be taken at 9512 Sawyer Street, Los Angeles, California, commencing at 9:00 a.m. on June 2, 20xx.

YOU ARE FURTHER NOTIFIED THAT:

The deponent is not a party to this action. So far as known to the deposing party, the deponent's address and telephone number are: 604 24th Street, Santa Monica, CA 90078,

(310) 222-4567. This deponent has been served with a Deposition Subpoena. A copy of that Deposition Subpoena is attached to and served with this notice.

DATED: <u>May 12, 20xx</u>   <u>*David A. Binder*</u>

                                                      David A. Binder
                                                      Plaintiff in Pro Se

PROOF OF SERVICE BY MAIL

STATE OF CALIFORNIA, COUNTY OF LOS ANGELES

I, the undersigned, certify and declare that I am employed in the County of Los Angeles, California; that I am over the age of eighteen (18) years and not a party to the within-entitled action. My business address is 405 Hilgard Avenue, Los Angeles, CA 90095-1476.

On May 12, 20xx, I served the foregoing document described as NOTICE OF DEPOSI-TION on the interested party in this action by placing a true and correct copy thereof in a sealed envelope addressed as follows:

Susan Prager
534 Olive Street
Los Angeles, CA 90095

I deposited such envelope in the mail at Los Angeles, California. The envelope was mailed with postage thereon fully prepaid.

Executed in the County of Los Angeles, State of California, on May 12, 20xx.

I declare under penalty of perjury under the laws of the State of California that the forego-ing is true and correct.

_____
SIGNATURE OF SERVER

NOTICE OF DEPOSITION OF A PARTY AND PROOF OF SERVICE BY MAIL
(This notice must be served on all parties by the party taking the deposition.)

David A. Binder
123 State Street
Los Angeles, CA
Plaintiff in Pro Se
Telephone (310) 204-5579

UNITED STATES DISTRICT COURT
FOR THE CENTRAL DISTRICT OF CALIFORNIA

David A. Binder	)	CASE NO.1234567
Plaintiff,	)	
	)	NOTICE OF DEPOSITION
	)	
V.	)	
	)	
Susan Prager	)	
	)	
Defendant	)	
	)	
	)	

TO EACH PARTY AND THEIR ATTORNEY OF RECORD IN THIS CASE:

YOU ARE NOTIFIED THAT: The deposition of Susan Prager will be taken at

9512 Sawyer Street, Los Angeles, California, commencing at 9:00 a.m. on July 2, 20xx.

DATED: May 12, 20xx

David A. Binder

David A. Binder
Plaintiff in Pro Se

PROOF OF SERVICE BY MAIL

STATE OF CALIFORNIA, COUNTY OF LOS ANGELES

I, the undersigned, certify and declare that I am employed in the County of Los Angeles, California; that I am over the age of eighteen (18) years and not a party to the within-entitled action. My business address is 405 Hilgard Avenue, Los Angeles, CA 90095-1476.

On May 12, 20xx, I served the foregoing document described as NOTICE OF DEPOSI-TION on the interested party in this action by placing a true and correct copy thereof in a sealed envelope addressed as follows:

Susan Prager
534 Olive Street
Los Angeles, CA 90095

I deposited such envelope in the mail at Los Angeles, California. The envelope was mailed with postage thereon fully prepaid.

Executed in the County of Los Angeles, State of California, on May 12, 20xx.

I declare under penalty of perjury under the laws of the State of California that the forego-ing is true and correct.

_____

SIGNATURE OF SERVER

NOTICE OF DEPOSITION OF A PARTY REQUIRING THE PARTY TO PRODUCE DOCUMENTS AT THE DEPOSITION AND PROOF OF SERVICE BY MAIL

(This notice must be served on all parties at least 35 days prior to the deposition by the party taking the deposition.)

David A. Binder

123 State Street

Los Angeles , CA

Plaintiff in Pro Se

Telephone (310) 204-5579

UNITED STATES DISTRICT COURT

FOR THE CENTRAL DISTRICT OF CALIFORNIA

David A. Binder		)	CASE NO.1234567
	Plaintiff,	)	
		)	NOTICE OF DEPOSITION
		)	AND REQUEST TO
V.		)	PRODUCE DOCUMENTS
		)	
Susan Prager		)	
		)	
	Defendant	)	
		)	
_____		)	

TO EACH PARTY AND THEIR ATTORNEY OF RECORD IN THIS CASE:

YOU ARE NOTIFIED THAT: The deposition of Susan Prager will be taken at 9512 Sawyer Street, Los Angeles, California, commencing at 9:00 a.m. July 2, 20xx.

YOU ARE ALSO NOTIFIED THAT:

The deponent, who is a party to this action, is required pursuant to FRCP 34 to produce the following documents, records, or other materials at said deposition[list]:

All correspondence received by Susan Prager from the Plaintiff.

DATED: <u>May 21, 20xx</u>   _David A. Binder_____

                                                         David A. Binder
                                                         Plaintiff in Pro Se

PROOF OF SERVICE BY MAIL

STATE OF CALIFORNIA, COUNTY OF LOS ANGELES

I, the undersigned, certify and declare that I am employed in the County of Los Angeles, California; that I am over the age of eighteen (18) years and not a party to the within-entitled action. My business address is 405 Hilgard Avenue, Los Angeles, CA 90095-1476.

On May 21, 20xx, I served the foregoing document described as NOTICE OF DEPOSITION AND REQUEST TO PRODUCE DOCUMENTS on the interested party in this action by placing a true and correct copy thereof in a sealed envelope addressed as follows:

Susan Prager
534 Olive Street
Los Angeles, CA 90095

I deposited such envelope in the mail at Los Angeles, California. The envelope was mailed with postage thereon fully prepaid.

Executed in the County of Los Angeles, State of California, on May 21, 20xx.

I declare under penalty of perjury under the laws of the State of California that the foregoing is true and correct.

_____
SIGNATURE OF SERVER

REQUEST FOR PRODUCTION OF DOCUMENTS AND PROOF OF SERVICE BY MAIL

(This request may be sent only to a party and the request must be served by the requesting party on all other parties at least 35 days prior to the date indicated for the production of the documents.)

David A. Binder
123 State Street
Los Angeles, CA
Plaintiff in Pro Se
Telephone (310) 204-5579

UNITED STATES DISTRICT COURT

FOR THE CENTRAL DISTRICT OF CALIFORNIA

David A. Binder	)	CASE NO.1234567
Plaintiff,	)	
	)	REQUEST TO PRODUCE
	)	AND INSPECT
V.	)	DOCUMENTS PURSUANT
	)	TO FRCP 34
Susan Prager	)	
	)	
Defendant	)	
	)	
_____	)	

Plaintiff David A. Binder requests defendant Susan Prager produce and permit plaintiff to inspect and to copy each of the following documents:

(1) All correspondence received by Susan Prager from the Plaintiff.

(2) [List all other documents to be produced.]

Plaintiff requests that these documents be produced for inspection and copying at 1414 22nd Street, Los Angeles, California, at 9:00 a.m on July 30, 20xx.

DATED: <u>May 21, 20xx</u>

<u>*David A. Binder*</u>

David A. Binder

Plaintiff in Pro Se

PROOF OF SERVICE BY MAIL

STATE OF CALIFORNIA, COUNTY OF LOS ANGELES

I, the undersigned, certify and declare that I am employed in the County of Los Angeles, California; that I am over the age of eighteen (18) years and not a party to the within-entitled action. My business address is 405 Hilgard Avenue, Los Angeles, CA 90095-1476.

On <u>May 21, 20xx</u>, I served the foregoing document described as REQUEST TO PRODUCE DOCUMENTS PURSUANT TO FRCP 34 on the interested party in this action by placing a true and correct copy thereof in a sealed envelope addressed as follows:

Susan Prager
534 Olive Street
Los Angeles, CA 90095

I deposited such envelope in the mail at Los Angeles, California. The envelope was mailed with postage thereon fully prepaid.

Executed in the County of Los Angeles, State of California, on <u>May 21, 20xx</u>.

I declare under penalty of perjury under the laws of the State of California that the foregoing is true and correct.

_____
SIGNATURE OF SERVER

INDEX

A

Abusive questioning, 4/14

Accountant-client communications, 7/7

Accuracy, of deposition testimony, 4/4–6

Admissions, 12/13

    See also Request for Admission

Admonitions, 2/8, 5/2–9, 11/9

    correcting inaccurate testimony and, 4/6

    examples, 5/3–9

    expert witnesses, 8/15

    guessing, 4/7, 5/5

    origin of, 5/3

    purposes of, 5/2–3

Advance notice, 1/5

Adverse witnesses. *See* Hostile witnesses

Alabama, discovery/deposition rules, A2/3

Alaska, discovery/deposition rules, A2/3

Answers

    Motion to Compel Answers, 12/17, 12/19–21

    See also Instructions not to answer; Questions, responding to

"Any notary" agreement, 4/25

Argumentative questions, 4/13–14, 10/16–17, 12/7

Arizona, discovery/deposition rules, A2/3

Arkansas, discovery/deposition rules, A2/3

Asked and answered response, 12/15

Assuming facts not in evidence objection, 10/14, 12/5

Assumptions, questions containing, 10/14

Attendees, 1/9–14

    See also Deponents; Expert witnesses; Nonparty witnesses; Parties

Attorney-client privilege, 1/14, 3/7, 7/4–6, 10/15

Attorneys. *See* Defending attorney; Deposing attorney; Lawyers

Authentication of documents, 10/20, 11/21, 12/11–12

B

Background questioning, 6/2–9, 11/9

    educational background of deponent, 6/7–8

    employment history of deponent, 6/5–7, 8/16

    expert witnesses, 8/15–17

    hidden agendas, 6/2–4

    of lay witnesses, 8/15–16

    legitimacy of questions, 6/4–5

    written interrogatories, 3/12–13, 9/2, 9/6, 9/8–11, 9/11–12, 11/4, A1/13, A1/17–18, A1/23

Bench warrant, 9/8

Bias, 8/24–25, 11/18

Breaks, 4/20, 4/23, 5/6, 12/26, 14/13

Businesses, as adversaries, 9/9, 11/5

Business records

    requests for, 3/7, A1/18

    reviewing prior to deposition, 3/13

C

California, discovery/deposition rules, A2/3

Calls for speculation, objection, 10/20, 12/10

CD-ROM, converting videotaped depositions to, 14/8

Chronology of events, 8/18–19, 11/7, 11/13–14

Clergy, penitential communications as privileged, 7/7

Coaching, by defending attorney, 12/22–27

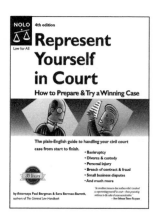

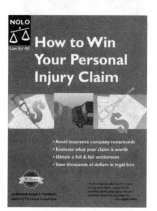

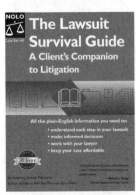

Remember:

Little publishers have big ears.
We really listen to you.

Take 2 Minutes & Give Us Your 2 cents

Your comments make a big difference in the development and revision of Nolo books and software. Please take a few minutes and register your Nolo product—and your comments—with us. Not only will your input make a difference, you'll receive special offers available only to registered owners of Nolo products on our newest books and software. Register now by:

PHONE
1-800-728-3555

FAX
1-800-645-0895

EMAIL
cs@nolo.com

or **MAIL** us
this registration card

---------------------fold here---------------------

NOLO Registration Card

NAME _____ DATE _____

ADDRESS _____

_____

CITY _____ STATE _____ ZIP _____

PHONE _____ EMAIL _____

WHERE DID YOU HEAR ABOUT THIS PRODUCT? _____

WHERE DID YOU PURCHASE THIS PRODUCT? _____

DID YOU CONSULT A LAWYER? (PLEASE CIRCLE ONE)   YES   NO   NOT APPLICABLE

DID YOU FIND THIS BOOK HELPFUL?   (VERY)   5   4   3   2   1   (NOT AT ALL)

COMMENTS _____

_____

_____

WAS IT EASY TO USE?   (VERY EASY)   5   4   3   2   1   (VERY DIFFICULT)

We occasionally make our mailing list available to carefully selected companies whose products may be of interest to you.

☐ If you do not wish to receive mailings from these companies, please check this box.

☐ You can quote me in future Nolo promotional materials.
  Daytime phone number _____.

DEP 3.0

Nolo in the NEWS

"Nolo helps lay people perform legal tasks without the aid—or fees—of lawyers."

—USA TODAY

Nolo books are ..."written in plain language, free of legal mumbo jumbo, and spiced with witty personal observations."

—ASSOCIATED PRESS

"...Nolo publications...guide people simply through the how, when, where and why of law."

—WASHINGTON POST

"Increasingly, people who are not lawyers are performing tasks usually regarded as legal work... And consumers, using books like Nolo's, do routine legal work themselves."

—NEW YORK TIMES

"...All of [Nolo's] books are easy-to-understand, are updated regularly, provide pull-out forms...and are often quite moving in their sense of compassion for the struggles of the lay reader."

—SAN FRANCISCO CHRONICLE

fold here

- -

Place
stamp here

Nolo
950 Parker Street
Berkeley, CA 94710-9867

Attn: DEP 3.0